What others have said about *The Russian Revolution*:

"A popular yet admirably written and absorbing narrative." —*Foreign Affairs*

"The style has the abrupt synoptic, intense quality of superb journalism . . . each theme is ingeniously conveyed by a gesture, a phrase, an anecdote. It seems unnecessary to add any praise to the book. It is a major reading event for the whole nonfiction public." —*Kirkus*

"The account [the author] gives of a complicated and controversial piece of history is fair and balanced." —*The New Statesman*

"A thoughtful and careful study . . ." —*The New York Times*

"It is well paced, well knit and admirably objective." —*The New Yorker*

Other books by Alan Moorehead:

Nonfiction:
Mediterranean Front
A Year of Battle
The End in Africa
Eclipse
Montgomery
The Traitors
The Villa Diana
Rum Jungle
Gallipoli
The Blue Nile
The White Nile
Darwin and the Beagle

Fiction:
The Rage of the Vulture
A Summer Night

THE RUSSIAN REVOLUTION

ALAN MOOREHEAD

Carroll & Graf Publishers, Inc.
New York

First Carroll & Graf edition 1987

ISBN: 0-88184-331-8

Carroll & Graf Publishers, Inc.
260 Fifth Avenue
New York, NY 10001

Manufactured in the United States of America

To Lucy

CONTENTS

ILLUSTRATIONS

A<small>N</small> ATTEMPT has been made here to give a brief, simple and straightforward account of the Russian revolution in 1917, and the events that led up to it. Quite clearly it cannot hope to please everybody; there is no more controversial subject on earth, and the passage of nearly half a century has not succeeded in quieting the strong feelings, the dissensions and the disagreements of those who lived in Russia at the time. Often commonplace facts are disputed by rival eyewitnesses and historians, and even the most devoted of scholars fall out over points of interpretation.

In the nature of things, then, this book cannot in any way pretend to be a definitive or exhaustive work. Its sole purpose is to provide for the general reader, as dispassionately and as objectively as possible, a description of a great political upheaval which is still too recent for history and yet, perhaps, too far off for him to remember with clarity from his own experience.

It may be of interest to mention here the unusual circumstances in which the book came to be written. Some ten years ago Dr. Stephan T. Possony, professor of international relations at Georgetown University, began with a small group of students to make a study of revolutionary techniques, in particular the technique of the Bolshevist conspiracy. Here was a theme which obviously overrode all others. It was the Russian revolution, probably as much as any other single event, that propelled the United States into world politics after the First World War; indeed, the revolution had its impact upon every country during the 1920's, and its influence is clearly visible in the depression and in the politics that led up to the outbreak of the Second World War. The Nazis' rise to power in Germany was intimately connected with the heritage that Lenin left behind; without Stalin's assurances of support Hitler would hardly have dared to plunge the world into another terrible conflict in 1939. America's present commitments in Europe and the Far East, the fall of China, the cold war, Korea, the endemic crisis in the Middle East, the missiles race—all these have their origin in the storm that swept away the Czar in Petrograd in 1917.

Dr. Possony and his associates concentrated their studies upon the peculiarities of the Russian Communist mind. How was it possible for a sincere Communist to overlook all the reversals of Bolshevik policy, to accept the slave camps, the treason trials, the repressive bureaucracy, and still remain loyal to the party? The answer seemed to lie in the 1917 revolution itself. To the devoted Communist the "October revolution" means almost as much as the resurrection of Christ means to the Christian. From that moment life began anew, and Lenin, the chief architect of the new order, is regarded to this day in Russia as the great hero of history, a prophet, a Messiah, an inspired genius whose motives were of a purity and altruism which are beyond all question. It will be seen that once this ikonization of Lenin and the revolution is accepted it is not difficult for the Communist to forgive the many errors the party leaders have committed: all these can be explained away as the temporary weaknesses and mistakes of individuals. The essential point is that the party itself remains sound, morally and intellectually infallible, certain to reach its preordained goal of human happiness in the end.

It seemed to the Possony study group that the time had come to challenge this orthodox Communist attitude toward Lenin and the revolution, and they decided to do this by going back as far as possible to original sources. A most profitable field of inquiry presented itself in the secret records of the German Foreign Office. These records in themselves have an interesting history. They were removed from Berlin during the last months of World War II, and stored in castles, schools and even mines throughout the countryside. Then, when the final collapse of Germany was imminent, the order came from Berlin for all official documents to be destroyed; and in fact the records of the German General Staff were burned. The remainder of the archives were saved by the personal courage of a

German official, Dr. Johannes Ullrich, at present the director of the Archives at the Foreign Office in Bonn. Dr. Ullrich defied the order from Berlin and managed to keep the bulk of the remaining documents hidden until the Allies arrived. They were then taken over by the British and transported to England for a preliminary examination. It was soon decided that the records which dealt with the period of the Nazis—that is to say from 1933 onward—should be officially published under the auspices of the French, British and American governments. Many of them were used at the Nuremberg trials. The rest of the documents, dealing with the years prior to 1933, were made available to the public in the form of microfilms. It was upon these microfilms that the Possony group began to work.

It was a slow and arduous business. There were hardly any indices. Many documents were missing; hundreds were meaningless or without importance. A web of code names that changed and changed again made a systematic search almost impossible. However, it soon became apparent in the secret correspondence between the German Foreign Office and its envoys abroad, and in the records of the Wilhelmstrasse itself, that the Germans had a close connection with the Russian revolutionary parties from 1915 onward. Revolutions cost money, and the Russian revolution had been a protracted affair. Where had Lenin and his friends found their money? Here at least was a partial answer: the documents revealed just what sums had been paid to certain agents to organize and finance subversive movements inside Russia. Naturally Germany was not the sole source of the Russian revolutionaries' funds, but there was enough fresh information here to encourage Dr. Possony to press forward with his investigation. There was, however, little hope of making real headway through the vast mass of records—the group was without funds and each member of it worked in his spare time on a voluntary basis —until in 1955 the Foreign Policy Research Institute of the University of Pennsylvania came forward with a grant. Then in 1956 the editors of *Life* Magazine offered to finance the project.

It was now possible to work efficiently and upon a wide scale. A staff of collaborators was set up to examine all available diplomatic records, not only in Germany but throughout Europe and even in countries as far afield as Turkey and Japan. In all about two dozen libraries and archives were searched, approximately 20,000 feet of microfilm or 100,000-odd documents were perused, some 800 books were read, and very many people who had connections with the Bolshevik leaders were interviewed.

This exhaustive research has established, I think beyond all reasonable doubt, that the Germans played an important role in bringing Lenin and the Bolsheviks to power, and it has made clear that the revolution itself was not quite the uncorrupted epic the Communists have made it out to be.

It was Dr. Possony's original intention to prepare an article upon his findings. The editors of *Life*, however, felt that the material should be expanded into a full-length book and at the end of 1956 I was invited to undertake the work. A lengthy summary of the research was made available to me and it has proved an invaluable addition to my own more general reading. This book, I hope, will serve as an introduction to the more detailed study of the Bolsheviks upon which Dr. Possony is working now and I would like to record my gratitude both to him and to the editors of *Life* for being given the opportunity of writing it.

For the rest, it will be seen from the short bibliography at the end of the book that my sources have been such as are available in any good library—in this case the London Library in England. I have drawn heavily upon such publications as Mr. Joel Carmichael's excellent translation of Sukhanov. I read these books without having any specialized knowledge of Russia or the revolution. This, perhaps, was not altogether a disadvantage, but I am well aware that my manuscript could never have been completed without the correction and the advice of Bertram D. Wolfe, Miss Laura Bell of *Life* and many others who have devoted years and even a lifetime to the study of the subject. In thanking them here I do not wish to say that they agree with all my conclusions or that I have accepted all of theirs; they may also dispute my presentation of the facts. No doubt many errors, or at any rate statements that are still open to debate, remain in the text. I can only ask the reader to believe that they have not been set down in malice or with conscious prejudice but are simply a part of that uncertainty which is bound to surround the Russian revolution, probably until the end of time.

ALAN MOOREHEAD

THE RUSSIAN REVOLUTION

CHAPTER ONE

Petrograd, 1916

SEPTEMBER and October are said to be the worst months of the year in Leningrad. A raw, damp wind blows in from the Gulf of Finland, fog and rain follow one another in a depressing succession of days, and everywhere mud and slush lie underfoot. It is often dark in the early afternoon and the cold night continues until nine or ten in the morning.

But then in November something perfectly wonderful happens: the heavy snow begins. It falls so thickly and so persistently that it blocks the view a few yards ahead, and sometimes in the course of a single night the whole city is transformed. The mud vanishes and the gold spires and colored cupolas now stand out against a background of dazzling whiteness. There is a kind of joy in the air. The temperature may stand well below zero, but in this dry sparkling atmosphere people get rid of their coughs and colds at last and can afford to smile. Traditionally, this used to be the moment when the droshky drivers exchanged their carriages for sleds and the coachmen, their beards frozen stiff, drove their horses along the quays at a tremendous pace. Out on the Neva workmen began to lay tramway tracks across the frozen water to the islands and the Vyborg side.

It is not impossible to envisage this scene as it was some forty years ago when Leningrad was still Petrograd,* a city of more than two

* Until August, 1914, when Russia was at war with Germany, the city was known as St. Petersburg. As a patriotic gesture it was then given the less

1

million people and the capital of Russia. In the winter of 1916 the Czar was still in his palace, a cosmopolitan aristocracy still revolved about the foreign embassies, the English Club, the churches and the opera. More than two years of war had made only superficial differences, at any rate to the outward scene. There were more military uniforms to be seen, and the street lights were faint and far between because of the fuel shortage and, later, the danger of Zeppelins coming over from Germany. Food queues were becoming longer and more frequent, and there was some anxiety about the increasing number of holdups and robberies in the streets. But the trams were still running, the long ornate corridors of the Admiralty and the Winter Palace were busier than ever, and the theaters were open every night including Sundays.

The prima ballerina Karsavina was dancing in Tchaikovsky's *Swan Lake* at the Mariinsky. Chaliapin was appearing at the Narodny Dom. Race meetings were being held at the Semenovsky parade ground, the Christmas circus had opened and the Stock Exchange remained calm and uneventful. Most of the better paintings in the Hermitage had been moved for safety to Moscow, but the fashionable shops and restaurants were crowded, and the war had not yet made it impossible for a duke or an ambassador to hold a reception in the grand manner. Nothing as yet had been bombed or damaged, and except for the snow and the massiveness of the buildings the city had a graceful italianate appearance that often reminded travelers of Venice.

In short, this was the world of privilege and established order, of a certain picture-book elegance which still seems vaguely familiar to us across all the commotions and upheavals of nearly half a century. One can recognize quite easily so many of these people and the parts they played, just as one recognizes and remembers the characters of some book, some play, some fairytale which stirred our imagination when we were very young. Thus, for example, we can picture the doorman standing before the palace in his pleated black coat and his military cap cocked a little sideways on his head,

---

Germanic name of Petrograd. In 1924 the Bolsheviks altered the name once more to Leningrad. This book is mainly concerned with the years that followed 1914, and therefore Petrograd will be used throughout to avoid confusion. The Western calender, which is twelve or thirteen days, depending on the century, ahead of the Russian, is also used throughout.

the Grand Duke with his medals, the Cossack leaning from his horse and the moujik in his blouse, the Duchess in white satin with her bird's-nest coiffure, her wasp waist and her décolletage, the droshky driver and his frozen beard, the professor at the university and the Orthodox priest with his stovepipe hat and his staff, looking like a prophet. And behind these figures there rises always the same theatrical background, the colonnaded ballroom, the tiers of boxes at the opera, the Russian eagle in the imperial coat of arms, the onion cupolas of the churches in a pale sky, the snow, the steppes, a straight railroad reaching endlessly into Siberia.

All this may be a trivial and novelettish recapitulation of Czarist Russia, and yet it does have a certain actuality in our memory, and these people and that background can often seem a good deal less strange to us than all the commissars, the committees, the factories and hydraulic projects and the million-headed blank-faced proletariat of modern Russia.

Perhaps it was the brilliance of the nineteenth-century Russian novelists that has fixed Czarist Russia so vividly in our minds, perhaps it was the very suddenness and completeness with which that world vanished, but at all events it was still there in the last days of 1916, and to a casual visitor arriving in Petrograd then it would by no means have been apparent that the Czar and his court, that the whole elaborate superstructure of feudal life which had been built up by the Russian monarchy for a thousand years, was about to disappear forever.

It was true that in December, 1916, there was a crisis in the government, that the antique machinery of the state and the army was in a desperate muddle, and that everybody talked about it; but no one as yet, not the foreign ambassadors, not the court or the ministers, not even the revolutionary leaders and certainly not the Czar himself, had comprehended fully just how explosive the situation was, how far it had drifted beyond all hope of remedy. Some of the people may have expected that a revolution was inevitable, but not the sort of revolution which was about to happen.

The war had exhausted the Czarist army. Something like 15 million men had been called up, and many of them had been sent into the trenches without proper clothing, without boots, even sometimes without a rifle. The dead were never accurately counted, and perhaps one can best gauge the enormity of this slaughter from a laconic note written by Hindenburg, the German commander, when it was all over.

"In the Great War ledger," he wrote, "the page on which the Russian losses were written has been torn out. No one knows the figures. Five or eight millions? We, too, have no idea. All we know is that sometimes in our battles with the Russians we had to remove the mounds of enemy corpses from before our trenches in order to get a clear field of fire against fresh assaulting waves. Imagination may try to reconstruct the figure of their losses, but an accurate calculation will remain forever a vain thing."

Now, for the moment, there was a lull in the long front line that stretched down for five hundred miles or more from the Baltic to the Black Sea, but such insensate killing had left many of the regiments without hope and without the power to recuperate. The front was still sound but there was talk of retreat in the air—of the necessity for falling back into the protection of the vast land mass of Russia itself —and although this policy might have had charms for some of the high commanders and the strategists it had precious little meaning for the infantryman on the spot. For him this was retreat, pure and simple, the end of any purpose in the war; and so the desertions began. By the end of 1916 hundreds of thousands of men had left their positions in the line, and many of them were now making their way back to their homes inside Russia.

Most of these soldiers were peasants, and it has been estimated that even in normal times their income never amounted to much more than about $150 a year. It was no unusual thing for a family to live in a single-room, thatched-roof cottage, with an earthen floor and a hole in the roof to allow the smoke of the cooking fire to escape. The farm animals often lodged inside as well. There were no bath-houses, no soap, no regular medical attention of any kind. A diet of bread and vegetables was varied only occasionally with meat, and although the supply of grain had actually increased during the war there were many areas where the peasants could not get enough to eat.

But even these conditions were probably better than the fate that was now beginning to overtake the workers in the city. Since 1914 wages had increased by 100 per cent, but in the same period prices had gone up by 400 per cent, and even then there was very little that could be bought in the markets and the food shops. The winter of 1916-1917 was particularly severe—at one stage no less than twelve hundred locomotives burst their frozen pipes and became immobile—and this contributed to the general confusion in the distribution of food. In Odessa people had to wait two days in line to get a little cooking oil. In Petrograd and Moscow bread queues formed throughout the freezing night, and it was hardly surprising that now, after two years of relative industrial peace, the workers were coming out on strike again. They were cold (there was of course an extreme shortage of fuel for heating), they were hungry, they were overworked (a ten-and-a-half hour day was the normal thing), and now they had had enough.

The educated classes, the civil servants, the merchants and shop-keepers, the politicians and the nobility, were still in 1916 insulated from the worst of these rigors. Yet they too had reached a point of exasperation and frustration which would long since have made itself felt in any other country. In the Duma some of the most respectable of the deputies had recently been making speeches which had come closer to treason than anything that had been heard before. Yet everybody knew that the Duma as an effective parliament never had a chance. It had no legislative powers of any consequence; it was a noisy "talking shop," and the Czar could and did dismiss it whenever he chose. There was a cabinet of a sort that was supposed to administer the country while the Czar was away at the front with the army, but it was without real control or responsibility. Something like a score of ministers had come and gone since the war had begun, and none had been much more than puppets.

Recently a certain A. F. Trepov, a run-of-the-mill conservative, had been put into the office of Prime Minister, but nobody—least of all Trepov himself—believed that he would last. The real power lay in one place only, and that was in the palace at Tsarskoe Selo, fifteen miles outside Petrograd, where the Empress was in residence; and behind the Empress, entirely dominating her, and through her the Czar, was the medieval figure of Rasputin.

The hatred surrounding this couple—the pious, German-born princess and the grotesque monk—had developed almost into hysteria in Petrograd, and it possessed the aristocracy quite as much as anybody else. In Petrograd society the Empress was universally referred to as "The German," and at least one plot was on foot to have her removed. As for the monk Rasputin, even the most vocal of the politicians and the nobles were finding it difficult to choose words to express their loathing and contempt. But it was contempt strongly mixed with fear. Under the protection of the palace he proceeded serenely on his course, dismissing the ministers he did not like, dropping a word to the Czar on how to conduct the war, and using his hypnotic powers to stir up the addlepated, superstitious mind of the Empress to the point where she hardly knew what she was doing any more.

The war had put a fearful strain upon the Czarist system, and Nicholas II was no Peter the Great to set things right again. It was really a race now to see which would come first: the ending of the war or the revolution. There was always a chance, of course, that the revolution might be staved off indefinitely provided that the war ended soon and victoriously; but in December, 1916, there was no sign of this. The Franco-British effort to break through the Dardanelles and come to the aid of their Russian allies had ended in disaster. The United States had not yet come into the war. France was hanging on desperately in the winter mud at Verdun, and at sea the Germans were about to launch their U-boat campaign, which was designed to starve Britain into surrender. Something like 160 Austrian and German divisions were now entrenched along the Russian front.

The war, then, as far as Russia was concerned, had subsided into a despairing stalemate. And yet, despite all this, it was difficult to see where the revolution was going to come from. A palace revolution, a rising of the nobles to replace the Czar, was quite feasible; but no single man either in Petrograd or among the generals in the army looked like being the leader of such a movement. Then too, there existed among the liberals as well as among the aristocracy an instinctive fear of what might happen if they upset the throne, if the illiterate masses, the "Dark People," followed their lead and raised a rebellion in the streets. Once let loose the mob and anything could happen; then all of them from aristocrats to shopkeepers might be swept away.

As for the left-wing revolutionary parties—the people who would accept rebellion at any cost—they too had been weakened by the war and driven underground. Most of the leaders were living in exile abroad or in Siberia: Lenin was in Switzerland, Trotsky was on his way to New York, Plekhanov, Axelrod, Martov, Dan and many others were scattered through Europe; and most of them were quarreling bitterly among themselves. None of them were planning to return to Russia, none had any idea that revolution was at hand. Lenin was even saying at this time that he did not believe he would ever live to see it.

And so a strange apathy rests over the scene, and it is something of a marvel that the Russian revolution, the most important political event of modern times, the event which has done more to shape our lives than anything else, should have entered in such an unexpected and rudderless way into history. It seems almost to have come in, as it were, by the back door, and although it was so much talked about beforehand it appears to have taken most of the main protagonists by surprise.

One has an entertaining glimpse of just how surprising the whole thing was from *Whitaker's Almanack*, the British reference book which has been issuing the vital statistics about the countries of the world year by year since the middle of the nineteenth century. In the volume dealing with 1916 everything is in order, and in its place, in the Russian section; the Czar is on his throne, the Duma is sitting, the imports and the exports are listed along with the figures dealing with the rainfall and the average extremes of temperature. But then in the next volume there is a sudden bewildered hiatus. In rather a shocked tone *Whitaker* reports that the Czar has been replaced by a M. Kerensky. "The newly-born freedom of the country," the book goes on, "has not up to the present proved an unmixed blessing as several opposing parties have arisen rendering any form of settled administration impossible." A certain "A. Oulianof Lenin" is believed to have seized the reins of power, and a "subaltern" has been named as commander-in-chief. Worse still, "the army is in a state of chaos and the allies are dispatching no more material aid to Russia." The note ends, "Any news coming to hand under the ruling conditions must obviously be looked on with the greatest suspicion."

And indeed how had it all happened? How in the space of these few short months from the first fall of heavy winter snow in 1916 to the beginning of the thaw in the spring of 1917 was a whole empire turned upside down?

"You will not find another such sharp turn in history," Trotsky says in his study of the revolution, "especially if you remember that it involves a nation of 150 million people." In ordinary times, he goes on, it is the state that makes history—the kings, ministers, bureaucrats, parliamentarians and journalists—and as a rule they leave records of their doings. But in a revolution the masses of ordinary people take over, and these masses are not accustomed to write things down, or explain themselves, either when they are in the slow process of boiling up to rebellion or when they are in the act of accomplishing it. The movements of their leaders and the revolutionary parties remain at the time very largely secret.

Clearly then, if we accept this—and it seems a valid proposition—there are two lines of inquiry into the truth about the Russian revolution. One line is the open and official one—the story as it is seen by the men in power and the heads of the established Czarist institutions, the generals and the judges, the leaders of the political parties, and finally by the Czar himself.

The other line concerns itself with the unofficial underground story, the maze of revolutionary intrigues, the devious fabric of emotions, of ideas and moods, which gradually, under the pressure of extreme hardship, possessed the majority of the Russian people and brought them to the point where they would accept any new leadership provided it offered some hope of taking them out of the hated world they knew into at least the prospect of something different.

In December, 1916, this revolutionary undercurrent was not quite ready to break through to the surface. Through long-ingrained habit the majority of Russians still looked up to the Czar, or at all events their idea of the Czar, as the main source of authority, either for good or evil. He was still the symbol that held the state together, and it seemed to many people that he could still lead them out of the chaos in which they were wandering; and it is one of the aberrations of history that Nicholas himself felt this too.

Since the Soviet government has been in power in Russia it has become the practice of Russian historians either to ignore Nicholas or to treat him as some vague remote ogre like Abdul the Damned, more of a legend than a man, and in any case of no account. But in

1916 Nicholas counted very much; he more than anyone else represented the system the revolutionaries were revolting against, and the idiosyncrasies of his nature are vital to the story.

In particular one needs to know just why he behaved in the way he did in this crisis; just how it was that he, of all the would-be mild martyrs of the world, should have been given such power at such a vital moment. The revolution slips by him almost accidentally. With all his intelligence and long experience, never at any stage during the revolution's long approach nor at the moment of its outbreak does he seem to have understood what was happening. In the end he leaves the tragedy in much the way he entered it in the beginning, terror and violence all around him, handsomely and honorably knowing nothing. This is an enigma that can only be unraveled by going back to Nicholas's origins in the last half of the nineteenth century. The following pages therefore are an account of the approach of the revolution from the Czarist point of view. Thereafter we will turn to the underground revolutionary movement itself.

CHAPTER TWO

The Divine Right of Kings

EVEN NOW in a world grown familiar with dictators and ruling cliques it is a little difficult to comprehend fully just how absolute was the power of the Russian Czars at the time of Nicholas's birth in 1868. The Czar took his position as the head of the state as naturally as a father will assume responsibility for his family, and the idea of the divine right of kings was something more than a survival from medieval times; it was a living faith that was passionately believed in and not only by the imperial family itself. To the great bulk of the Russian people outside the court it was just as much dogma—unalterable and absolute dogma—as the *Communist Manifesto* and the theses of Lenin were to the Bolsheviks later on.

The Mongol tradition was still surviving very strongly in the 1860's, and the very nature of the Russians themselves—the indolence and laziness of the peasants, the lack of culture among the nobility—may have made it inevitable that there should have been a central ruler, and that he should have ruled by force and violence. It might be said, of course, that this backwardness was forced on the Russians, that it was the tyranny of the Czars which had turned the majority of them into a race of nameless slaves, but the fact remained that this was a predatory state which the Czar and a small group of noblemen and bureaucrats ruled for their own exclusive benefit. The peasant was a serf who could not have any ambition other than to die early and peacefully, or to survive with a minimum of work, taxes, hunger and beatings. The ruling group owned all the wealth, enjoyed all the privileges and monopolized all the political power, and it did not intend to give up any of its prerogatives. It considered the peasants (some 95 per cent of the population) to be little better than animals who could not be trusted with the slightest responsibility.

By the time Nicholas was born a century or more had gone by since Peter the Great had set up the Russian state as though it were a sort of private domain, a country estate of the Romanov family, or perhaps just simply a school for mentally backward children. Beneath the Czar there were three great institutions, the bureaucracy, the army and the Holy Synod, and the officials within them were as tightly organized as ants in an anthill. Year by year, according to his ability, his character and his luck, the government servant crept up the fourteen established ranks, each rank with its appointed uniform, its privileges and its pay, until he reached retirement and his appointed pension at the end. It was a vast civil service. A tenth of the urban adult male population was in it. The peasants were ruled by the police, who were responsible to the county officials, who were responsible to the local governor, who was responsible to the Minister of the Interior, who was responsible to the Czar; and the Czar was responsible only to God.

"Thus, long before Marxian socialism was so much as dreamed of," Bertram D. Wolfe writes in his *Three Who Made a Revolution,* "the Russian state became the largest landowner, the largest factory owner, the largest employer of labour, the largest trader, the largest owner of capital, in Russia, or in the world. . . . This brought into being the world's largest apparatus of bureaucracy."

There were no elections and no parliament existed. All power filtered downward from the Czar above. He had a council of ministers to advise him, but they were all appointed by himself and held office at his pleasure (which was sometimes capricious and short). There was no such thing as free speech, and every published book, magazine or newspaper was censored (though not so drastically as at present).

All this, at any rate in its broader aspects, had been faithfully preserved down to the time of Nicholas's birth, together with its inevitable accompaniment: the discontent, the frustration, and finally the indignation of the people who hated such a way of life. Here

again it is almost impossible for anyone brought up in a democracy
to understand completely the hunger that there was in nineteenth-
century Russia for an elected parliament, a constituent assembly, in
which there would be free speech and some power at least in framing
and exercising the law. This is the dream that in the end survives all
others, the slogan which, at one time or another, is taken up by all
the revolutionary parties, right, left and center, the Bolsheviks included. Basically the Russian revolution is the story of the life and
death of this idea of a constituent assembly.

The stand of the Czars on this issue was very simple: Russia was
not Western Europe. It was not yet ready for democracy. If you
slackened the control too rapidly the illiterate millions might rise
and overwhelm you; then only chaos would result.

Nicholas's grandfather, Alexander II, was at least willing to go a
certain distance in making reforms, in fact rather further than any
of his predecessors. In 1861, against monumental opposition from
the landowners, the officials and the court, he liberated the serfs. As
things turned out, his system of liberation was bondage of another
kind, and the peasants eventually found themselves in some ways
rather worse off than they were before. Half the landlords' land was
handed over to them, but they had to pay for it, and they were
obliged to work it not as individuals but in community groups. In
practice this meant that they had to live off half as much land as they
had before, and since individual ownership did not exist there was
very little inducement for the peasants to effect improvements.
Still, it was the principle of the thing which was thought to be important, and it is useful to remember that Alexander here was not so
far behind the times. Slavery was not peculiar to Russia; 1861 was
also the year when civil war began on this issue in America.

Alexander's other major reforms were the creation of the zemstvos
—the rural councils that provided a form of local self-government—
and an overhauling of the antique legal and military systems (up to
this time peasants were obliged to serve up to twenty-five years in
the army, and penalties for misdemeanors, particularly flogging, went
beyond all humanity).

All in all it was a serious advance toward freedom, and for the
time being it left Alexander in a mood of caution. The Dark People
did not seriously abuse their new privileges, such as they were, but

on the other hand there was still no real internal peace. The peasant risings continued. Universities still talked sedition. The attempts made on the Czar's life grew, if anything, more frequent—and there were attempts made from the educated class as well as from peasant terrorists. One sympathizes with Alexander's cry: "What have these wretches got against me? Why do they hunt me down like a wild beast?"

For fifteen long years, from 1864 to 1879, Alexander made no further effort to relax his traditional control. But then at the end of the 1870's he began to stir himself again. Under the Czar's authority a plan for a constitution was drawn up. This was still a long way from providing an elected parliament on the European model, but it was something new in the Russian scene, a definite limitation of despotism. The ukase was signed and was merely awaiting publication when on March 13, 1881, all these plans and much else besides came to an abrupt and savage end.

In the early afternoon of that day Alexander was returning in his carriage to the Winter Palace along the Catherine Canal in Petrograd, and a young man named Rysakov threw a bomb. The Czar escaped untouched but some of the Cossacks in his escort were wounded, and he got down to speak to them. At this moment a second terrorist, a twenty-five-year-old Polish student named Ignacy Grinevitsky, threw a second bomb between his feet. Alexander was fearfully mutilated and they carried him half-unconscious into the palace to die.

There ensued then one of those awesome Russian death-chamber scenes which one associates with Tolstoyan novels: the ornate crowded bedroom, the ikons, the relatives coming up one by one to take their last agonizing farewell of the dying man. Nicholas, now twelve years old, was there in a blue sailor suit, with his father, the future Alexander III, and his Danish mother, Maria Feodorovna, who had come running in from the imperial gardens, a pair of ice skates still in her hand. Princess Yurievskaya, who probably loved the Czar more than anyone else (she had been his mistress for many years before becoming his wife only nine months previously), threw herself onto the bed in an extremity of grief and the Czar's blood stained her dress. For three-quarters of an hour the priests and the doctors gathered round, and then it was over. Nine of the Romanovs in that room, Nicholas among them, were themselves destined to die such a death, and never for very long in the years to come were they allowed to forget the prospect of it.

It seems only fair in following Nicholas's hesitating career to remember this. The terrorists, with all the law against them, were often safer than he was; they lurked in secrecy and he was out in the open. Not all the bodyguards nor the great palace fortresses, nor even the simple passage of time, could altogether remove him from the fear of violence. One hardly wonders that he became a fatalist so soon, or that he should have grown up with an instinctive sense of isolation and uncertainty. "Whatever I try," he once said, "nothing succeeds. I am out of luck." His birthday fell on May 6, the feast of Job, and he was fond of quoting the prophet: "Hardly do I have a fear than it is realised, and all the misfortunes that I dread fall on me."

The assassination of Alexander II had, however, quite another importance besides the gloomy influence it exercised on Nicholas's character; it was a clearly discernible landmark in Russian history. For the time being it brought to a stop all question of political change in Russia, and from this point onward it was inevitable that the boy should have been brought up in an atmosphere of extreme political reaction, of autocracy pure and simple.

Nicholas's father, Alexander III, was in many ways an ideal man to take advantage of the reaction against liberalism which followed the assassination. He looked like a Czar and behaved like one. He was a huge man, bearded and confident, and he was possessed of quite extraordinary physical strength; he was even said to be able to straighten a horseshoe with his bare hands, or conversely, tie an iron poker into knots. There is indeed a good deal about him of the Victorian country squire, the tough amiable autocrat who is perfectly satisfied with his inheritance, and who intends neither to change it nor look beyond it. He had no ambition for foreign conquests nor any liking for international intrigues. He wished quite simply for things to stay as they were. His closest advisor was the jurist Konstantin Pobedonostsev, a diehard reactionary of the purest water. It was Pobedonostsev's contention that liberty of any kind was a menace —a peculiar kind of menace that proliferated itself like a disease— and ended only in chaos since it could have no fixed objective. Con-

THE DIVINE RIGHT OF KINGS

structive policies could only be made by the "central will of states-men."

"Parliament," he wrote, "is an institution for the satisfaction of the personal ambitions, the vanity and the personal interests of the deputies. . . . God forbid that fate would give Russia the ominous present of an all-Russian parliament."

The new Czar himself, Alexander III, was quite ready to forbid it. His first act on taking power was to tighten up police supervision everywhere and then, having given the proposed constitution a brief, unfriendly glance, he abandoned it altogether. Autocracy was back on the throne again, and during the next thirteen years Alexander spent much of his time on his various country estates resolutely pretending that, so far as Russia was concerned, time was standing still.

In reality, however, a great deal was happening. A vast change was overtaking Russia. The government may have been marking time but the economy of the country was not. By the late 1880's trade was beginning to move on a colossal scale. In the Donets Basin a new mining industry was expanding, and peasants were migrating there in thousands in search of better wages and conditions than they could ever get on the land at home. Others pushed eastward toward the undeveloped areas of Siberia. Foreign capital was beginning to flow into Russia, and a whole new range of industries was springing up around the principal cities. In 1891 the Trans-Siberian Railway was begun, and it was by some way the biggest project of its kind the world had ever known, since it was to link China with Europe and open up markets that could not have been dreamed of before. Moscow was brought within eight days of the Pacific.

Everywhere a new class of factory workers was coming into being, and although they were underpaid, lacking in skill and overworked (mothers brought their children to the factories with them), it was the start of a new world of an industrial, "westernized" character.

The chief architect of these changes was Sergius Witte, one of the most interesting men in Russian politics, for he was a realist with an extraordinary adroitness in effecting changes under the dead hand of Pobedonostsev and the Czar. Witte, though of noble birth, began life as a railroad clerk in Tiflis, and by 1892 had worked his way up to the head of the ministry of communications. It was Witte who had launched the Trans-Siberian Railroad, and later as Minister for Finance he overhauled the archaic Czarist economy. He negotiated huge loans from France and welcomed private capital from abroad. Under Witte Russia was put on the gold standard and the government secured one of the most lucrative sources of national income—a monopoly on the sale of vodka. The Russian government, in fact, was rapidly becoming rich.

The other important figure in Petrograd through these years was Vyacheslav K. von Plehve. Plehve was a bureaucrat of the extreme kind, with a touch of ruthlessness added. He accepted as a matter of course all the paraphernalia of autocracy; the censorship of the press, the suppression of the liberty of the universities, the pogroms against the Jews, the rule of the police. While Witte worked outward toward Europe and the Western world, Plehve worked inward upon Russia. It was as Director of the State Police that he had hunted down the leaders of the successful plot against Alexander II in 1881, and now in the early nineties he was steering a course, skillfully and ruthlessly, toward the key post of Minister of the Interior. Witte and Plehve, not unnaturally, loathed one another.

Between these three, then, Pobedonostsev the diehard intellectual, Witte the state financier and Plehve the policeman, Alexander III's government continued on its inflexible course, and not even the three years' famine that began in 1891 could shake it. For a period of something like thirty years no reform of any consequence had been carried out, and no adjustment other than increased repression had been made to meet the new conditions of the country's economy or the unrest gathering from below.

Nicholas grew up through these years in the approved fashion of young princes in the nineteenth century; it was a world of countless relatives and retainers, of tutors and religious services, of uniforms and parades, of holidays in the Crimea and hunting in the woods, of visits to Uncle This or Cousin That in the royal palaces of London and Berlin. None of it came near to the real issues in Russia. His only contact with the revolutionary elements which were already forming about him was of the most violent kind. Barely seven years after his grandfather's assassination he was nearly killed in a railroad smash; the imperial train was derailed at Borki, and although Nicholas was unhurt—Alexander with his huge bulk held back the splintered timbers of their coach to enable the boy to crawl out of the wreck—twenty-one others were killed. This accident was not actually the work of terrorists, but in the previous year, 1887, a definite plot had been uncovered at the last moment. This was an inept and crazy affair organized by university students, yet it had its place in history, since the coming revolution brushed very close to Nicholas here: one of the ringleaders was Alexander Ulyanov, Lenin's elder brother. He was hanged. Then again a few years later, when Nicholas was in Japan, he just escaped death when a fanatic rushed at him with a samurai sword.

Yet for the rest it was a sheltered and a spartan life. Alexander III seems to have been something of a martinet inside his family, and he saw to it that Nicholas slept on a camp bed and was roused at six in the morning. His lessons were followed by a rigid training in the open air. Nicholas cannot have minded particularly. He adored the out-of-doors, hard riding and hard walking, the camp life of the army (he walked, it was said, "faster than a horse," and once, later on, he made a forced march of ten hours to try out a new infantry kit for the army). There seems to be no doubt he wanted to do well, to fulfill honorably his place in the world; and that place was made abundantly clear to him by Pobedonostsev and his father. Indeed, this side of his education was one long essay in the arts of absolute rule, of the unassailability of his own position. Nicholas loved and revered his father. He wanted to be like his father in everything.

Yet he grew up very differently. He was slight, gentle and quiet. His contemporaries remember his "tender, shy, slightly sad smile," his "frank blue eyes," his really infectious charm of manner. He was strikingly good-looking in the bearded, cultured, slightly withdrawn way of his first cousin King George V of England, whom he so closely resembled. An engaging photograph exists of the two young men standing side by side, each with his identical yachting cap, his nautical jacket, his white duck trousers, his trimmed Vandyke beard. Theirs is a world of immense distinction and prestige; they are so serious, so young and handsome, a vision in a Victorian parlormaid's dream of royalty in the flesh. There is even a ballet dancer in this early part of Nicholas's life—the famous Kshesinskaya, who later was to skip through the revolution in such a curiously symbolic way —but his affair with her does not appear to have been very serious.

His serious attachment, and it was probably the most important event in Nicholas's life, began in 1889, when Princess Alix of Hesse visited Petrograd. The affair seems to have lagged somewhat in the beginning; Nicholas's elegant and formidable mother, the Empress Maria, did not approve of it, and Nicholas himself, then aged twenty-one, did not think he stood a chance; the girl was too beautiful, he thought, too inaccessible. He went off on a trip around the world with nothing decided and no plans made for their meeting in the future.

Almost too clear and intimate a light falls on this young couple's courtship and their subsequent private life together. Nicholas was an ardent diarist of the intensely personal kind, and we can assume he would never have been so naïve as this, so unwary and spontaneous, had he known that his jottings were ever going to come to light. Then too, we have Alix's letters to him, and the act of writing these letters was to her a communion, a confession of the soul.

Yet for all our knowledge of lovers and their writings Alix still needs a little explanation, for she belongs to a world which is too dated for immediate sympathy and still not far enough away to have an aesthetic and historical quality of its own. She was one of the younger daughters of the German Grand Duke of Hesse-Darmstadt, who had married Princess Alice of England, and thus she was a granddaughter of Queen Victoria. She was four years younger than Nicholas, and when she was six her mother had died. At once she had been plucked up by her English relatives and brought up under Queen Victoria's eye in Kensington Palace, London. By the time she met Nicholas in Petrograd she was the perfect expression of an aristocratic Victorian upbringing: a girl of seventeen, blue-eyed, fair-haired, complexioned like a rose and delicate and beautiful in all her features except just possibly her chin, which had rather a determined mold. She was shy and modest and naturally romantic; and the Victorians had fixed in her (as only they knew how) a touching and absolute faith in her Protestant religion. She loved and believed in the mystic power and beauty of the Church to the exclusion of almost all else. And now this wonderful young man Nicholas had appeared.

"O Lord," he wrote in his diary, "how I want to go to Ilyinskoe."

Ilyinskoe was the country home near Moscow of his uncle, the Grand Duke Sergius, who had married Alix's sister Elizabeth, and

Alix was on a visit there. The date was now 1891, but the courtship was still not advancing very rapidly. In January of the following year we find Nicholas writing forlornly, "My dream is someday to marry Alix H. I have loved her for a long while, and still deeper and stronger since 1889 when she spent six weeks in St. Petersburg."

The chief obstacle was not the Empress Maria's coldness toward the matter, but the fact that in order to marry the heir to the Russian Czar Alix would have to exchange her Protestantism for the Orthodox Russian faith; and this by no means could she bring herself to do. But there were powerful parties interested in the marriage; the German Kaiser was not against it, Queen Victoria was quite ready to see her granddaughter on the Russian throne, and Alexander III had been won over by Nicholas's pleadings. In April, 1894, the Kaiser, Queen Victoria, the young couple themselves and various relatives gathered at Coburg in Germany to see what could be done.

We can follow the negotiations through Nicholas's diary. "Heavens, what a day!" he writes on April 17. " . . . She [Alix] looked particularly pretty but extremely sad. They left us alone and . . . we talked till twelve, but with no result; she still objects to changing her religion. Poor girl, she cried a lot. We parted more calmly."

Queen Victoria, however, was not so easily put off, and within three days the girl was won round.

"Wonderful, unforgettable day in my life," Nicholas wrote in his diary on April 20, "the day of my engagement to my darling, adorable Alix. [Nenaglyadnaya, the Russian for adorable, could also be translated 'I cannot look enough at her.'] . . . O God, what a mountain has rolled from my shoulders. . . . The whole day I have been walking in a mist without fully realizing what has happened to me. Wilhelm [the Kaiser] sat in the next room and waited with the uncles and aunts till our talk was over. I went straight with Alix to the Queen [Victoria] and . . . the whole family was simply enraptured."

And in a letter to his mother: "The whole world is changed for me; nature, mankind, everything; all seem to be good and lovable and happy."

It was probably the best time Nicholas ever knew. Queen Victoria swept him off to England so that he could be a little longer with Alix—they picnicked beside the Thames at Walton—and plans went forward for the wedding. It was celebrated even sooner than they expected. Alexander III had fallen ill at Livadia, his estate in the Crimea, and in the autumn of 1894 his condition rapidly worsened. He was only fifty, but he had received severe internal injuries in the Borki train crash six years before; and it was not within his nature to put much trust in doctors or follow their advice.

Alix was hastily summoned from England to meet her future father-in-law while there was still time, and the official betrothal took place in the Czar's bedroom a few days before he died on November 1. Five weeks later, while the court was still in mourning, the marriage took place. Nicholas was twenty-six, his wife twenty-two.

"Never," she wrote in her husband's diary (the diary that like all else had now become a mutual possession), "did I believe that there could be such utter happiness in this world, such a feeling of unity between two mortal human beings. I love you—those three words have my life in them." A day or two later she wrote again, "No more separations. At last united, bound for life, and when this life is ended we meet again in the other world to remain together for all eternity. Yours, yours."

There was too much feeling here to be contained, too much inexperience and excitement. Ideally, as in one of Marie Corelli's novels (and Alix was an avid reader of them), the story should have ended on this highly charged note, and the young couple should have subsided into the mediocrity of some provincial little state like Hesse. Neither of them, even if they had been alone and unhappy, was equipped to handle the fantastic power of the autocracy in Russia. Nicholas was frightened by it. His wife had no time for it; merely to be with him was all the world she wanted.

And so she began now, almost from the moment of her marriage, that long series of retreats into the whims and raptures of her private life, which in the end was to do almost as much as any other single factor to bring on the revolution in Russia. The metamorphosis of little blue-eyed Princess Alix into the woman she subsequently became is, in its way, as incredible and as unexpected as the emergence of the chrysalis into the butterfly, but at least it has the merit of being consistent. There were just two themes in this life, Nicholas and religion, and for much of the time the two were a good deal mixed up together in her mind. The young Empress took on her new faith in the Russian Orthodox Church with all the transports, the utter missionary conviction of the convert who has reached his faith by a terrible inner struggle. The very fact that she had resisted the change so strongly in the beginning made her surrender all the more complete. She had been born with a deeply religious cast of mind, and now, gloriously, the Orthodox Church had all the answers for her. Like her love for Nicholas her faith was exclusive and extreme; from this time onward in her religious devotion she was more Russian than the Russians.

Nicholas's mother, now the Dowager Empress, may have foreseen something of all this, and perhaps it was the reason why she had originally opposed the marriage. At all events, the first symptoms of Alix's inadequacies as a public figure quickly began to show. She found that she could not stand the round of elaborate receptions and banquets at Petrograd. She had no taste for parade of any kind; she even went so far as to draw the blinds on the imperial train when it came to a halt, so that she would not be faced with the officials and the dull adoring provincial gentry waiting outside on the station platform.

It was left to the Dowager Empress to make good these deficiencies; it was she who stood with her son at the palace receptions while Alix remained in her private apartments waiting for Nicholas to return. Alix was not liked by the court itself. She hated the inevitable intrigues, the posturing and the place-seeking round her husband, and instead of making at least a casual effort to accept these people she did the thing that was most calculated to make them loathe her; she ignored them. She let it be seen that she despised them.

Even the great occasion of the coronation (when she did sincerely try and do what was expected) conspired against her. It took place at Moscow in May, 1896, and as part of the ceremonies there was to be the customary giving out of little presents to the crowd on the Khodinka Field. A huge mass of people assembled, the presents were displayed on stands—rubles, handkerchiefs and cups—and suddenly the word got about that there were not enough presents to go round. A frantic rush began, and in a moment thousands of screaming people, many women and children among them, were pressed headlong into some open ditches that ran across the field.

Many hundreds were suffocated or crushed to death.

There was a ball given by the French Ambassador in Moscow that night, and it was thought strange that, at this of all times, the young Czarina should have chosen to dance the whole night through. Probably neither she nor Nicholas knew much about the tragedy; probably, in any case, the etiquette of the court required them to go through with the fixed program. But this made no difference; the story was soon going the rounds that the new Czar was an ill-starred man, and that his young wife, a foreigner, was callous and anti-Russian as well. One can almost hear him murmuring, "Whatever I try nothing succeeds. I am out of luck."

The other source of the Empress's unpopularity was more unjust and more serious. Russia needed a male heir to the throne and Alix could produce nothing but girls. Year by year they arrived until there were four of them in all: Olga, Tatiana, Maria and Anastasia. Alix herself was bitterly disappointed, and in her distress she began to give way, almost as a drug addict will give way, to the superstition that was always latent in her nature. She was a natural quarry for any quack, provided he had a religious tinge to his make-up. A procession of dubious priests, astrologers, faith healers and spiritualists began to find their way to the palace at Tsarskoe Selo outside Petrograd, where she spent most of her time. She was fascinated by the story of an obscure dead monk who was credited with the gift of predetermining sex, and used her influence to have him made into a saint—a move that was not at all liked by the Church. Once too a French "lay doctor" actually succeeded in persuading her that she was about to have a son, and she went through the painful experience of hysterical pregnancy.

Through all this Nicholas seems to have attended her patiently and kindly. He too had a side to his nature that was increasingly beguiled by horoscopes and soothsayers—the element of luck—and with the years he had grown to rely upon his wife more and more, as a counselor, as the one companion he could really trust. She soothed him and consoled him; she gave him the thing he really craved, a sense of confidence in himself.

In the end they were rewarded. On August 12, 1904, a son was born, and while the bells were ringing all over Russia they christened him Alexis Nicholaievich. But luck had not quite reached them yet.

The boy had inherited from his mother the besetting curse of so many of the royal families of Europe, the disease of hemophilia. Extreme care would have to be used in his upbringing, and it was not expected that he would live beyond his eighteenth year.

Through these first ten years of her marriage the Empress intervened very little in public affairs; Nicholas, with Pobedonostsev at his elbow, was left to go his own way, and he lost no time at all in indicating what that way was going to be. It was customary on the accession of a new Czar for minor officials to come up from the provinces and present addresses of congratulation to the throne. There was still a great deal of good will toward Nicholas at his coronation; he was young and good-looking, his recent marriage, an obvious love match, had given him a certain aura, and it was thought not impossible that his reign would open up a better future for everybody. One of these addresses of congratulation, however— it came from the zemstvo of Tver, a town outside Moscow—contained a hint of criticism. It expressed the hope that "the voice of the people's need will always be heard from the height of the throne," and "the rights of individuals and public institutions will be firmly safeguarded."

Left to himself Nicholas would no doubt have accepted this mild word of advice, but Pobedonostsev seems to have pounced on it, and one can hear his voice in the royal reply, Nicholas's first major statement of policy. These ideas of the zemstvos interfering in internal administration were, he declared, "senseless dreams"; and he added, "I shall maintain the principle of autocracy just as firmly and unflinchingly as it was preserved by my unforgettable dead father."

There is a record by an eyewitness of the scene at which this pronouncement took place: "A little officer came out," this eyewitness says; "in his cap he had a bit of paper; he began mumbling something, now and then looking at that bit of paper, and then suddenly he shouted out: 'senseless dreams;' here we understood that we were being scolded for something. Well, why should he bark?"

It could be argued that Nicholas's downfall really begins from this moment, for it was not the revolutionaries he was alienating here (they were implacably against him anyway) but all serious liberal feeling throughout Russia. The liberals could only answer with a despairing sigh—and turn reluctantly toward the left. Why should he bark?

For the time being there was very little anyone could do to save the situation. Alexander III had handed on the autocracy as a going concern to his son, the state police were powerful everywhere, and the mass of the people just as backward and leaderless as they were before. The important new fact in the situation had not yet become apparent, the fact that Alexander III was a dominating character and Nicholas was not. Nicholas was a weak man, well-intentioned and perhaps personally courageous, but weak, and there was no strength in him for compromise. He had a natural aversion to an argument, he hated to hear anything unpleasant, and his instinctive reaction to a problem was to procrastinate, to turn aside from it and do nothing, to escape into the simplicities of his family life in the country.

Trotsky, an adept at ruining his own case by malice, has a ferocious chapter on Nicholas in his *History of the Russian Revolution*.

The Czar's diary is the best of all testimony [he writes]. From day to day and from year to year drags along its pages the depressing record of spiritual emptiness. "Walked long and killed two crows. Drank tea by daylight." Promenades on foot, rides in a boat. And then again crows and again tea. . . .

Nicholas was not only unstable, but treacherous. Flatterers called him a charmer, bewitcher, because of his gentle way with the courtiers. But the Czar reserved his special caresses for just those officials whom he decided to dismiss. Charmed beyond measure at a reception, the minister would go home and find a letter requesting his resignation. That was a kind of revenge on the Czar's part for his own nonentity.

Nicholas recoiled in hostility before everything gifted and significant. He felt at ease only among completely mediocre and brainless people, saintly fakers, holy men, to whom he did not have to look up. . . . This "charmer" without will, without aim, without imagination, was more awful than all the tyrants of ancient and modern history.

This is, of course, absurd, and yet the first ten years of Nicholas's reign are very largely the story of his tendency to evasion, of the workings of the brain of a man who would have made an admirable constitutional monarch but who was hopelessly unfitted to understand and control the gathering forces of revolution in Russia.

There is a good deal in Trotsky's contention that Nicholas disliked men who were abler than himself. Witte, his best minister, soon found himself in trouble, and Plehve, who was a better courtier, was firmly in control of the Ministry of the Interior by 1902. It was Plehve's ambition to convert Russia into even more of a police state than it was before, and he was not unsuccessful. Increasing waves of strikes, street demonstrations, and peasant risings broke against his police machine, and achieved nothing very much except more and more arrests, more exiles in Siberia, more repression of the Jews, and more support for the revolutionary movement underground.

A kind of brittle lethargy hangs over these first years of the twentieth century in Russia. Everyone sees the danger, no one is content; yet nothing is done, nothing is decided, until in the end it required a foreign war to bring things to a crisis.

The Russo-Japanese war of 1904-1905 was the last of the Romanov private expeditions, a purely expansionist affair, an attempt at a land grab. It left the mass of the Russian people quite indifferent, and even the bureaucracy and the educated classes were divided about it; some of them in fact wanted their own army to be defeated so that in the ensuing political upheaval the Czar would be forced to introduce reforms at home.

Nicholas's part in the matter has never been entirely disentangled but there is no doubt that, unlike his father, he was attracted by the idea of military conquest. As a young man—and he was still only in his middle thirties—he had traveled in Japan and Siberia, and the Germans did all they could to egg him on since they wanted to keep Russia out of Europe and the Middle East. "Russia," Bismarck had once said, "has nothing to do with the West; she only contracts Nihilism and other diseases; her mission is in Asia: there she stands for civilization." The Kaiser was even more explicit. In 1902 when he attended the Russian naval maneuvers in the Baltic he sent a farewell message to Nicholas: "The Admiral of the Atlantic greets the Admiral of the Pacific."

Then too the Far East was the easy way for the Russians to go. The Czarist armies had had no great success in their campaigns in the West in the latter part of the nineteenth century, but primitive China and the Pacific seaboard were anybody's game—or so it seemed. The Trans-Siberian Railway had already provided the Russians with a convenient springboard. Originally the line had run through to Vladivostok—the name incidentally means "Ruler of the East"—entirely on Russian territory. In order to do this it had skirted past the north of Manchuria, which was a Chinese possession, and this had meant a detour of about six hundred miles, or one and a half days' traveling through uninhabited territory. Recently, however, the Russians had obtained from China permission to build a direct link across Manchuria to Vladivostok, and this meant that the Russians had to police the area with their own troops since it was infested with robber bands and outlaws. Little by little in a camouflaged and unobtrusive way Manchuria had become a Russian protectorate, and the plan now was to expand still further into the peninsula of Korea. Already a group of Russian businessmen who were known to be close to the Czar had obtained a mining and timber concession on the Yalu River in northern Korea.

All this looked extremely menacing to the Japanese, and they protested. They were prepared in certain circumstances to accept the Russian protectorate of Manchuria, but Korea was quite another matter, and by the middle of 1903 both sides were getting ready for war.

Powerful interests in Petrograd were ranged both for and against the expedition. Plehve, the army commanders and the Yalu business group were all in favor of it; Witte and the foreign office against. Between these two opposing camps the Czar wavered uneasily for a time. He tried to bargain with the Japanese for the Yalu concession, and he did this not through the accepted channel of his foreign office but through serving officers and other private envoys; and so Russia spoke with two voices, and neither in Tokyo nor in Petrograd did anyone know precisely where they were. Immense intrigues festered round the court in Petrograd, where much money and many reputations were involved. In the midst of this, in August, 1903, Nicholas took the opportunity of getting rid of Witte, whom he never liked, and it became increasingly clear in Tokyo that the Czar had no real intention of giving up his plans in Korea. In the second week of February, 1904, while the exchange of diplomatic notes was still going on, the Japanese struck with a naval attack at Port Arthur in the Yellow Sea. As at Pearl Harbor, thirty-seven years later, there was no warning.

The eighteen months' war which followed was one long catalogue of Russian disasters. At least one major scandal was involved; the Russian commander of Port Arthur, which was supposed to be an impregnable fortress, sent out his white flag to the Japanese when he still had some two million rounds of ammunition and four months' supply of food.

The campaign finally came to a crisis when the Russians dispatched their Baltic fleet around the world in the last desperate hope that it would destroy the Japanese navy in the Yellow Sea. It was a fantastic plan, more of an emotional gesture than a studied act of war, and very few people in Petrograd believed that the ships had the ghost of a chance. The Baltic fleet was weak and overaged, and it was manned by inexperienced crews. One has the feeling that it was flung into the struggle in much the same way as a gambler, having lost steadily throughout the game, will suddenly risk all that remains to him in a single throw which will either recoup his losses or ruin his fortunes entirely.

The ships set out in October, 1904, and ran into trouble at once; believing that they were about to be attacked on the Dogger Bank at night, they opened fire on some British fishing boats, and this did not dispose the British (who in any case supported the Japanese) to be helpful about opening the Suez Canal. Some of the Russian ships were forced to make the long haul round Africa and proceed by way of Madagascar and the Indian Ocean to the coasts of China, and it was May, 1905, before they finally reached their destination. Japanese agents had reported on their approach at every step of the way. On May 27, off Tsushima Island, the massacre occurred. The Japanese steamed at a range of seven thousand yards across the leading Russian ships, and in three-quarters of an hour it was all over. By some freak of chance three Russian vessels managed to disengage and make port.

With this the war was over, and both sides were now ready to accept President Theodore Roosevelt's offer to mediate for peace. Witte was the Russian representative at the conference at Portsmouth, New Hampshire, in September, 1905—he had been summoned back by the Czar at this low moment in the country's affairs—and he contrived to get very reasonable terms from the Japanese: Korea was to be left to them as a zone of influence, and Russia was

to evacuate southern Manchuria. No indemnity was to be paid by
the Russians.

Nicholas had lost here upon almost every count: in Russia's prestige in the world, in the damage to his armed forces, in the explosion
of his dreams of a new empire in the East. But these were obvious
losses. They can be put aside and forgotten in the face of a much
more serious and sinister thing which this war had brought upon
his head: it had created the conditions for revolution inside Russia.
It had broken or at any rate loosened his autocratic hold on the
country, and, just for a few short months, it provided an ominous
glimpse of what lay ahead. In brief, the thing that Nicholas feared
more than anything else now happened: the Russian underground
came to the surface, the Dark People appeared in the streets, and
they marched up to the gates of the Winter Palace in Petrograd.

CHAPTER THREE

The New Man

THE REVOLUTIONARY movement in Russia was a growth like no other in the world, and it may be that one can only understand its bewildering contradictions by keeping firmly in the back of one's mind a picture of the physical nature of the country itself: the long dark winter, the spells of intense cold and heat, the vast expanse of flat land that leads on, like the sea, to endlessly receding horizons. A human being is a midget in this boundless landscape. One can sympathize with the Russian's desperate need to establish his own identity there, his desire, by some outcry, some act of defiance, to reassure himself that he is not nothing in the world. There is no easy comfort to be had. It is a climate and a topography that call for extremes and idealism, not for liberalism or compromise. Half measures are no good in this wilderness any more than a leaking boat is any good in an ocean. One needs certainty, a sense of security, something solid to hold on to in the dangerous void—and it has to be absolutely solid.

This absolutism is at the core of the Russian revolutionary mind; it has to go the limit, to be utterly wrong or utterly right but in any case utterly committed; and there is a kind of mystical joy in this complete abandonment. It must be all or nothing, chaos or heaven, and in the meantime the existing world must be swept away. "Nihilism was born in Russia," Dostoevsky declares. "We are all nihilists."

"Blood will flow in streams," Alexander Herzen cries. "And the upshot? . . . It is enough that . . . there will perish the world which oppresses the new men of the new time. . . . Long live chaos, therefore, long live destruction! *Vive la mort.* . . . We are the executioners of the past." And Mikhail Bakunin has his vision of "a tornado of destruction."

In the nineteenth century Russia was almost as isolated as it is now from the main stream of human thought in the West. Foreign books were hard to come by, especially if they dealt with such vaguely subversive subjects as philosophy and political science. Even if the university student did succeed in getting hold of a few smuggled or illegally printed pamphlets he was up against a serious difficulty; he had no real knowledge of the broad culture of the West nor any clear idea of how to adapt that culture to the Russian scene. Often too he had no training in acquiring education, and he was not patient; he might gallop through half a dozen abstruse philosophical tracts from Germany and it was enough to turn him into a zealot. Here at one swoop he thought he had discovered the blinding truth about everything, and it was not in the Russian character to accept contradiction very easily. He might sit up having interminable discussions through the entire night, but he would continue to be resentful of other opinions. His opponents he regarded as heretics and enemies.

The Russia in which Nicholas II had grown up was filled with all kinds of "believers" who swallowed the queerest creeds, ranging all the way from minor religious deviations and sects who expected salvation from the drinking of milk to less harmless people who specialized in drunken sex orgies, violence, collective torture, self-mutilation and sometimes collective suicide.

The very passion with which these believers believed made it inevitable that vendettas should spring up between the rival groups, and these vendettas naturally expanded into the revolutionary movement as well. Here again the backwardness of Russia made things far worse than they need have been. In a country without a parliament there was no tradition of responsibility, no rules as to what was fair play and what was not, no skill in negotiation, no moderation anywhere. Ferocious tirades took the place of argument, and physical violence was never far away from anybody's mind. This was a world of opposing maffias, and of an interpretation of the idea of loyalty that simply bewilders the Western mind; in fact, it is hardly loyalty at all but more like downright treachery. Presently we shall meet a really sinister character in this eddying scene—the man who betrays his friends, the police spy, the *agent provocateur.*

All of this of course does not mean that there were not distinguished and high-minded men among the many groups fighting for self-expression: this was the age of Tolstoy, Dostoevsky and Turgenev; or that the revolutionary movement was basically corrupt. It was unformed, it was crude, it was sabotaged by illiteracy and it was fighting against overwhelming odds. It was also bedeviled by the enormous gulf that lay between the educated man and the peasant. They were almost like foreigners speaking a different language and knowing very little of one another's lives. And so from the very beginning there is a two-sided aspect to the Russian revolutionary movement; more often than not the peasants rose of their own accord, and it would be a local and leaderless affair, a spontaneous angry outburst of the mob. Meanwhile the revolutionary intellectuals continued in the universities with their endless cerebral debate, and it was punctuated only from time to time by isolated acts of terrorism.

To some extent the theme of the Russian revolution is the bridging of this gap between the universities and the peasants, the combination, as in some chemical formula, of the intellectuals and the masses, and this was the point where the revolution became really explosive.

Looking back, one sees that in the end revolution in Russia was probably inevitable. It was the perfect model of a state that was prone to revolution, and the very misery of the age made it impossible for Czarism to continue. Like Fabrizio in Stendhal's *La Chartreuse de Parme* the revolutionaries were bound to break out of their bonds because they were more often thinking of ways to escape than their jailers, the Romanovs, were thinking of imprisoning them.

The origins of this struggle—one might almost call it an underground civil war—go back at least as far as the eighteenth century, when the Cossack Pugachev raised a rebellion that lasted sixteen months and had as its war cry "Land and Liberty." Voltaire, Diderot and d'Alembert all were widely read in Russia during the reign of Catherine the Great (1762-1796), and the first Russian revolutionary book soon followed. It was written by a nobleman, Alexander Radishchev, with the title *Journey from St. Petersburg to Moscow*, and it was inspired by Sterne's *Sentimental Journey*. It criticized the bureaucracy and serfdom and it appealed for agrarian reform. Catherine knew how to make short work of this sort of thing; Radishchev was arrested, condemned to death and finally sent to Siberia. He managed to return after Catherine's death and was employed in drafting government laws, but soon committed suicide in a fit of melancholia. It was the Napoleonic Wars, however, which gave the right-wing revolutionaries their first real impetus. Many of the Russian officers who pursued the French army to Paris were deeply impressed by what they saw in France, and they came back to Russia with a program for the abolition of serfdom and the setting up of a republic. The Dekabrist rising in 1825 was the result, and when it was broken up 121 of the conspirators were condemned to death or sent to Siberia. During the next twenty years—the years of Nicholas I's reign—there were 556 separate peasant risings in Russia, and the intellectual revolutionary movement began in earnest. Both Herzen and Bakunin were writing from the safe sanctuary of Western Europe by the second half of the century; Herzen with his demand that the revolutionary movement should cease being romantic and instead turn toward socialism, atheism and individual freedom; and Bakunin with his anarchist thesis of the destruction of both state and church.

In the 1850's and 60's nihilism arrived—the word was invented by Turgenev—the cult of believing in the destruction of all constituted authority, and it was accompanied by the idea that the way ahead lay not through art but through science; science now was to be the great panacea. These also were the years of the first serious attempts by the intelligentsia to combine with the peasants. The Narodnik movement was an intensely Russian affair, a going down to the peasants rather than an effort to raise them up. The Narodniks believed that the revolution would be based upon the workers on the land, and that their instinctive communism would legitimately form the new Russian state. Out of these beginnings one of the two great left-wing parties—the Social Revolutionaries—grew up.

Meanwhile, a technique for the physical act of revolution, for terrorism and all the business of secret cells and underground communications was developing. A new man was conceived, the professional revolutionary, a man who regarded himself as expendable, who followed blindly the leader and the party line, and who if need be would lie, cheat and murder to gain his objective. He was possessed neither of patriotism nor of pity; his only faith was in the revolution itself, and in this he was a fanatic. This idea was first put forward by Serge Nechaev and later developed by Peter Tkachev, and it made strong claims on the Russian mind. Tkachev indeed is a predecessor to Lenin, for he envisaged a communist state on utopian lines which would be created by a small resolute group of these supermen. It was Turgenev, however, in the following fragment, who best put into words this Russian mania for extremism, for perfection and for martyrdom:

"To you who desire to cross this threshold, do you know what awaits you?"

"I know," replied the girl.

"Cold, hunger, abhorrence, derision, contempt, abuse, prison, disease and death!"

"I know, I am ready, I shall endure all blows."

"Not from enemies alone, but also from relatives, from friends."

"Yes, even from them . . ."

"Are you ready to commit a crime?"

"I am ready for crime too."

"Do you know that you may be disillusioned in that which you believe, that you may discover that you were mistaken, that you ruined your young life in vain?"

"I know that too."

"Enter!"

The girl crossed the threshold and a heavy curtain fell behind her. Fool! said someone gnashing his teeth. Saint! someone uttered in reply.

Here then one has terror added to the missionary vision. The end—the destruction of autocracy—justifies all things, including bombs; even more than that, it justifies itself even if proven wrong. The self-immolation of the victim is the important point.

Turgenev was not imagining things. Already in the 1860's a series of devastating fires swept through the wooden buildings of Petrograd and other cities, and these may well have been the work of revolutionary incendiarists. The bomb which killed Alexander II was but one incident in a spate of bomb throwing. There were even subterranean schools where the weapons were made and the arts of detonating bombs were demonstrated to beginners. The terrorists now were professional terrorists, not nobles and guards officers, but university students who lived in a world of passionate idealism and passionate hate. Violence was beginning to beget violence in a vicious and never-ending circle, and it was destroying the possibility of any reasonable approach to reform. The young men, on fire with the idea of personal sacrifice, despised liberalism; socialism—the redistribution of wealth and the end of Czardom—was their direct aim, and it became for them a sacred trust. And so, gradually, by the 1880's a definite revolutionary doctrine can be seen to be taking shape: the belief in "the people," socialism, materialism, science, the idea of the ruthless "New Man" breaking down the past and turning his back on it.

As yet, however, this is a new religion without procedure, without ceremony and without a church. Not even its faith is really formed. The various conspiratorial groups have not yet become political parties, and they have no hierarchy of officials, no settled meeting place, and no established creed. There is no question, as yet, of united action; each man works underground, illegally, and in place of a constructive program there is a confused belief in idealistic terrorism for its own sake.

The year 1883—which is also the year that Karl Marx died in London—sees the beginning of the end of all this; the first major Marxist figure arrives on the Russian scene. Georgi Valentinovich Plekhanov occupies a strangely muted place in Russian history. It was nothing extraordinary that later on the Bolsheviks under Stalin should have distorted and suppressed his reputation—they did that with nearly everybody—but even in the books written by his contemporaries Plekhanov continues to be an uneasy ghost. There is a certain colorlessness about him; he occupies a place which can be compared not too fancifully to that of the Venerable Bede in English literature; he is acknowledged as the pioneer, the founder figure, but with a kind of perfunctory reverence. Revolutionary history hurries on to the great name of Lenin, just as in England the unfortunate Bede lurks as a pale shade under the eminence of Chaucer.

Yet Plekhanov, the man who now is accorded just a few inches of type in the encyclopedias, was not only the founder of the Russian Marxist movement: he dominated it for more than twenty years. During most of that time not Lenin nor Trotsky nor any of the others would have dreamed of challenging his intellectual superiority. They sat at his feet, eager to pay homage and to learn. It was upon his ideas that they fed.

Plekhanov was the son of a prosperous country gentleman in the Tambov province (many of the revolutionary leaders came, not from the cities, but the great plains), and was destined for the army, but turned instead to politics in his student days (and here again this follows a fairly general pattern). When he was not yet twenty he was demonstrating in the streets of Petrograd with the Narodniks, but he turned against them soon afterward because of their terrorist tactics and emigrated abroad to Switzerland. A group of companions and followers went with him, the chief of whom were Vera Zasulich and Paul Axelrod. In 1883, when Plekhanov was still only twenty-six, they founded in Geneva a party called the Liberation of Labor. This was the first Marxist group in Russian history, and its principal object was to apply Marxism systematically to the Russian scene.

It was Plekhanov's belief that the revolution in Russia would develop upon European lines; that is to say, Russia would have to become industrialized and would have to produce a proletariat, a working class, before Czarism could be overthrown. Only the workers could produce a revolution: "In Russia," he said, "political freedom will be gained by the working class, or it will not exist at all. The Russian revolution can only conquer as a workingman's revolution—there is no other possibility nor can there be."

For the next thirty-five years of Plekhanov's life—and he spent almost all of it in exile—this was one of the major points debated by the Russian underground. Others saw a different solution. The Narodniks, for example, the back-to-the-peasant group, did not believe that Russia was destined to have a capitalistic and industrial phase before the revolution could occur: they held that she could proceed directly from serfdom to socialism.

One starts to see here the beginnings of a future rivalry; the

Marxists with their emphasis on the industrial worker, the Narodniks with their emphasis on the peasant. It was Plekhanov, presiding over his revolutionary court in Geneva, who most rapidly began to gain ground. In his writings he urged that terrorism was a secondary weapon; the main object was to set up a socialist organization among the working class in Russia, to train agitators, to stimulate strikes and demonstrations, and to spread Marxist ideas through the illegal printing press. Soon small groups of his followers began to form in the principal cities in Russia. They called themselves Social Democrats.

Through all this period the Russians were very small fry in the international revolutionary movement. The Germans were far more active. When in 1889 Plekhanov went to attend the initial congress of the Second International in Paris (the First International had been organized by Marx and Engels in the seventies) he was very much in the minority. Neither Marx nor Engels, moreover, had thought very highly of the Russians. Marx was particularly trenchant about them. "I do not trust any Russian," he once wrote Engels. "As soon as a Russian worms his way in all hell breaks loose." Russia, in any case, Marx thought, still had a long way to go before it achieved socialism; he had much better hopes of the United States, where "the masses are quicker."

Yet Plekhanov and his friends continued to gain supporters, especially inside Russia. The famine of the early nineties helped their cause, and in 1898 a conference was held in Minsk to unify all the Marxist groups inside Russia. They formally adopted for themselves the name of the Russian Social Democratic party, and from this time forward its underground organization continued steadily to expand.

So now, at the turn of the century, when the revolutionary movement had been in existence for something like a hundred years, and orientated toward socialism for fifty years, Marxism became a leading revolutionary ideology in Russia. The Social Democrats had at this stage just one main rival: the Narodnik party, who soon adopted *their* official name, and it had rather more of an explosive sound: the Russian Social Revolutionary party.

In the welter of party names that unavoidably lies ahead in these pages it is as well to keep these two firmly in mind, for they repre-

sent the basic grouping of the Russian left wing: the Social Democrats whose gospel is Marx and *industrial* socialism, and the Social
Revolutionaries whose main idea is to work through the peasants to
agrarian socialism.

Most of the revolutionary splinter groups which are now about
to appear fit into one or other of these two categories, and although
they seemed important at the time they soon become lost in the
general onrush toward rebellion. Liberal ideas, of course, existed
everywhere, but there were still no coherent political parties of
the center or the right unless the Czar and his court and his vast
bureaucracy be considered a party; with all its fantastic complica-
tions it was at this time pretty well a straight issue between these
revolutionary groups and autocracy.

An underground web was now spinning itself across Europe into
Russia, and it was dominated by Plekhanov and the Social Democrats. They had their newspaper, *Iskra,* the Spark (taken from
Pushkin's "The Spark shall ignite the Flame"),* their couriers running it into Russia along with other subversive literature; their
printing presses inside Russia itself; their terrorist section; their
underground for taking care of political refugees; and their own
tenuous system of finance.

The chief concern of Plekhanov and his friends now was to get
some sort of coherence into this scattered and uneven organization,
especially coherence of thought; it was essential that they should
all know where they were going, what precise ends they had in
view. Principles had to be laid down—the written creed of the
new religion—and tactics agreed upon. And in order to do this it
was essential to hold a conference somewhere outside Russia where
the delegates could talk freely without danger of arrest. It was a
long business getting this conference together; the party leaders
were not only scattered through Russia or in exile in Siberia but
dispersed through Europe as well, chiefly in England, Switzerland
and Germany, and almost everyone had different views on the
agenda and on how it should be presented. By 1903, however, the
matter was arranged, and Brussels was chosen as the meeting
place. This was the culmination of twenty years of effort by
Plekhanov, and even in the hard revolutionary world it was perhaps
a little too hard on him that this moment of his triumph should also

* See, later, Lenin's part in *Iskra.*

have been the moment of the beginning of his downfall. A new man had appeared on the scene.

Upon one thing at least all the accounts of Lenin agree: he was not handsome, or even particularly interesting to look at. He was a short, plumpish man with a reddish-gray beard who had gone bald very early, and his clothes were cheap and baggy. "At first glance," Bruce Lockhart says, "he looked more like a provincial grocer than a leader of men."

But he was not vain. "Lenin was one of the most selfless of great men," Edmund Wilson writes. "He did not care about seeing his name in print, he did not want people to pay him homage; he did not care how he looked, he had no pose of not caring about it."

As an orator Trotsky describes Lenin as "flat," and Sukhanov, one of the most intimate observers of the revolutionary scene, says that he was neither emotional nor witty; toward the end of his short life he became downright monotonous. Yet at his prime, Sukhanov says, "he was an orator of enormous impact and power, breaking down complicated systems into the simplest and most generally accessible elements, and hammering, hammering, hammering them into the heads of his audience until he took them captive."

Lenin, like most concentrated men, was extremely simple and well-disciplined in his habits. Vices like drinking certainly never allured him. We are told that he enjoyed chess and music and even occasionally such sports as skating and hunting; but all were given up because "they hindered his work." He was not morose or gloomy: Trotsky speaks of him as being positively gay on occasion, in a teasing and bantering kind of way. On the other hand, if he was crossed, he could get himself into a state of cold and ruthless fury.

Probably the most effective description of Lenin by a contemporary is that which has been given by an out-and-out admirer, the American reporter John Reed. This is how Reed describes his hero at one of the extreme crises of the revolution:

A short stocky figure with a big head set down on his shoulders, bald and bulging. Little eyes, a snubbish nose, wide generous mouth, and heavy chin; clean-shaven now, but already beginning to bristle with the well-known beard of his past and future. Dressed in shabby clothes, his trousers much too long for him. Unimpressive to be the idol of a mob, loved and revered as perhaps few leaders in history have been. A strange popular leader—a leader purely by virtue of intellect; colorless, humorless, uncompromising and detached, without picturesque idiosyncrasies —but with the power of explaining profound ideas in simple terms, of analysing a concrete situation. And combined with shrewdness, the greatest intellectual audacity.*

Vladimir Ilyich Ulyanov, to give him his real name, was of Russian-German extraction. He was born in 1870 at Simbirsk (now Ulyanovsk) of a Russian father who was a schoolteacher of physics and mathematics and a mother who was the daughter of a Russianized German family named Blank. Simbirsk, on the Volga, was a sleepy place of thirty thousand people living for the most part in wooden houses. No railway ran to this provincial backwater; travelers remembered it for its apple and cherry orchards, its nightingales, and for the fact that when the winter snow melted the river flooded over its banks.

Lenin was the third of seven children, one of whom died at birth, and he had a happy country boyhood. Certainly he never experienced poverty. His father rose steadily in his career until he became a provincial inspector and superintendent of schools, a rank that gave him the title of "Actual State Councilor," which was equivalent to Major-General in the army; he was addressed as "Excellency."

The Ulyanov children did well at school; Alexander, the eldest boy, won a gold medal, and Lenin, who was four years younger, soon followed suit. They were a religious, hard-working family, and none of the children received any revolutionary notions from their serious-minded parents. Alexander, we are told, had a liking for Dostoevsky and Lenin for Turgenev; there is no mention whatever of Marx. It was the year 1887 that set their new life in motion; that was the year when Alexander, who had gone up to Petrograd to continue his studies, took part in the students' plot against Czar Alexander III. It was a sad and terrible thing from every point of view. At the Petrograd University Alexander Ulyanov had become a blazing fanatic against Czardom—he never recanted or pleaded for mercy at his trial—and he and six fellow conspirators

* *Ten Days That Shook the World*, published 1919 by Boni & Liveright, 1926 by International Publishers.

were very young. They never threw their bomb (the police picked them up while some of them were carrying it down the Nevsky Prospekt), and it was perhaps an excess of severity that the Czar should not have given them another chance. He signed the warrant condemning young Ulyanov and four of the others to death, and they were hanged on May 20, 1887.

Józef Pilsudski, who was later to become the leader of the new Polish state, was also involved in the plot, and that in itself is enough to give this tragic incident an historic importance. But what we are concerned with here is the effect of it upon Lenin, who had just turned seventeen, and this apparently was considerable. From this moment he does not look back. He strikes out with absolute determination toward the revolutionary left, and never relaxes until his death. There is also a special aspect to all this: Lenin's father had died suddenly of cerebral hemorrhage in the previous year, and his mother had had to go up to Petrograd alone to plead for her son's life. None of the respectable neighbors in Simbirsk would accompany her; it was socially bad and even perhaps politically dangerous to be associated with a case of this sort. The widow sat through the court hearing, saw her son for the last time before he died, and when she returned home she and her family were to some extent socially ostracized. It seems not impossible that some of Lenin's black hatred and contempt for the property-owning classes, whether conservative or liberal, may have dated from this time.

At all events he plunged without delay into revolutionary activities at the University of Kazan on the Volga, where he had been sent to study law. Within three months of his entering the university he was involved in a students' protest meeting, was arrested and expelled. He went off to join his eldest sister Anna on their mother's country estate at Kukushkino, and later, on another property outside Samara, where he made a halfhearted attempt at managing a farm.

Through these years he read tremendously. In 1890, in response at last to his mother's petitions to the authorities, he was allowed to take up the study of law again in Petrograd. In twelve months' intensive work there he covered the four years' course in jurisprudence, and in the examinations of 1891 passed out on top. The following year finds him practicing law in Samara, and the year after that he is back in Petrograd again; and there he met Krupskaya, his future wife. They were both Marxists and followers of Plekhanov and the Social Democrats, both active among the workers in Petrograd, both children of reduced noble families. He was twenty-four and already growing bald. She was twenty-six, and in her strong, clear beautiful face there is a certain resemblance to Lenin's mother, though it is less marked by suffering and by patience. They were devoted to one another.

There exists a photograph taken about this time of Lenin surrounded by his closest friends. There they sit in the photographer's studio, potted palms and columns behind them, tassels on the chairs, their hair carefully brushed, and they look more like a university study group than a gang of revolutionaries. Lenin sits firmly in the center with a serious and professorial air.

However, his health was not good; he went down with pneumonia in 1895, and he was eager to get abroad partly to recuperate and partly to make contact with the Russian exiles whose writings he already knew so well. In the summer of 1895 the authorities finally allowed him to go, and for four months he toured France, Germany and Switzerland. His meeting with Plekhanov, Zasulich and Axelrod in Geneva does not appear to have been entirely successful—even at this early stage they seem to have had some doubts about a hard uncompromising streak in the young man—but they were delighted by his vigor and his intelligence. They accepted him as a disciple, and in early October he came back to Russia to continue his work in the underground. Russian police spies had noted Lenin's activities in Europe (as the brother of the notorious Alexander Ulyanov he had been on the police lists for years) but the customs officers appear not to have made any special examination of his baggage, nor to have discovered that one of his suitcases had a false bottom. It was filled with seditious literature.

There now began the flood tide of Lenin's revolutionary activities in Russia, the only sustained work he was to do inside the country until the last few years of his life. He formed the illegal League of Struggle for the Liberation of the Working Class. He traveled to Moscow and other centers. He wrote pamphlets and he helped to organize a strike. And in December, barely three months after his return, when he was on the point of publishing a revolutionary newspaper, he was arrested. He was given away by a dentist whom he had regarded as a colleague, but one feels that he could not have escaped the police much longer anyway. A strong tendency to recklessness—almost a desire to be persecuted—marks all the early revolutionaries. There must also have been a certain pleasure in the game of outwitting the police, in all the exciting business of false-bottom suitcases, of elaborate codes, of messages hidden in the spines of books, of certain significant letters in the books marked with dots, of conspiratorial names (Lenin was not Lenin as yet, but simply Vladimir Ilyich or Ulyanov), and of disappearing inks, like milk which, when dipped into tea and heated, reappeared in a brownish color.

Lenin was a great practitioner of these devices. He wrote to Axelrod in Geneva about this time: "You must write in Indian ink. It would be better if you were to add a small crystal of potassium bichromate ($K_2 Cr_2 O_7$); then it would not wash off. Use *thinner* paper." And again: "It is essential to use liquid paste; not more than a teaspoonful of starch to a glass of water (and moreover, potato flour, not ordinary flour which is too strong)." His first letter out of prison was directed to his landlady and it was in code.

Lenin took to life in the cells as only a monk, an ascetic and an avid reader of books can take to it. That is to say, he accepted it; he did not attempt to escape (in which he differs from so many of the other more physically active and emotionally impatient revolutionaries). His day was neatly portioned out: so many hours for reading one kind of book and so many hours for another; politics in the morning, fiction at night; so many hours for writing, for translation, for the study of languages, and (very important) regular periods of physical exercise. He found that the best way of getting warm in his icy cell was to prostrate himself fifty times, reaching his hands down to the floor as in religious prayer. He recalled later: "I was not in the least perturbed that the warder, on peeping through the little window, would wonder in amazement why this man had suddenly grown so pious when he had not once asked to visit the prison church."

Prison in any case was not too hard on political offenders in those days. He had access to the prison library and an abundant supply of books from outside. His mother and his sister Anna sent him food and winter clothing. He had no difficulty in smuggling out the revolutionary tracts that he wrote. He does not appear to have been discontented. After fourteen months—there was no question of a trial—he was informed that he had been sentenced to exile for a further three years in Siberia.

Exile in Siberia under the Czars was not nearly such a drastic tragedy as it has since become. If the prisoner had permission and the means to pay for his own passage he proceeded like a normal traveler to his destination. There were no guards; he simply reported to the authorities on his way and at the journey's end he set up his own household in the Siberian village to which he was assigned. He could not move about Siberia without permission, but within his own province he was more or less a free man. He could take jobs, get married, visit his friends, and the only prison walls were the vast distances which isolated him from the outer world. By the time Lenin arrived Siberia had become a training ground for the revolutionary intellectuals; almost all of them spent at least several years of their life there, and as a rule they profited very much from it. They had time to think and write and scheme. Usually their health improved (Siberia has not altogether a bad climate); and although they may not have actually welcomed the experience it provided them with a certain toughness for the struggle that lay ahead.

Lenin set off in February, 1897, and proceeded by train and horseback on a series of leisurely stages to the east. It was not until late March that he arrived in Krasnoyarsk, and there he waited another month for the ice to break up so that he could proceed by river steamer to the village of Shushenskoye, which had been assigned as his place of detention. It was a primitive community of fifteen hundred people, plagued by hordes of mosquitoes in the summer and shut in by snow and ice throughout the winter. The Sayan hills rose up in the distance. Here Lenin spent the next three years. He went out shooting a good deal—his letters are full of references to duck and snipe and the difficulty he had in getting a well-trained dog—and in the summer he bathed in the Yenisei River. He visited his friends who had been sent into exile in the neighboring towns. But most of all he worked. He translated Sidney and Beatrice Webb's *History of Trade Unionism*, he completed his own first major work, *The Development of Capitalism in Russia*, he wrote articles for socialist journals, and he kept up a steady correspondence with Plekhanov, Axelrod and other revolutionaries living abroad. More than ever books filled his life. Letter after letter went off to his mother and his sisters asking for parcels to be sent, and anything was acceptable: political tracts, dictionaries, grammars (he was advancing fast in his knowledge of English, German, French and Italian), histories, novels and philosophy. The dullest of statistics seemed to give him a special delight.

Early in 1898 Krupskaya was arrested in Petrograd and sentenced to three years' exile in Siberia. She arrived in May at Shushenskoye looking ill and worn but she found Lenin much plumper and sunburned. They were married soon afterward.

"At the beginning of my exile," Lenin wrote about this time, "I decided never to touch a map either of European Russia or even of Russia; it would mean too much bitterness as I looked at those various black spots. But it is not so bad now."

With only another year of his sentence to run he begins to look ahead. His letters abroad take on a sharper tone and he argues fiercely over the interpretation of Marx; and with two other exiles, Julius Martov and Alexander Potresov, he starts to make plans for the publication of *Iskra,* the new revolutionary paper which is to rally the Social Democratic party and unite all Marxists everywhere.

When in February, 1900, his exile came to an end he had to leave Krupskaya behind; she still had another year of her sentence to run, and with all his pent-up energy he threw himself into the *Iskra* plan. He settled first at Pskov near the Estonian border, and the others joined him there to organize agents for the distribution of the new paper. Through the spring and early summer Lenin traveled about Russia on this work (he was arrested when he made an illegal visit to Petrograd and was lucky to get off with a few days' imprisonment), and in July he found his way at last to Geneva.

There appears at first to have been some argument there. Plekhanov, Zasulich and Axelrod were now the old guard of Russian Marxism, and Lenin and his young friends did not always agree with them. Lenin in particular was against any revision, any sort of watering-down of the orthodox Marxist program. He did not want to waste too much time on such reforms as the eight-hour day; the revolution itself was his object and he wanted it to be controlled and organized by a small group of professionals at the top. These professionals in his view could never be elected democratically by the workers; they were to be self-appointed men, men who felt their vocation as a priest feels his vocation, and they were to have a priest's utter determination about their faith; any deviation from this faith was heresy. This clearly was a dictatorship of a kind, and the old guard did not altogether like it.*

In the end, however, a compromise was patched up: *Iskra* was to be edited by a board, with Plekhanov, Zasulich and Axelrod representing the old school, and Lenin, Martov and Potresov representing the younger group. Lenin saw to it that arrangements were made for the printing of the paper in Germany, where he himself proposed to live (partly, one feels, in order not to be too closely under Plekhanov's eye), and when Krupskaya joined him there she was made secretary of the enterprise. The underground organization in Russia, moreover, remained in Lenin's hands.

The funds for *Iskra* and the Social Democrats came from a number of different sources. It is known that two thousand rubles were provided by Alexandra Kalmykova, the owner of a bookshop in Petrograd and Lenin's publisher. The German Social Democrats may have contributed. And funds may have come from still another Russian in exile—Alexander Helphand. Helphand, who used the underground name of Parvus, is an odd and somewhat sinister figure in the Russian revolution, a two-sided figure. He had arrived in Germany in the 1890's, and he was embarked upon a successful career as a businessman and financier; one of his many ventures was a publishing house which translated and printed Maxim Gorky's works. The other side of him was the Marxist economist and writer who was very well in with the German socialists. In brief, he followed the ancient course of dining with the right and voting with the left, and he was everywhere. With his knowledge of German politics and his printing works he probably helped *Iskra* through its early difficulties, and he was rather on Lenin's side.

The first issue of the paper that came out in December, 1900, never reached Russia; it was seized at the border by the police, but after this the underground workers grew more efficient. Merchant seamen were found who were willing to smuggle copies aboard ships bound for Petrograd in the Baltic and Batum in the Black Sea; there was even a system by which the paper was bundled up in waterproof sheets and dumped overboard at prearranged points, and other routes were opened up through Austria, Egypt, and Persia.

---

* For a fuller discussion of the differences between Lenin and Plekhanov see Bertram Wolfe's *Three Who Made a Revolution.*

Eventually most of the copies got through. To the underground inside Russia *Iskra* had almost a mystical importance; here was the shining word of their leaders in exile abroad, the spark that would set fire to the revolution at last, and soon the contributors to the paper became famous names, Lenin's perhaps most of all. From the first he set out to build up a reputation around this "Lenin"* as a source of ideas and leadership. Rather grandly he used the third person in his articles: he would write, "As Lenin said in our last issue . . ." It was a technique the revolutionary world was soon going to know very well, the ex-cathedra pronouncement from on high. Lenin's pamphlet *What Is to Be Done?*, which was developed from his *Iskra* articles, had just the right note of quiet, persistent, infallible authority.

And now there began for the conspirators, especially Lenin and Krupskaya, a roaming rootless life which was to continue for the next seventeen years. They move from Munich to London, from Paris to Zurich, from Brussels to Cracow; and nearly always it is the same thing, the same backroom in some nondescript boarding-house, the same revolving haze of intellectual argument. Three knocks on the door are the sign that Comrade X or Y has arrived by the underground route from Russia bringing news, letters from party cells, and perhaps a little money. Trotsky recalled such an arrival in London in 1902. He reached the city in the middle of the night and took a horse cab to an address he had been given in Finsbury. His three knocks on the door brought Krupskaya running downstairs to let him in, and presently he found himself in the presence of the legendary Lenin of whom he had heard so much and whose articles he had so often read. Lenin was much taken with this young disciple—Trotsky was nine years younger—and would have got him on the editorial board of *Iskra* had Plekhanov permitted it. They used to go walking in the London streets, and Lenin pointed out the landmarks of the town: "That is *their* parliament house; that is *their* Westminster Cathedral." It took Trotsky a little time to realize that by "their" Lenin did not mean the British: he meant the capitalist class. With Lenin you had to get used

---

* Formerly he had used the pseudonym "Ilyin," which seems to have been a contraction of his real name, Vladimir Ilyich Ulyanov. "Lenin" may have come from "Ilyin."

to the idea of never relaxing, of never diverting your attention from
the great class struggle that lay ahead.

Lenin was often poor. Once during this period he was in agony
with shingles, and since they could not spare a guinea for an English
doctor Krupskaya sat up through the night painting him with iodine.
By day he went regularly to the Reading Room in the British
Museum. Wherever he happened to be, it was always some library
that was the focus of Lenin's life. Had he kept a diary it would
have read rather differently from the jottings of the Czar Nicholas in
Russia: "Wrote letters," he might have noted. "Walked to the
library. Read Adam Smith's *Wealth of Nations* and Locke. Walked
home." And then again more letters, more books.

He excited no comment, did nothing outwardly extraordinary,
passed nameless and unnoticed in the crowd. There is an apocryphal
story told in London of how, many years after the revolution had
come and gone, inquiries were made about Lenin at the Reading
Room of the British Museum. An elderly attendant there pondered
for a moment and then said: "A little man with a red beard? Bald,
shabbily dressed? A foreigner? Yes, of course I remember. Now I
wonder what ever became of him." The story could be true. Outwardly at least Lenin was as unremarkable as that.

His tigerishness, his unrelenting concentration, was directed
through these days upon the coming Social Democratic congress in
Brussels. Like Plekhanov, he saw here the first really vital crisis of
the party, the crossroads at which its future direction would be
decided; and he was quite determined that his own will was going
to prevail. When in April, 1903, just prior to the Congress, Lenin
moved down to Geneva from London, he was approaching an open
breach with Plekhanov. He radically edited Plekhanov's draft for a
party program which was to be presented to the congress and produced one of his own which was less elegant but more practical.
Meanwhile, with the help of Krupskaya, who had now become a
kind of chief-of-staff for the Social Democratic party, he went pains-
takingly through the list of delegates, ensuring that as far as possible
his own followers would be sent. All this was the work of many
months and much patient argument.

When finally the congress assembled at Brussels in July, 1903,
some sixty delegates were present, and some of them had been

hanging about for weeks waiting for the proceedings to begin. They were a remarkable collection: a minority group who had contrived to make their way out of Russia through the underground, three or four workmen, the rest chiefly intellectuals gathered from the émigré colonies scattered through Europe. The meeting was supposed to be secret, but nearly sixty exuberant Russians, shouting and arguing through the day and night, were not easily disguised, and soon all Brussels knew about them. The congress opened at last on July 30 in a flour warehouse draped in red cloth, with Belgian police prowling round the alleyways outside. The weather was hot. Plekhanov took the chair and made the opening speech, and he had with him on the platform Lenin and another of the *Iskra* group. Almost at once quarrels broke out, and they were carried to such a pitch that by the end of the first week in August the Belgian police had had enough; they ordered a section of the delegates to leave the country within twenty-four hours. At this the whole congress left in a body for England, arguing fiercely on the boat all the way over, and from August 11 to August 23 they continued the meeting in London.

In the endless cross-currents of debate there was, as Lenin had foreseen, just one central issue: was the party to organize itself as a democracy which anyone could join, or as a small dictatorship? Was everyone to share the power and have a hand at policy making, or was the control to be given to one central committee?

Lenin himself was in no doubt whatever; he wanted the *Iskra* group to have control and he himself wanted to control *Iskra*. He is described as being beside himself through these days. He barely slept or ate; he was in a rage to have his way. When early on he saw that there was no chance of rallying the whole congress to his views, and the vote actually went against him, he set himself quite deliberately to split the party in two. His tactics in building up his own faction had at least a certain ruthless clarity about them. He contrived to lock opponents out of committee meetings, he lobbied tirelessly among waverers, and finally he so angered the important group known as the Jewish Bund its members walked out of the congress. Then, seizing his chance very quickly, he got a majority vote of two. This was an historic moment for the party, and for Russia, since Lenin at once proclaimed that he and his followers were the majorityites—Bolsheviks—and his opponents the minorityites—the

Mensheviks. It was a distinction which was hardly true at the time and still less true when he was outvoted later on.

However, in the last days of the congress he succeeded in forcing through a series of vital decisions; the party's constitution was written in such a way that the editors of *Iskra* were able also to control the central committee of the party inside Russia. As for the *Iskra* editorial board itself, Plekhanov was the only representative of the old guard on it to survive. The new board was to consist of just three people: Lenin, Martov and Plekhanov.

And so finally in the last week of August, 1903, when the Czar was wandering into war against Japan, this congress, which had taken two and a half years to prepare, and was designed to unify them all, broke up in sheer exhaustion, its members utterly divided. Inevitably within a matter of months Lenin's artificial victory came to nothing, and the reaction against him was astonishingly intense. Trotsky, the brightest of his disciples, abandoned him and became if not an outright Menshevik at least a camp follower in that direction. Martov, Lenin's closest friend, refused flatly to serve on the *Iskra* board, and soon Plekhanov felt strong enough to insist that both Axelrod and Vera Zasulich must be brought back onto the paper. Even in Russia Lenin's following began to fail, since many of the rank and file of the party were disgusted at his tactics at the conference; and before long his funds began to dry up. No doubt too he began at this time to suffer from the besetting malaise of all political exiles, the feeling of rootlessness, of futility, of being out of touch.

Lenin, an expert in the arts of retiring in order to fight better on another day, accepted defeat, or at any rate he gave the appearance of doing so. He resigned from *Iskra* and his other offices in the party and went walking with Krupskaya in the mountains of Switzerland.

The year 1904 slipped by with Lenin utterly absorbed in his quarrel with the Mensheviks. The Japanese attack on Port Arthur on February 8 occurs and he scarcely lifts his head to observe it. On July 28 Plehve, the ruler of Russia under the Czar, is assassinated and he takes no notice. On January 1, 1905, Port Arthur falls, but beyond noting with approval that the "progressive Japanese" are doing well he is not interested.

The Japanese were very active in attempting to provoke a revolution in Russia during this period, and they were in touch with most of the revolutionary leaders, Lenin included. It was a devious business, and it was handled with great determination and skill by a Colonel Motoziro Akashi. Akashi turned up in Stockholm early in 1904 as a Japanese military attaché, and he made contact there with a wealthy Finnish agitator of strong anti-Czarist views named Konni Zilliacus. Between them these two produced a grandiose plan which aimed not only at running munitions into Russia but also at rallying and financing the anti-Czarist movement everywhere. They worked so persistently that by October, 1904, they succeeded in convening a meeting of thirty revolutionary leaders in Paris, and a plan of sabotage and corruption inside Russia was agreed upon. The Japanese found the money, and at one time or another, consciously or unconsciously, the most heterogeneous people were inclined to support them: respectable Russian liberals like Milyukov and Shipov, Frenchmen like Georges Clemenceau, Anatole France and Jean Jaurès, American sympathizers like Mrs. Ella Hall, a wealthy widow who assisted the gun running with her yacht, and most of the leading Social Democrats.

Lenin's part is obscure. It is known, however, that he obtained money at this time, for in December, 1904, he was able to finance his new newspaper *Vperyed* (*Forward*), which was to be a counterblast to *Iskra*. He himself was the editor, and he had one clear policy in view: to defeat the Mensheviks and win back control of the party. The revolution itself (and certainly the Japanese interest in it) was almost a secondary affair.

Vperyed, as with all Lenin's propaganda activities, was a success from the start, and he soon began to gather a new and powerful group of adherents around him: Anatole Lunacharsky, an atheist who believed in the religion of man, Meyer Wallach, who was known as Maxim Litvinov, A. I. Rykov, who later was to be one of the leaders of the Soviet Council of People's Commissars, and the philosopher-economist A. A. Bogdanov.

All these rallied to *Vperyed,* and Lenin was engrossed in his new campaign to split the Social Democrat party when suddenly and unexpectedly there arrived news from Russia that was to change not only his but everybody's life: the Japanese war had created a crisis in Petrograd. The revolution had broken out.

Now finally the time had come for the Czar and the underground to meet in the open.

CHAPTER FOUR

The Rising of 1905

TRADITIONALLY revolutions followed wars in Russia. The liberation of the serfs had been made inevitable by the Crimean War in the middle of the nineteenth century; the assassination of Alexander II was the sequel to the war against Turkey in 1877; and now the Japanese war had precipitated the most serious revolution the country had ever experienced. By the beginning of 1905 Nicholas was in much more danger from his own people than from the foreign enemy in the east. Eleven months of unsuccessful campaigning had broken the morale of the Russian army, and in the cities civilians were sick of working at pressure and in miserable conditions for a war they did not support or understand.

Both the police and the more solid section of the bourgeois community saw the trouble coming, and each in its own way tried to head it off. Through the closing months of 1904 many of the leading businessmen in Moscow joined forces with the liberal politicians—the intellectuals in the universities, the zemstvo officials, and the professional classes—and they held meeting after meeting to urge reforms on the government, only to be met with a blank uncompromising no. The zemstvos, the Czar repeated, must mind their own business; autocracy was to remain inviolate. He indicated, however, that he himself had plans for certain new political laws which he would introduce in his own good time. It was a promise of a sort but something more than promises was needed.

51

The Ministry of the Interior, on its side, was trying to meet the emergency by other methods. As far back as 1901, S. V. Zubatov, a chief of the Moscow Okhrana, the secret police, had hit on the idea of the principle of the safety valve as a means of preventing unrest. He formed a government-sponsored union, the Society for Mutual Aid for Working Men in the Mechanical Industries. It encouraged the workers to air their grievances, to set forth their demands for higher pay and a shorter working day, but at the same time the police took good care to ensure that the meetings were conducted in an atmosphere of reverence and loyalty toward the Czar. There was also a religious side to the proceedings. The psychology behind the scheme was very well expressed by General D. F. Trepov, chief of the Moscow police: "In order to disarm the agitators," he wrote, "it is necessary to open and point out to the worker a legal solution of his difficulty, for we must bear in mind the agitator will be followed by the youngest and boldest of the crowd, while the average worker will prefer the less spectacular and quiet legal way. Thus split up, the crowd will lose its power."

And it had almost worked. Police socialism was tried in a number of different areas, and soon there were official unions in all the main industries. But now at the end of 1904, under the pressure of war, the system was rapidly breaking down. With every week that went by it was becoming apparent to the workers that they were simply wasting their breath in concocting pious petitions that never received an answer from the authorities: they needed direct action and a leader. And they found both in an Orthodox priest named Father Georgi Gapon.

Gapon is an odd figure in the Russian revolution. He was one of those dedicated minor characters with a zeal for remaking the world who would have done very well had he been allowed to continue in a small way. It was his fate, however, to be catapulted into the center of national affairs which were quite beyond his range; he flew too high, and because his motives were so good his subsequent disillusionment was devastating. He is a little like Icarus and he is heroically absurd. Gapon came from a peasant family in the Ukraine, and as a young man he had been much moved by Tolstoy's conception of nonviolence and of a mild and loving anarchy as the solution for the problems of the world. He had entered the Orthodox Church, but he was really more of a social reformer than a priest. He abhorred drinking and gambling, and lectured the workers strongly about vice—he was an effective orator —and while he agitated for better conditions in the factories he also reminded his followers of their religion and their duty to the Czar. If Father Gapon had had a political slogan it might have been "God Save the Czar and the Eight-Hour Day." In 1905 he was a striking-looking man of thirty-two, with a pointed black beard and a thin and holy face, and he had become a popular idol. His Union of Russian Factory Workers was a national movement.

The police were not at all opposed to Father Gapon: with his piety and his nonviolent notions for reform he was just the man they wanted. They supported him; they regarded him as one of their agents and they do not seem to have been disturbed by the fact that he was also in touch with Maxim Gorky and other leaders with revolutionary ideas. This was the man who set the 1905 revolution alight.

Early in January the Petrograd metal workers came out on a four-day strike, and when this had no effect Gapon decided to adopt more forceful tactics:

On January 21 he wrote to the Czar:

Sire!

Do not believe the Ministers. They are cheating Thee in regard to the real state of affairs. The people believe in Thee. They have made up their minds to gather at the Winter Palace tomorrow at 2 p.m. to lay their needs before Thee. . . . Do not fear anything. Stand tomorrow before the people and accept our humblest petition. I, the representative of the workingmen, and my comrades, guarantee the inviolability of Thy person.

                                                            Gapon

This was not just another simple petition from the moujiks. Gapon had a tremendous following in the huge Putilov workshops in Petrograd, and he really did have the power to lead a mass demonstration into the streets. Whether or not he could control it was another matter, and the Ministry of the Interior was in a difficult position. The man they had promoted had got altogether too big for them, too far to the left, and on the night of January 21 it began to look as though there might be serious rioting in the city. Already two days previously a sinister incident had occurred during the Epiphany ceremony; the customary salute of guns had been fired from the fortress of St. Peter and St. Paul but at least one of the shells was live and it had landed near the Winter Palace. This may have been simple negligence on the part of the gunners, but no one could be quite sure; and now it was decided to head off the demonstration by putting Gapon under arrest. Gapon, however, could not be found, and nothing then remained to be done but to bring as many police and soldiers as possible into the city, and to wait and see what the next day would bring forth.

Meanwhile Nicholas had left Petrograd. If he got Gapon's letter he did not answer it, and in any case he never had the slightest intention of receiving a mob of demonstrators at the palace. He packed up his family and moved to Tsarskoe Selo, fifteen miles outside the city. He never again returned to live in Petrograd.

At the appointed time on January 22, some 200,000 men, women and children gathered on the snowbound streets, carrying ikons and pictures of the Czar, and with Father Gapon at their head converged on the Winter Palace. They sang "God Save the Czar" as they moved along. Gapon carried in his hand their petition for an eight-hour day, a minimum wage of one ruble a day (about fifty cents), no overtime and a constituent assembly; and this he hoped to hand personally to the Czar while the crowd waited in the snow outside the palace.

When Peter the Great built Petrograd he paid careful attention to the question of its defense. Broad boulevards like the spokes of a wheel reach in to the Admiralty Building and the Winter Palace on the banks of the Neva, and consequently both these strongholds have a clear line of fire along the main arteries of the city. Such a street plan also made it possible for parades and political demonstrations to be seen to their best advantage, and this vast crowd of hymn-singing, ikon-bearing workers must have looked very impressive as it debouched in five separate columns onto the great square before the Winter Palace. It might also have looked rather threatening.

At all events, something like panic seems to have seized on the military officers who had been left by the Czar to deal with the situation, and they called on the marchers to stop and disperse. But you could not break up a crowd of this size very easily; the workers were in an exalted state of mind and they were convinced that they had only to reach the Czar for their case to be understood. When they came on again the soldiers of the palace guard opened fire. They fired from a distance of only ten or twenty yards straight into the screaming, struggling mass of people, and there was horrible carnage; more than five hundred were killed and several thousand wounded. Afterward the thing that the survivors remembered so well was the red blood on the snow, and from now on it was rubbish for Nicholas to indulge himself in the sentimental idea that he was really loved by his simplest and humblest subjects; they remembered this Bloody Sunday and the bodies lying in the streets of Petrograd.

Nicholas no doubt was appalled at what had happened, and there was an attempt to make amends; he contributed to the fund raised for the families of the dead and wounded men, and later on he did receive a hand-picked deputation of workers—but none of this made much impression. After Bloody Sunday there was a steadily rising crescendo of strikes, demonstrations, disorders and open terrorism. On February 17 the Grand Duke Serge Alexandrovich, the Governor of Moscow, was assassinated outside the Kremlin; and by the end of the year more than fifteen hundred government officials had been killed.

Father Gapon escaped arrest after Bloody Sunday by fleeing across the border to Finland, whence he addressed a bitter letter to Nicholas: "The innocent blood of workers, their wives and children, lies forever between thee, oh soul destroyer, and the Russian people. Moral connection between thee and them may never more be. . . . Let all the blood that has to be shed, hangman, fall upon thee and thy kindred!"

Bloody Sunday had turned Gapon into a revolutionary if not an outright terrorist, and his first act on arriving in Switzerland (where he was greeted as a hero) was to call on the embattled political exiles. He urged them to sink their differences and unite in raising an immediate rebellion in Russia; and he might just as well have been baying at the moon. Both Plekhanov and the Mensheviks and Lenin and the Bolsheviks were busy with plans for holding rival party conferences in Europe, and neither was disposed to move.

Trotsky, however, saw things differently; he set out at once for Petrograd.

In the annals of the Russian underground 1905 must certainly be judged to be Trotsky's year. He rises above all the others; he assesses what is happening more accurately than they do; he emerges from the party rivalry; he is the intellectual who is also the man of action.

Trotsky was one of the youngest of the exiles (he was twenty-six at this time), but he had suffered and experienced as much as any of them. He was the son of a well-to-do Jewish peasant farmer, and he had grown up on the steppes. He had not reached twenty when he had been arrested in Odessa, and he had spent two and a half years in Russian prisons before being exiled to eastern Siberia. Unlike Lenin, he was an escaper, and the fact that he had married and had two daughters had not deterred him. His wife had rigged up a dummy in his bed, and while she staved off the police for four days, saying he was too ill to be disturbed, he made his way back to Russia with a false passport. He had now abandoned his real name, Lev Davidovich Bronstein, and with his own peculiar brand of irony had adopted the pseudonym Trotsky, which was the name of one of his jailers in Odessa. No one had been more active in the Russian underground. He had organized revolutionary cells, he had written for *Iskra*, and finally in a peasant cart he had smuggled himself out of Russia into Western Europe.

It had been a tremendous thing for young Trotsky to meet his heroes, Plekhanov, Axelrod and Lenin, to learn from them and take orders from them; but now that they were sunk in their arid intellectual brawl he left them behind in Europe and became the effective leader of the party inside Russia itself.

Trotsky reached Petrograd in the spring of 1905 by way of Kiev to find that the situation had not quite ripened into crisis, and the Czar's police soon hunted him across the border into Finland. (Finland was an invaluable haven for the revolutionaries; although nominally part of the Russian empire the country had its own government, and its rights were not often violated by the Czar. Here safely over the frontier, only twenty miles from Petrograd, the revolutionaries could keep in close touch with the underground inside the city.) Soon Parvus arrived from Germany and joined Trotsky in hiding, and together the two men made their plans while they watched and waited for events to come to a climax.

The crushing Russian naval defeat at Tsushima on May 27 was the first of a chain of explosions; within a month the sailors on the battleship *Prince Potemkin* had risen in rebellion. For a few days they terrorized the Black Sea, until at length they sailed on to the Rumanian coast and were interned. Almost at once there were nationalistic risings in Poland, the Baltic States and the Caucasus, and everywhere throughout Russia itself there were reports of the looting and burning of farmhouses by the peasants. Jewish pogroms, inspired and perhaps organized by the authorities (the Jews were widely thought to be responsible for the revolutionary disorders), added to the confusion. In September, when the humiliating peace with the Japanese was signed and the disillusioned and semi-mutinous soldiers were drifting back from the east, the unrest spread into the cities. The trouble began in Moscow with a fairly innocuous dispute in the printing trade over whether or not the printers on piecework should be paid for punctuation marks. This "comma strike" brought the workers in other trades out in sympathy, and all at once the railways were engulfed. It was almost as if Russia had been waiting for this signal; all kinds of improbable people now came forward to demonstrate against the government. The corps de ballet in Petrograd went on strike. Employers who had their own reasons for a showdown handed out strike pay to their men. In Petrograd there were no newspapers, no streetcars, no telegraph or postal services, and no bakers willing to bake bread. Overnight revolutionary posters appeared on the streets, and crowds came out to demonstrate with ominous red banners. Lawyers refused to transact business; banks closed down. Almost the entire adult population of the capital stopped work; it was one of the most complete general strikes in history.

The exiles abroad had by now begun to stir themselves at last. Lenin had been studying textbooks on street fighting in the Geneva libraries, and he sent a stream of instructions to his followers in Russia. "I see with real horror," he wrote, "that we have been talking bombs for more than half a year and not one single one has been made"; he went on to give some forceful advice on the use of "rifles, revolvers, bombs, knives, brass knuckles, clubs, rags soaked in oil to start fires with, rope or rope ladders, shovels for building barricades, dynamite cartridges, barbed wire, tacks against cavalry. . . ." Funds could be raised, he suggested, by breaking into the banks, and he gave details of how old men, women and children could play their part in the struggle.

Meanwhile the practical business of gun running was taken over by Father Gapon, Litvinov and others who appear to have been supplied with money by the Japanese and wealthy sympathizers in the United States and elsewhere.* The incident of the *John Grafton* is a lurid example of the excitement that was now besetting all their minds. Litvinov managed to buy a considerable quantity of arms in Europe by posing alternatively as a South American officer and as an agent for outlaw bands in Macedonia; according to one account he secured four thousand bayonets, five thousand pistols, ten thousand rifles and over four million rounds of ammunition. The *John Grafton,* a British boat of seven hundred tons, was chartered to run the consignment into Russia through the Baltic, and in late July she set sail. However, as it so often happened in these affairs, the Czar's agents knew all about her, and she was intercepted by the Russian warship *Asia* in Finnish waters and forced to run herself aground. The arms were seized, but some devious business with the captain of the *Asia* followed, and in return for a heavy bribe he was induced to hand his booty back to the revolutionaries. Some of it was used in the Moscow street fighting before the end of the year.

In the midst of all this two events of great importance took place in Russia. In Moscow Paul Milyukov, a distinguished historian, and Dmitri Shipov, the chairman of the city zemstvo, succeeded in rallying the more progressive liberals into a coherent political party which emerged finally with the name of the Constitutional Democratic party—usually shortened to the Cadets. The Cadets were semirevolutionary and nonsocialist: they wanted a democracy and a parliament along British lines, and as a means of forcing the Czar to grant a constitution they gave their support to the strike. From now onward the Cadets become one of the three main parties dominating the political scene. They stand well to the right of the

---

* There was a good deal of support for the revolution in America. "If such a government cannot be overthrown otherwise than by dynamite," Mark Twain wrote, "then thank God for dynamite."

Marxist Social Democrats (now divided into Bolsheviks and Mensheviks), and the Social Revolutionary party, the party of the peasants, but for the moment their main opponent is the Czar.

The other event concerns Trotsky. Directly the strike got under way in October, 1905, he came back secretly to Petrograd and joined in the work of organizing a general strike committee which was to act as a headquarters for the workers. Delegates, each representing five hundred men, were elected in the factories and sent to a central council or Soviet, and this Soviet now controlled the strike in Petrograd. It distributed arms and supplies, took charge of policy, issued its orders in the form of printed bulletins, arranged for guards and demonstrations, and acted, in fact, in much the same way as an army headquarters acts in the field. The idea of a Soviet was not new—Axelrod and others had canvassed it some time before—but this was the first actual experiment in giving the workers a central direction in an emergency, and although it only lasted a few weeks it set a pattern which was to be followed in 1917.

A similar body was set up in Moscow, but the Petrograd Soviet was the important one, and it was very largely controlled by the Mensheviks. Its first two presidents, Zubrovsky and Khrustalev-Nosar, followed more or less along the Menshevik line, and Trotsky shared the practical leadership with Parvus. The Bolsheviks in Petrograd tried at first to boycott the Soviet—Lenin, whether at home or abroad, had no love for any organization which he could not control—but finally they came in when they saw which way the wind was blowing.

And indeed it was blowing too hard for the Czar. In the summer he had made a few tentative concessions in an effort to ward off the storm; he had given the universities, for example, freedom from state control; but still the opposition mounted, and now all Russia appeared to be united against him. His first instinct had been to call out the military to crush the strike, but at the end of October, with the industrial life of the country virtually at a standstill, events had gone too far for that. He gave way: under Witte's guidance he issued a manifesto which granted to Russia the first "constitution" in its history.

The October Manifesto was a cautious and anemic document. It authorized the setting up of an elected parliament, a Duma, but the Czar was still to be the supreme ruler. When later the terms of the new constitution were announced it was found that Nicholas still retained direct control of the army and navy, of foreign policy and of the Ministry of the Interior. Legislative power was divided between the Duma and an Imperial Council, half of whose members were to be appointed by the Czar. The government could also issue decrees when the Duma was not in session. This obviously was only a step toward democracy, yet even so it was a considerable break with the principle of autocracy, and it went a long way toward satisfying Milyukov and the Cadets. It did even more than that: it broke the strike. Directly the manifesto was published the Cadets withdrew their support of the Soviets, since they were not interested in the wider aims of the revolutionaries, and the government gradually began to get control of the situation again.

There were still some tense moments. No sooner was a mutiny at the Kronstadt naval base suppressed than trouble blew up again in the Black Sea. The hero of this adventure was a Lieutenant Schmidt, and he had a certain dizzy success for a day or two. Schmidt led a mutiny among the sailors in Sevastopol; he seized the cruiser *Ochakov*, ran up the red flag and signaled to Nicholas: "I assume command of the fleet. Schmidt." It was not altogether absurd; very soon the mutiny spread along the docks, and to eleven other vessels as well, and it was not until the mutineers were defeated in a naval engagement that they gave in. Schmidt was executed. Other revolts among the garrisons in Vladivostok, Kiev, Voronezh and Chita were subdued more easily.

Nicholas now was in a position to move against the Soviet in Petrograd. On December 9 its president, Khrustalev-Nosar, was arrested, and Trotsky took over. He contemplated calling for an armed rising in the city, but in the end settled for a scheme put forward by Parvus: the workers were asked to refuse to pay taxes and to start a run on the banks. They were to withdraw their savings and demand payment in gold. It was an effective stroke; under this pressure the government agreed to some, at least, of the workers' further demands.

Lenin and Krupskaya now belatedly came winging back from abroad, along with Father Gapon and one or two other leaders of the Social Democrats. But already they were too late. Petrograd had grown tired of disturbances, and the Soviet's second call for a general strike on December 16 came to nothing. By now Trotsky was under arrest, and presently Parvus and most of the Soviet deputies followed him into jail.

Moscow struggled on for a little longer. Financed by revolutionary funds and encouraged by Lenin the workers put up a bitter fight in the icy streets at the end of December, but the army turned its artillery onto the strikers and they were driven off their barricades. By the last day of the year the country was subsiding fast into an uneasy and apprehensive peace.

It had been a tumultuous year that had taken everybody by surprise, and it left the revolutionaries rather worse off than they were before. Lenin visited Moscow and hung on for a few months into 1906, but in the end he was forced to leave for Finland and he narrowly escaped arrest. Plekhanov never set out for Russia at all, and Axelrod and Martov turned back when the strike collapsed. Out of the 300 members of the Petrograd Soviet who were arrested, 284 were eventually released. Trotsky and Parvus, however, were detained, and after many months in prison were sent into indefinite exile in the coldest and remotest corner of Siberia. Father Gapon drifted abroad, only to end his days as a police agent and a sort of lobbyist of the revolution. In 1906 he was murdered in Finland.

Practically the only advantage the revolutionary movement could claim from its brief twelve months' career in the light of day was that it had been able to close its ranks in an emergency, and Trotsky was very largely responsible for this. The rank and file had not liked the split between the Bolsheviks and the Mensheviks, nor the quarrels that divided the Social Democrats from the Social Revolutionaries; they wanted the whole movement to combine, and in this Trotsky had been their leader.

There was another, more subtle effect which also made this 1905 uprising a dress rehearsal for 1917; the Soviet, or at any rate the Menshevik part of it, had had for a few short weeks a potent whiff of power, and they were left with a feeling that they were not yet capable of handling it. It had been too confusing and bewildering. They needed more trained men before they could launch the Dark People into government. The obvious course, the Mensheviks felt, was to move more slowly; to bring in first a liberal bourgeois government of the Cadets before they advanced directly upon Marxist socialism. This was a matter that was going to keep the revolutionaries safely divided for many years to come: the years when they subsided once more into the underground.

As for Nicholas, he appears to have survived the upheavals of 1905 with remarkable aplomb. Nothing that had happened had in any way changed his views or weakened his faith in autocracy. In a crisis he had been forced to make concessions. But now the crisis was passed. He went forward into the new year quite determined to take back, at the earliest suitable opportunity, as much as he could of the power that he had been so roughly obliged to give away.

CHAPTER FIVE

The Trial of Democracy

THE NEXT eight years in Russia, 1906 to 1914, have become overshadowed by the First World War and the Bolshevik revolution, and so to a certain extent they have been neglected and forgotten. And yet in many ways this period is one of the most vital in Russian history. The country was more prosperous than it had ever been before; the budget was balanced and even showed a surplus; the vast railways network was expanded at a greater rate than any subsequent Communist government has been able to achieve, private trade was booming, and from all over the Western world firms like International Harvester and the Singer Sewing Machine Company began to set up their own establishments in Russia. Then too, these were years of good harvests, and the heavy industries like mining broke all records in production. After 1906 both strikes and terrorist activities steadily diminished, and by 1911 the revolutionary movement was virtually at a standstill.

There was another aspect that was still more important: for the first time democracy was given a trial in Russia. Judged by Western standards it was a bumbling and erratic sort of democracy, yet the experiment was made, and the fact that it ended in revolution is no reason for thinking that it was bound to fail. It might very well have succeeded. Its struggle against the enormous backwardness of Russia was never entirely hopeless, and at least it demonstrated beyond all doubt that the Russians like any other people can be governed by other means than those of the police state.

It would be absurd, of course, to pretend that this was some kind of a golden age in Russia—both workers and peasants were still living in conditions that would not be tolerated for ten minutes in a modern democracy, real freedom of the individual was still a dream, and the Czarist bureaucracy still lay on the country with its old leaden weight—yet it was a bright chapter, the best there had ever been. Perhaps the most telling evidence of this is that Lenin himself gave up hope. More than once at this time he used the phrase: "I do not expect to see the revolution."

One could draw a simple graph to illustrate these years. It would show two lines, one representing the fortunes of the Russian government, and the other of the revolutionaries, and as the one line went up so the other would go down. After 1906 the government's reputation rises steadily until it reaches its peak with the prime ministership of Peter Stolypin in 1909; and thereafter it falls again (with a short recovery in 1914 and early 1915) into the final and fatal chaos of the war; and this is the point where the revolutionary movement emerges from the depths and breaks through permanently into the open.

It is the Duma, Russia's first parliament, which is the touchstone of these events, and in the whole Russian tragedy there is nothing sadder or grimmer than the way in which this one white hope of the situation was sabotaged and beset from every side, dragged down by the very people it was designed to save. There were even occasions when the Duma deputies themselves seemed to have been intent upon their own destruction.

Yet it would be unfair to judge the Duma in the light of present-day parliaments established in the West. The Duma was only just beginning, it was emerging almost at a bound from the feudalism of the past, and the new deputies had to find their way with no experience to guide them. They had enemies on every side: Nicholas and the court, who loathed the whole idea, the revolutionary parties, most of whom boycotted the elections, and the bureaucracy, which would have preferred to go on running the country in its own autocratic way without criticism or interference.

It might have been judged an impossible situation; a Czar at the top who is determined to keep as much of his power as possible; beneath him a subservient council of ministers, men of the Czar's own choosing holding all the key posts. And now this new untried undisciplined body of amateurs clamoring to get their share of the government.

All this was bad enough, but Nicholas made matters a good deal worse by dismissing Witte from the presidency of the council of ministers on the eve of the Duma's first meeting. He had never liked Witte; he regarded him as a rival and he could not forgive him for forcing the creation of the Duma in the first place. He waited just long enough for Witte to extract a huge loan from France—it was the equivalent of $400 million—and then he had him out. Witte, one feels, might at least have made an effort to work with the Duma, but his successor as president of the Council, an aging bureaucrat named I. L. Goremykin, proposed to do nothing of the kind. Nobody to the left of the Czar, which is to say practically the whole Russian nation, seems to have had a good word to say about Goremykin. He is described as insignificant, wily, cynical and sycophantic, and the last adjective is certainly not unfair, for the new president held very strongly to the view that the Czar was always right, and that the ministers, whatever their private views might be, were simply there to interpret his will.

The Duma which assembled for the first time in the Tauride Palace in Petrograd in May, 1906, was not at all a revolutionary body. The Cadets, with more than 150 seats, were by far the largest party, and in both appearance and ideas they bore some resemblance to the respectable frock-coated liberals of Gladstonian England, an England which, incidentally, they admired very much and were determined, if they could, to re-create in Russia. The next largest party was an offshoot of the Social Revolutionaries, a labor group known as the Trudoviks, with over a hundred seats, and although it represented the working classes and the peasants it was not absolutely hostile to the Czar. The elections in fact had been a creditable event; neither crackpots nor extremists had swept the poll; the electors really had tried to return the ablest and most serious candidates, men of the kind who had been running the local zemstvos.

The proceedings opened with an "Address to the Throne" on the lines of English tradition. In it the Duma asked for a series of reforms which in any democracy would have been regarded as no more than reasonable. There was a short silence from the throne, and when Nicholas did decide to answer he did not appear himself. He sent Goremykin down to the Tauride Palace and Goremykin announced flatly that the Duma's demands—especially the demand dealing with land reform—were, quite simply, "inadmissible." Upon this the Duma passed a vote of censure on the government.

"So far," writes Bernard Pares, the historian of this period who was also an eyewitness there, "everything had proceeded on the English model, and after the vote of censure presumably the Government [i.e., Goremykin and the council of ministers] ought to resign. It did not do so, and the Government and the Duma sat looking at one another, each wondering what step it dared to take, and what support it would receive from the country."

As far as the Duma was concerned this was a losing game, since they were bound to make some sort of move to justify their existence; and the only move that was open to them was to go on making angry speeches against the government. Nicholas stood it for two months, and then put a stop to all further argument by declaring that the Duma was dissolved. He did this by surrounding the Tauride Palace with troops, and when the deputies arrived there on July 22 they found the doors bolted and barred against them.

There was an outcry: a number of Cadets and Trudoviks decamped across the border to Finland and issued the "Vyborg Manifesto," an appeal to the public to defy the government by refusing to pay their taxes or to serve in the army. But it was not an outcry which could expect much response; the events of 1905 were too recent and the famous Russian lethargy had taken possession of the masses again.

And so, at this earliest moment of the experiment in democracy, a pattern is set, and it is to be repeated again and again through the next ten years. The Czar's council of ministers struggles along until it feels it must get popular support, and it calls the Duma together again. It works with the Duma for a little while—and the elections are so rigged that the deputies as far as possible are chosen from the right-wing parties—only to discover that the deputies are still intractable; however right-wing the rightest of them are, they still find the Czar and his council perched far away on the distant peak of autocracy. And so the Duma is dissolved, or silenced, or ignored, and exasperation festers everywhere.

There is however one brief and important respite from this dismal round; Nicholas soon found that Goremykin was altogether unequal to his job, and Stolypin was put in his place. Peter Stolypin was no blind lover of the Duma—he allowed a second election of deputies to take place and then quickly got rid of them—but he saw that it was folly to crush the Duma entirely. The sensible thing was to manage it, to find ways of working with the more sober parties while at the same time putting through his own program of reform.

Stolypin was a remarkable man, the best Prime Minister Russia ever had. The thing that is chiefly remembered about him by his contemporaries is his directness; he came from the provinces, and he brought a fresh country air into the sophisticated and antiquated atmosphere of Petrograd. Even the Czar was impressed at first. "I cannot tell you," he wrote to his mother, "how much I have come to like and respect this man." Bernard Pares, who knew Stolypin, says he "had none of the ambiguities of promoted bureaucrats. It was the first time that the cabinet had, not a mere chairman like Goremykin, or a dictator like Witte, but a real leader." Izvolsky (the Foreign Minister) describes him as "gifted with a very clear and healthy turn of mind."

Moreover the new premier looked the part. He was large, black-bearded, a direct looker-in-the-eye, and there was something reassuring and very sensible in his manner. Also he was brave. During the 1905 disorders he had been in charge of the most difficult of all the Russian provinces, Saratov, and he handled it coolly and well. Neither the bombs nor the bullets could shake him—and one of them was to injure his daughter for life. It was the sort of personal bravery that makes for ruthlessness; almost his first act on gaining power was to set up a number of tribunals which sentenced to death every terrorist he could lay hands on. After that rough start he opposed every effort of the Czar to suppress the Duma entirely, and embarked resolutely on his program of agrarian reform which was to become the chief monument to his career.

It was an admirable scheme and it was desperately wanted. Briefly, his plan was to make it possible for the peasants to own their land outright, instead of sharing it with others on a communal basis. Immediately there was an improvement; men began to take a pride in their farms and worked hard to buy more land and to increase the yield. In other words, Stolypin set up a new class of peasant landowners, and he was lucky enough to get the scheme off to a good start with a run of good seasons. By 1916, six million two hundred thousand peasant families were settled on their own property. By 1917, when the Bolsheviks were parading the slogan "All Land to the Peasants," the peasants under the Stolypin plan already had three-quarters of it.

In a certain sense, then, Russia was transformed by Stolypin's work, and Lenin, ever a realist, saw great danger in this, the danger that the revolutionary spirit might die out among the peasants. "If this [Stolypin's land reform] should continue for very long periods of time . . ." he wrote, "it might force us to renounce any agrarian program at all. It would be empty and stupid democratic phrase-mongering to say that the success of such a policy in Russia is 'impossible.' It is possible!" Trotsky too respected Stolypin; it is a notable thing that in all Trotsky's endless tirades against the Czarist ministers he has nothing really scathing to say about this forceful man.

But it was not Lenin or Trotsky or any of the revolutionaries who made the most difficulties for Stolypin during this hopeful time; by 1909 his chief, or at any rate his most insidious opposition, came from a most unexpected quarter, from the Empress Alix herself. One must again go closely into her private life in order to understand it.

Since the birth of her son in 1904 the Empress had retired more and more from public life, and when she did appear at court functions she was abrupt and restrained. Various ambassadors have recalled with a shudder in their memoirs that whenever they attended some dinner or reception at the palace they had the uncomfortable feeling that their hostess, with her cold eye and vague manner, was simply waiting and longing for the moment when she could get them to go home. She was obsessed about the baby's health, the threat that at any moment the slightest knock could bring on fatal internal bleeding, and this had caused her to develop a nervous heart disease. For long periods she scarcely let the child out of her sight, and the 1905 disturbances had naturally added to her neurosis. She had one ruling thought in her mind—the defense of the royal family against the mob—and it was not a passive defense; let any politician threaten or disturb her husband and she rose up in a perfect blaze of rage and contempt.

Meanwhile, within the palace walls and the gardens of Tsarskoe Selo the young family was growing up entirely insulated from the ordinary life of Russia. Even in late adolescence the four girls still spoke and behaved more like children of ten or twelve. Those few outsiders who met them describe them as uncommonly dutiful and attractive in an artless way; they had their pet names for one another, their needlework, their readings from improving books and their games with Papa or Mama in the evening, and, above all, their great religious devotion. It was the prescribed Victorian upbringing, a blending of innocence and spartan duty (a cold bath every morning was the rule inside the family), and there is no question whatever that they loved one another very much indeed.

Few intimates were admitted to this closed circle; indeed, when all the scores of relatives and close retainers have been passed by (and except for the tutors and nurses none of them were really intimate), just two names remain. One was Anna Vyrubova, to whom the Empress seems to have felt a sense of personal and indulgent responsibility since she had encouraged her in a disastrous marriage. When the marriage collapsed Anna Vyrubova came to live in a little house in the palace grounds, and she fitted naturally into the role of the poor and permanently grateful relative. She is described as the lame duck of the family, and was always with them. Outsiders found her evasive, kittenish and irritating.

The other denizen of this nook, and the direct cause of the Empress's hate for Stolypin, was Rasputin.

Gregory Efimovich Rasputin has been so blackened and discredited in the forty-odd years since his death that it is almost impossible to see him any more. Like Richard III of England, or Italy's Cesare Borgia, he is all villain, the pure quintessence of wickedness, a monster with the cunning of Iago and the brutishness of Caliban. Nothing is good about him; he seldom washed and he smelled vilely; at the table he plunged his greedy hands into his favorite fish soup, he was the kind of drunkard who smashes the furniture, he was blasphemous, vicious and obscene, and his lechery had a barbaric Mongolian quality that made him more like a beast than a human being. "I had in my possession," wrote Rodzianko, one of the presidents of the Duma, "scores of letters from mothers whose daughters had been dishonored by this insolent rake."

Without denying a word of all this one still feels that the picture is incomplete; one still needs to know, for example, how such a demon got into the royal palace and remained there cherished and honored until he became the virtual ruler of Russia. It is not enough to say that the Empress was unbelievably gullible and superstitious; others accepted Rasputin too, and not only when he was the favorite of the court, but long before, when he was nothing more than an itinerant fakir wandering the countryside. They thought they found something supernatural in this peasant, something that lifted him up above other men and put him in touch with mystical forces which were either satanic or divine. And in fact the more one learns about Rasputin the more one realizes that he was not at all bogus. According to his own perverse code he was entirely consistent; he never recanted, he had no mumbo-jumbo of mystical signs and ceremonies, no horde of robed disciples, he did exactly what he said he was going to do.

His real crime, of course, in the eyes of society was that he broke the conventions, he outraged their way of life. He had a sadistic glee in showing up the pretentiousness, the pomposity and the silliness of his wealthy patrons. Petrograd society was very corrupt and Rasputin knew it. He could degrade and humiliate the sycophants around the Czar precisely because they were sycophants, and therefore venal as well as frightened. Rasputin himself was not exactly venal, at any rate as far as money was concerned. He never amassed wealth, he simply enjoyed the business of living dangerously, of indulging all his appetites to the limit; to put it bluntly, he didn't give a damn. He was, moreover, very shrewd. His casual observations about people (Nicholas, for example, he said "lacked insides") were extremely revealing, and he could handle back-stairs politics rather more ably than most of the bureaucrats in Petrograd. Finally, he was a superb actor; he played his role as though he believed in it absolutely, and perhaps he really did.

Rasputin was three years younger than Nicholas, a year younger than Lenin, and he began life in the way he intended to go on. Like his peasant father before him, he was a rowdy in his village of Pokrovskoe in the Tobolsk province of Siberia, a drinker, an idler and a debaucher of the local girls. He had no education (he never did succeed in writing properly), and until the age of thirty he loitered in the abysmal backwater of Russian peasant life, known only to the local people as a horse stealer and as a wild eccentric with erotic appetites and immense physical strength. Somewhere around the turn of the century he abandoned his wife and three children and went wandering off as a kind of mendicant holy man, a *starets,* one who though not an ordained priest had seen the true light of God. There were many such in Czarist Russia, but few voyaged so far as Rasputin did; he is said to have been at least once to Mount Athos in Greece and to Jerusalem. Moreover, he had a convenient faith of his own; one must first sin, he claimed, before you could obtain forgiveness. He declared he could save people in this way, especially women, provided they became united with him both in soul and body; and no doubt there were many who succumbed to that gleaming hypnotic Ancient Mariner's eye and were convinced.

At the end of 1903 Rasputin turned up in Petrograd, a ragged peasant of average height, with a long tangled beard and dirty hair falling over his shoulders. Some little fame had preceded him —he was said to have predicted droughts and other natural disasters before they happened—and he was taken up by the monks to whom he went for shelter. There was a cult of mysticism in Petrograd at this time, and Rasputin's fanatical eyes and outlandish appearance obviously helped his reputation. Quite soon he was passed on to the Grand Duchess Militsa, a great practitioner of occult ideas, and from the Duchess to Anna Vyrubova, who just at that time was about to get married. She consulted Rasputin about this step, and Rasputin told her, quite rightly, that it would end in disaster. Anna Vyrubova was Rasputin's entrée to the court. In November, 1905, Nicholas wrote in his diary, "We got acquainted with a man of God, Gregory, from the Tobolsk province."

It can hardly have been because of the illness of the Czarevich that Rasputin was first accepted at court; the child was only fifteen months old at this time. He must have impressed himself directly on Nicholas and his wife from the beginning. They seem to have felt that through this strange uncouth peasant they were in touch with the "real" Russia, the masses of the Dark People; he was the means by which they could short-circuit the scheming politicians in the Duma and go directly to the heart of their subjects. Later, however, the bond between them was absolutely sealed when it was discovered that Rasputin had strange powers over the boy; he had only to gaze into the child's eyes, murmuring soothing words—or even speak over the telephone—and all would be well, the pains subsided and the boy went to sleep. So many extravagant stories are told about Rasputin's hold over the Czarevich, of the way in which he alone could make the boy recover from his bleeding attacks, that one hardly knows what to accept as true. But the fact remains that until the day he died the Empress believed absolutely that Rasputin and Rasputin alone could keep her son alive.

Given her highly religious nature, it was enough to convert her into a blind follower of this grubby prophet. She adored him; nothing he did, nothing that was proved against him, disturbed her confidence in the least; black became white, criticism was written off as spiteful jealousy, every doubtful act was whitewashed. "They accuse Rasputin of kissing women, etc.," she wrote once to the Czar. "Read the apostles; they kissed everybody as a form of greeting."

It has not been suggested that the Empress had an illicit affair with Rasputin; her feelings were too ethereal and highly charged for that. Yet her devotion could reach a startling pitch. In 1909, when Rasputin was temporarily under eclipse, she wrote to him:

My beloved unforgettable teacher, redeemer and mentor! How tiresome it is without you! My soul is quiet and I relax only when you, my teacher, are sitting beside me. I kiss your hands and lean my head on your blessed shoulders. Oh how light, how light do I feel then! I only wish one thing: to fall asleep, to fall asleep, forever, on your shoulders and in your arms. What happiness to feel your presence near me. Where are you? Where have you gone? Oh I am so sad and my heart is longing. . . . Will you soon be again close to me? Come quickly, I am waiting for you and I am tormenting myself for you. I am asking for your holy blessing and I am kissing your blessed hands. I love you forever. Yours, M.

M stood for Mama.

Such excess was not perhaps altogether harmful so long as it was confined to a private relationship between the Empress and Rasputin. But it was not; already in Stolypin's time Rasputin was beginning to express his notions about politics, and they were accepted by the Empress as divine inspiration, the more especially as Rasputin took good care to support the principle of autocracy. She begged Nicholas to listen to her mentor and to accept his advice.

Stolypin, on his side, was quite aware of this new breeze blowing from the court and he did not like it; he had enough troubles with the Duma without having to contend with a hostile bloc in the palace as well. In the police files there was ample evidence of Rasputin's extramural activities in Petrograd, and they were a long way from being saintly as the Empress supposed. The Starets was now being lionized by society, and he reveled in the opportunities it gave him for seducing wealthy and titled women whom, he said, he preferred to peasants since they "smelled better." Perhaps there was something in Rasputin's very brutishness that made him attractive, perhaps it was his known intimacy with the Empress, but at all events a large number of hostesses had him to their houses or visited him in his own rooms. Between these escapades he caroused at the gypsy establishments on the outskirts of the town, and night after night he was violently drunk.

Police spies followed him everywhere, and their reports became almost monotonous: "He returned today 5 o'clock in the morning completely drunk"; "On the night of the 25-26 the actress V. spent the night with Rasputin"; "He arrived with the Princess D. at the Hotel Astoria", "Rasputin came home with Princess Sh. very drunk."

He was completely reckless. The Princesses' governess was forced to protest against his wandering into the girls' bedroom in the palace, and even this did not prevent him from seducing the Czarevich's nurse. When these things were reported to the Empress she brushed them aside as utterly absurd.

By the beginning of 1911, however, Rasputin's name had become an open scandal in Petrograd, and Stolypin ordered him out of the city. These were still early days in Rasputin's rise to power, and although the Empress hated Stolypin for this move and never afterward forgave him she was still not strong enough to get the banishment revoked. The Starets returned to his native village in Siberia.

So now in the summer of 1911 Stolypin had enemies on every side. The revolutionaries were against him both on general principles and because with the success of his land reforms he was ruining their plans. The Duma was against him because he fought their every attempt to gain more power. With Nicholas he was already quarreling because he was breaking down the autocratic rule; and now, with Rasputin's banishment, he had acquired in the Empress his bitterest opponent of all. "Never mention that man to me," she said later. "He was overshadowing his Emperor."

Stolypin was ill, tired and disillusioned. He wanted to resign but was kept in office as the only possible man for the job, and was drifting again into another breach with the Czar and the Duma when, on September 14, 1911, the thing that they may all have half wished for in their hearts actually happened: he was murdered.

It was a particularly horrible crime. Nicholas had gone down to Kiev on a ceremonial visit, and Stolypin was with him when he attended a performance of Rimsky Korsakov's *Tsar Saltan* in the opera house. The Prime Minister was shot by a terrorist named Dmitri Bogrov during an intermission. Nicholas himself in a letter to his mother gives the best account of the scene:

Olga and Tatiana [his two eldest daughters] were with me at the time. During the second interval we had just left the box, as it was so hot, when we heard two sounds as if something had been dropped. I thought an opera glass might have fallen on somebody's head and ran back into the box to look. To the right I saw a group of officers and other people. They seemed to be dragging someone along. Women were shrieking and, directly in front of me in the stalls, Stolypin was standing; he slowly turned his face towards us and with his left hand made the sign of the cross in the air. Only then did I notice that he was very pale and that his right hand and uniform were bloodstained. He slowly sank into his chair and began to unbutton his tunic. . . . People were trying to lynch the assassin. I am sorry to say the police rescued him from the crowd and took him to an isolated room for his first examination. . . . Then the theatre filled up again, the national anthem was sung, and I left with the girls at eleven. You can imagine with what emotions!

Count Vladimir Nicholaievich Kokovtsov, the new prime minister, was a long way from being another Stolypin. Still, he was an able administrator, he had been a close associate of Stolypin, and in a cautious way he managed to keep the same policies going through the last few years of European peace. But already there were signs that the revolutionary movement was beginning to revive. The death of Leo Tolstoy in the previous November had been made the occasion of great street demonstrations in Petrograd, and by 1912, with every month that went by the number of strikes steadily increased. In April there was a serious flare-up; the miners at the Lena gold fields stopped work and an irresponsible police officer ordered his men to open fire on them. It was another Bloody Sunday in a small way, and from this moment there is a definite acceleration in disorders and disturbances of every kind. The official statistics give a very clear idea of the way that things were moving. After 1905 the number of men and women taking part in political strikes each year drops from nearly two million to about half a million in 1907. In the following year the figure is ninety-three thousand. In 1909 it is eight thousand; and then abruptly in 1912 we are back to half a million. By 1914 the total is climbing over the million mark once more.

In 1912 the fourth and last Duma was elected, and here too one can watch the political temperature rising. Year by year the deputies grow a little bolder in their attacks on the government and upon Nicholas himself. After the Lena gold fields affair they sent one of the new members, a bright young lawyer named Alexander Kerensky, to investigate the miners' grievances, and the experience produced in him a further swerve to the left. At the same time the Duma insisted on an official inquiry into Rasputin's activities, and while the Empress raged in private the deputies openly debated and denounced his influence at court. "Hanging is too good for him," she said of one of the more outspoken members. She begged Nicholas to dissolve the Duma, to clamp down a new censorship on the press, and actually succeeded in getting several anti-Rasputin ministers and officials dismissed from their posts.

The *Starets* meanwhile was wandering between his home in Siberia and his rooms at 64 Gorokhovoy in Petrograd. He could not now openly appear at Tsarskoe Selo, but he kept in touch through Anna Vyrubova. In October, 1912, there was an incident that made the Empress more than ever determined to have him back: the Czarevich slipped in getting into a boat and at once started an acute internal bleeding. The child was in great pain. Anna Vyrubova telegraphed the news to Rasputin in Siberia, and he replied calmly,

"The illness is not as dangerous as it seems. Don't let the doctors worry him." It was a brilliant shot in the dark. No sooner had the message arrived than the boy began to recover. To the Empress once again it was clear beyond all doubt that Rasputin was the instrument of God.

Much of her rancor was now directed toward the new Prime Minister Kokovtsov, since it was he who was primarily responsible for allowing the official investigation of Rasputin to take place. Kokovtsov had been rather a favorite at court, and it had been the practice of the Czar sometimes to embrace him. "Remember, Vladimir Nikolaievich," Nicholas once said to him, "the doors of this study are always open to you at your first wish." Now, however, at official receptions the Empress passed by Kokovtsov with averted eyes, and in February, 1914, he went the way of all Nicholas's prime ministers who were lucky enough to escape assassination; charmingly, affectionately and abruptly he was dismissed. Goremykin, the faithful butler of Czarist politics, was brought back in his place. Goremykin was now seventy-four, and not very willing; still, he knew his duty.

Nicholas was feeling very strong. Even against Rasputin's advice he gave his support to the anti-Jewish laws, and none now but the most reactionary followers were appointed to government posts. Early in 1914 he contemplated a plan for weakening the Duma and finally suppressing it altogether. It was the most unreal of policies; the Duma had done very well through these years, it had gradually learned the business of parliamentary debate, and it had in fact become a vital part of the Russian government. Even the most rabid of monarchists at the court were forced to advise the Czar that he could do nothing against the Duma without raising a serious disturbance; and the idea was dropped.

Nicholas had now been twenty years on the throne, and still the steely mildness remained, the same adamant dream of the divine right of kings. So far as he was concerned, Lenin and the other scheming exiles might just as well have been living on the moon.

CHAPTER SIX

The Exiles

THE 1905 RISING was a botched and unrehearsed affair, and yet it did something to harden the revolutionary movement, to professionalize it and give it a technique that had been lacking before. It left the Social Democratic party very weak, but now at least it was something more than just a band of outlaws; it was an accepted part of the political scene. A man could make a career in the party and even represent it quite legally in the Duma. In other words, the party was beginning to develop a sense of responsibility in place of its earlier desperation; it was turning toward less violent ways of gaining its objectives.

There was a definite sign of this at the third Social Democratic conference held at Stockholm in the spring of 1906. It was called a "unity congress," and the Mensheviks at least were all for unity. They had emerged as the strongest group in the party; they, not the Bolsheviks, had controlled the Petrograd Soviet in 1905, and in 1906 they possessed, Lenin admitted, "more money [than the Bolsheviks], more literature, more transport, more agents, more 'names,' more collaborators." Now they wanted to sink their differences with Lenin and his group so that they could reorganize the party on more solid and practical lines. As a first step toward this at Stockholm they carried a majority vote against the use of expropriations.

This was a major break. Expropriations were becoming an important means of obtaining money for the revolution. The idea of expropriations—they were known as "exes"—of carrying out robberies with an altruistic motive—was as old as Robin Hood, but it was given a special twist in Russia: party members raided banks, government offices and merchants and paid over a part at least of the money they got to the Central Committee of the party. It was a highly profitable business—in one raid alone in 1906 some 800,000 rubles were taken from the Bank for Mutual Mercantile Credit in Moscow—but sometimes it also led to a terrible loss of human life. Bombs were the usual weapons in these raids, and they were often thrown indiscriminately in crowded streets.

It was not usually the Social Democrats themselves who performed the physical acts of terror. This was left to various groups of specialists, but they were supplied, aided and hidden by the Social Democratic underground organization. And now at the Stockholm conference the Mensheviks, with a solid majority behind them, decided to call a halt: in future they would conduct the struggle in a less ruthless way. Plekhanov even criticized the workers in Moscow for fighting in the streets at the end of 1905.

Lenin disagreed emphatically with all this. The only mistake the Moscow workers had made, he said, was in not fighting harder and more skillfully. Violence was the essence of the revolution: it was unavoidable. He argued strongly against the ban on expropriations, but the best he could do was to get the conference to agree to set up a small group known as the Military Technical Bureau, which, ostensibly, was to act only in self-defense; its business was to fight a militant gang of the extreme right in Russia known as the Black Hundreds. Apparently suspecting nothing, the conference allowed Lenin to take charge of this bureau. And here Lenin saw his chance: if the Mensheviks wanted to throw away this gold mine of expropriations then so much the worse for them, he would take it over for himself. He used his newly won authority to call another conference consisting of his own close followers, and then set about doing the thing the conference had expressly forbidden him to do: he reanimated the expropriation raids in Russia, and the money he received never reached the central funds of the party; Lenin converted it directly to his own use. He had one broad design in view, and neither now nor later did he ever forget it: to win back control of the party. To do this he needed money to start a new newspaper of his own, and to win over new Bolshevik recruits in Russia.

His plans appear to have been very carefully made. Within a short time Lenin's small group had its own network of Bolshevik agents in all the larger cities, and expropriations were flourishing more strongly than ever. Lenin himself remained in Finland, but he had in Russia itself several really able lieutenants who carried out operations on the spot, notably the philosopher-scientist Alexander Bogdanov and Leonid Krassin. Krassin is a remarkable man in the revolutionary movement, a perfect specimen of the double life. So far as the authorities were aware, he was a well-to-do engineer; secretly he was a Bolshevik agitator who operated in a very large way. He ran an illegal press, collected money from sympathetic liberals, passed agents to and fro across the Russian border, and as a side-line manufactured bombs for the terrorists; and still he found time to carry on intellectual discussions with Lenin on the meaning and practice of Marxism. The two men quarreled later, but at this time they were close friends, and together they pumped money into the Bolshevik cause for all they were worth.

During 1906 and 1907 violence became almost part of daily life in Russia: it is estimated that in these years alone some four thousand people were murdered. In June, 1907, a desperado known as Kamo made a really sensational coup in Tiflis; with a small band of men and women accomplices, he waylaid a bank coach in broad daylight and got clean away with 340,000 rubles* for the cause. A part of this money found its way to the Bolsheviks.

Lenin had one other source of income. It happened from time to time that wealthy supporters left money to the Social Democratic party in their wills, and on several occasions—there was one particularly turgid affair involving a Moscow millionaire—Lenin found ways of steering this money into his own pocket.

Meanwhile his name was becoming better known. His new paper *Proletarii* was appearing regularly, and he could count on some thirty thousand followers inside Russia. In the spring of 1907 a new

* These figures must be regarded as approximate since accurate records of the expropriations do not exist. It is certain, however, that at the contemporary exchange rate of two rubles to the dollar very large amounts were involved.

party conference was due to be held in London, and he was ready for a trial of strength. Lenin put in an enormous amount of work in his preparations for these conferences. He wrote letter after letter to his followers, patiently arguing, explaining and insisting, making himself absolutely sure of their loyalty. In 1907 he was able to do something more; he selected a number of reliable men who he knew would vote his way and he supplied them with money to enable them to travel to London.

In the long and deadly serious record of Russian party conferences the 1907 gathering stands out as a lively and even a colorful affair. It was the greatest array of revolutionary talent that had yet been assembled. Just over three hundred delegates arrived from inside and outside Russia—about two hundred of them intellectuals and the remainder working men—and they must have presented an interesting spectacle: some straight out of Russia in sheepskin hats and workers' blouses, others in the business frock coats of the period, others again disguised by beards and shaven heads, and all of them very noisy. Plekhanov was there with his trusties of the old guard, Vera Zasulich and Axelrod, and he numbered among his Menshevik companions such men as Martov, Dan and Tseretelli, who were already becoming legendary figures in the movement. Maxim Gorky arrived from Italy, where he conducted a school for Russian revolutionaries on the unlikely island of Capri, Lenin came in from Finland, and Trotsky inevitably made his appearance.*

Lenin could count now on the support of a new and formidable group of lieutenants who were almost all destined to play a leading part in the revolution: Bogdanov, the intellectual doctor, Kamenev and Zinoviev, two of the younger veterans of the struggle inside Russia, who were perhaps closer to him than anybody, Litvinov, the future Commissar for Foreign Affairs, Voroshilov, the future field marshal, Yaroslavsky, Rykov, Nogin and others. There was also a

---

* Trotsky had been sent by the Czarist police to a place called Obdorsk well within the Arctic Circle in remotest Siberia. The nearest railway line was one thousand miles away. "Every day," he had written to his wife on his journey there, "we ascend one degree farther into the Kingdom of cold and barbarism." But this had not deterred him. While a fellow exile set up a false trail which delayed the police for several days Trotsky, covered in furs against the biting cold, secreted himself under a load of hay on a reindeer sleigh and got away. He had gold coins hidden in the heels of his boots to pay his way, and he soon contrived to cross the border into Europe.

minor supporter from Georgia, Joseph Vissarionovich Djugashvili who later was to use the pseudonym Stalin, but who was not yet senior enough in the party to have a vote.

In the usual way the conference got off to a slow and ragged start. The delegates assembled first in Copenhagen, but they were soon ousted by the police and eventually straggled across to London. Here Ramsay MacDonald, the British socialist leader, was of some help to them; he managed to obtain the use of the Brotherhood Church in Whitechapel in the east end of London. It belonged to a severe religious sect known as the Christian Socialists, and the agreement was that the Russians should hold their meetings in this odd place for a period of three days. Three weeks later the Christian Socialists were still pleading with their guests to leave the building just long enough for them to get in for their Sunday prayer meeting. Gorky meanwhile kept some of the more needy delegates going by raising funds from his English friends; he had one sum of £3,000 from a wealthy soap manufacturer.

Gorky's own reminiscences of the conference are most revealing. The uproar was apparently continuous, and Lenin was in the thick of it.

When we were introduced [Gorky says], Lenin shook my hand heartily, and looking me over with his keen eyes and speaking like an old acquaintance he said jocularly: "So glad you've come. I believe you're fond of a scrap. There's going to be fine free-for-all here." I hadn't expected Lenin to be like that. Something was lacking in him. He rolled his r's gutturally, and had a jaunty way of standing with his hands poked up somehow under his armpits. He seemed too ordinary, did not give the least impression of a leader. . . . But now Vladimir Ilyich [Lenin] hurries to the pulpit and cries *Comrades!* in his guttural way. He seemed to me to speak badly, but after a minute I and everybody else was absorbed in his speech. It was the first time I had heard complicated political questions treated so simply. . . . No striving after eloquent phrases . . . but every word uttered distinctly, and its meaning marvellously plain. . . . He was interrupted by shouts of hatred. One tall bearded individual kept jumping up from his seat and stuttering: "Little p-plots . . . p-playing at little p-plots!" . . . These hostile thrusts had no noticeable effect on him.

Pokrovsky, the Russian historian, also gives an effective picture of Lenin's powers in argument:

There was above all his enormous capacity to see to the root of things, a capacity which finally awakened in me a sort of superstitious feeling. I frequently had occasion to differ from him on practical questions, but I came off badly every time. When this experience had been repeated about seven times, I ceased to dispute and submitted to Lenin even if logic told me that one should act otherwise. I was henceforth convinced that he understood things better and was master of the power denied to me, of seeing about ten feet down into the earth.

The whole of the first week went by in electing a chairman, and finally Plekhanov by the narrowest of margins was defeated by Lenin for the post. For the rest the conference was an inconclusive and rambling affair which left the delegates, if anything, more divided against themselves than ever. The Mensheviks would have liked very much to have censured Lenin over his terrorist activities, but they had no way of getting at the facts.

A more fundamental cleavage was now becoming apparent, and however blurred and confused it was at every step of the way it served finally to drive almost every man toward either the Menshevik or the Bolshevik side. The Mensheviks in a general way wanted to come out from the underground and fight their battles in the open. They wanted to enter the Duma and join forces there with the Cadets and the other liberals against the Czarist government. They wanted a large and legal party roughly organized upon democratic lines, and its hands clean of violence.

Lenin and some of the Bolsheviks (not all: some of his closest adherents began to leave him at this time) shifted their ground from time to time, but in principle they were implacably opposed to these ideas. They were all for continuing the struggle underground, and it was a struggle which they insisted had to be controlled by a small group of self-appointed professional revolutionaries at the top. They did not believe that any good would come from combining with the Cadets, because the Cadets, they thought, were weak and inevitably would make a compromise with the Czarist government.

These arguments came up again and again, as the conference went on, and were wrung out to the last drop of meaning, but it was always argument without power or responsibility behind it: they had no power. In 1907 the revolutionary movement inside Russia was running down. When the conference broke up in June nothing decisive had been settled.

One has a queer picture of the exiles over the next few years. They hunt in packs. They coalesce only to split up again and form new patterns in another way. The best of friends turn into the bitterest of enemies. They drift from conference to conference throughout Europe, and when they are not together they wrangle at a distance in their newspapers. And all of them from time to time suffer from the chronic melancholy of the exile: the ennui and frustration of never being on their native soil, of watching the years go by and nothing apparently accomplished. The need for money presses upon them continually, and every city where they pause briefly on their wanderings is like any other: the same back room in the same boardinghouse in the same back street. They live life at second hand, constantly talking about the Russia they cannot see and the revolution that has not happened, endlessly reading newspapers and awaiting news from Russia. But Russia keeps receding.

Lenin suffered from this demoralization as much as anybody, since his was a mind with a single objective, and he could not easily turn to other secondary affairs. He was exhausted after the London conference. We hear of him returning to Finland with his beard shaved off and a big straw hat on his head as a form of disguise, and he went off roaming in the woods of central Finland with Krupskaya. They camped out under the pine trees, and Krupskaya would make the two-hour train journey into Petrograd and be back in the evening bringing with her the proofs of the articles Lenin had written for the newspapers, and such news of the comrades as she could pick up in the city. There was a sudden alarm in the winter of 1907; Lenin heard that Russian security police were coming across the frontier to round up revolutionaries, and with a guide he bolted hastily across the frozen sea by night to an island in the Gulf of Finland where he picked up a steamer for Stockholm; and when Krupskaya joined him there they continued through Germany to Switzerland. Their next few years are a story of restless movement: visits to London, to Paris, to Berlin, to Austrian Poland, to Brussels, to Copenhagen and back to Switzerland again. Once Lenin found himself giving lectures at Gorky's school on Capri, but neither there nor anywhere else was he able to win the support he had had at the London conference. One by one his old followers were antagonized and dropped away. They opposed him, especially over the use of expropriations, and soon he was forced to drop that form of activity altogether. In 1909 he was at a very low ebb, and we find Krupskaya writing, "We have no party at all." It was worse than that; the full tide of the Menshevik reaction was setting against him. The truth about his former gun running and his support of the expropriation raids in Russia was beginning to come out, and the Mensheviks were disgusted at the way in which he had seized the party funds for his own use. He had too, they thought, brought the whole Social Democratic party into disrepute with his "dirty money" from expropriations—they were not criminals or common bandits—and now they demanded that Lenin should cease his endless bickering against the majority. The Bolshevik newspaper *Proletarii* must close down.

Lenin was too weak to do anything but acquiesce. He agreed to a scheme whereby *Proletarii* should be merged in *Pravda*, the more moderate paper which Trotsky was getting out in Vienna. He agreed to a party truce. Early in 1910 he wrote to his sister Anna from Paris:

Darling Anyuta,
We have had a very "stormy" time lately, but it has ended in an attempt at peace with the Mensheviks. Yes, yes, strange though it may seem: the factional organ [Proletarii] has been closed down and we are trying hard to move towards union. We shall see whether we shall succeed. . . .

The letter neatly reveals his skepticism, and in fact he did not try very hard, if indeed he tried at all. The Mensheviks were soon infuriated to discover that he was resuming his terrorist raids inside Russia, and that in his writings and in his attempts to build up new Bolshevik cells his opposition was as implacable as ever. In 1911 Martov—the Martov whom everybody respected and liked, and who was once one of Lenin's closest friends—published a pamphlet entitled *Saviours or Destroyers?* It was an indictment of all Lenin's secret methods. "The famous majority of the London Congress," Martov wrote, "was manufactured. . . . 'Voting units' were hastily formed with the aid of enormous pecuniary resources acquired by the editorial board of *Proletarii* in part by expropriations, in part by 'confiscation' of funds intended for the general aims of the party—

and these 'voting units' each possessed the right to send a delegate."

Lenin never answered these charges, but soon afterward he was compelled to give up a part at least of the money he had illegally acquired. Some of the banknotes from the Tiflis holdup were actually burnt along with a quantity of bank notepaper which was to have been used for counterfeiting.

It is Lenin's resilience—his ability by sheer persistence to wear the others down—which in the end astonishes one more than anything else about him. The year 1911 finds him apparently at the nadir of his career. He is discredited by the majority of the party, his money has gone, he has no newspaper to hold his Bolsheviks together, and Krupskaya, the one supporter whom he can count on to follow him anywhere, is suffering from ill health.

The following year, 1912, all is changed, or at all events rapidly changing; he bounds straight back into the front of the movement again. He was helped no doubt by the unrest in Russia, which increased steadily after the Lena gold fields shooting, and his underground network, though weak, had been ingeniously planted in the cities where it was in the best position to take advantage of strikes and demonstrations. But clearly it was his own personality which was the deciding factor, his absolute persistence, his ruthlessness and his marvelous ability for taking other people unawares. Perhaps too Martov's pamphlet stung him into action.

In January, 1912, he called a party conference in Prague. In point of fact it was not a party conference at all; few except Bolsheviks were either invited or attended, but it declared itself to be a representative gathering of the Social Democrats; and it proceeded calmly in the name of the party to expel Martov, to demolish the truce with the Mensheviks and to adopt in its entirety the Leninist program for revolutionary action in Russia. In the same autocratic manner the title of Trotsky's newspaper *Pravda* (*Truth*) was taken over and used for a new newspaper with a purely Bolshevik line. The new *Pravda* was the best read of the revolutionary publications, its circulation fluctuated between twenty and forty thousand copies, and Lenin's reputation grew with it. The paper was seized and banned by the Czarist police a number of times, but like Lenin himself it continued to bounce back under new names and disguises such as the *Northern Pravda* and the *Workers' Pravda*, until it was finally suppressed in 1914.

In order to maintain a stronger hold on these affairs Lenin in 1912 moved closer to Russia into Galicia in Poland, which was then under Austrian domination, and no doubt the Austrian police connived at this; in the international politics that preceded the First World War it was very much in the Austrian interest to keep the Russian revolutionary movement alive.

There was one other watcher of these addled events whom we must consider here—the Okhrana, the Russian secret police. The Okhrana was an astonishing phenomenon. Not even the revolutionary movement could surpass its sophistry, its treachery and its fantastic double-dealing. It operated as one would expect a secret service to operate, that is by its agents infiltrating the ranks of the revolutionary parties, but this was done on a scale which surely has never been attempted anywhere in the world except in modern Russia.

At the beginning of the century the Okhrana was a relatively small affair with some twelve thousand agents. But by this year of 1912 these numbers had swollen into an army of some twenty thousand men, some of whom actually held high office inside the revolutionary parties. It has been estimated that 10 per cent of the members of the revolutionary groups were Okhrana agents. They swarmed everywhere, not only inside Russia, but in all the haunts of the revolutionaries in the capitals of Europe. They attended all the party congresses, wrote for the party newspapers, and took an active part in the gun running, in the smuggling and even in the acts of terrorism. If they did not entirely succeed in corrupting the revolutionary movement they certainly retarded it, weakened it and confused it extremely. It was not at first the aim of the Okhrana to break up the revolutionary parties altogether; it followed the classic strategy of dividing and ruling. It encouraged the antagonism between the two chief groups, the Social Revolutionaries and the Social Democrats, and on the whole it rather favored the more cerebral Social Democrats on the grounds that they were less given to terrorism. Inside the parties its agents were active in promoting every split and disagreement. Year by year their reports poured into the files in the Okhrana's headquarters in Petrograd.

All this was complicated enough, but it became ten times more complicated when, in some cases, Okhrana agents turned traitor to their employers and joined the revolutionary movement outright; and a hundred times more complicated still when rival factions set up within the Okhrana itself, each seeking to do down the other, even to the point of murder.

Even the briefest glimpse at the career of the celebrated Evno Azev gives one an idea of the bizarre lengths to which these dealings could go. Azev was the son of a poor Jewish tailor, and he was born in Grodnensky province in 1869. By trade he was an engineer. By temperament and by ability he was one of the outstanding double-dealers in history; he was both a senior member of the Okhrana and a founder of the Social Revolutionary party, in which his particular job was to lead the terrorist section. Committing murder and selling information came all alike to Azev, and in 1904 he achieved the supreme distinction of conniving at the murder of his own employer, Vyacheslav Plehve, the Minister of the Interior. The reasons for his doing this are not clear—perhaps it was because he believed that Plehve had carried out pogroms against the Jews—but what is clear is that Azev was not tried or condemned. Far from it; he continued in the employ of the Okhrana, and when, years later, the revolutionaries discovered his real identity—it was a major scandal at the time—they went no further than going through the form of condemning him to death. But he was not shot or hanged.

It is also a notable fact that when the Bolsheviks seized the Okhrana files after 1917 they did not proceed very far in tracking down the agents whose names they found there. The excuse given was that in most cases pseudonyms had been used and it was a difficult business establishing correct identities. It may also have been that some of the senior Bolsheviks did not wish to have an investigation.

Azev was not an ordinary traitor, and Bertram Wolfe probably comes near to the truth when he writes, ". . . he took funds from both police and revolutionaries, deceiving and cheating both. He betrayed the plans for many acts of terror, prevented many intended assassinations, delivered many of his comrades into the hands of the authorities. But other projects he permitted to be carried out, even planned some and saw to their success. His motives? To raise the price of his services to the police, to retain the confidence of his associates, to serve the obscure intrigues of one official against another, to settle grudges, even to satisfy his own strangely ambivalent personal convictions. In the end he scarcely knew himself whether he was a terrorist spying upon the government or a police agent spying upon the terror." Shortly before his death in 1918 Azev was interviewed by a member of the German Foreign Office and he declared himself to be, at heart, an antirevolutionary.

The other notorious Okhrana spy who concerns us here, and rather more closely than Azev, is Roman Malinovsky. He was less spectacular than Azev but very nearly as devious, and there is something almost comic about the very shamelessness and boldness of his career. Malinovsky was a good deal younger than Lenin—eight years divided them—and he is described as an attractive, rather ruddy and excitable man, a fluent conversationalist and orator. The Russian police pictures of him—and police photographs are hardly calculated to flatter—show a round Russian head, thick close-cropped hair, a drooping mustache and intelligent confident eyes; in all a handsome man. He had a reputation for being a heavy spender and a heavy drinker, and in his early career he was several times convicted for petty crimes. His origins were both Russian and Polish and not distinguished; he was a metal worker, and in 1907 was secretary of the Metal Workers' Union in Petrograd. Somewhere about this time the Okhrana got hold of him and he began in a small way as a police agent spying on his colleagues. Soon, however, he was given a regular wage by the Okhrana and promoted to the important work of splitting the Social Democratic party.

Lenin met him for the first time at the Prague Conference in 1912, where he turned up as an enthusiastic Bolshevik representing the Moscow trade unions. From the beginning Lenin seems to have been captivated, and he promoted Malinovsky's election to the Duma as a Bolshevik representative. The Okhrana was much in favor of this move—the higher Malinovsky stood with the Bolsheviks the better—and they were able to aid his election in the most practical way by the simple device of putting his rival candidates under arrest. Malinovsky now became the Okhrana's highest-paid spy, with a salary of five hundred rubles a month, and he appears to have lived his double life to the full. He sent copies of his Duma speeches for approval both to Lenin and to the police. Sometimes Lenin, Kamenev or Zinoviev would write the speeches for him, and these he dutifully forwarded to the Okhrana for inspection before he delivered them. His financial position prospered; his Okhrana salary was raised to seven hundred rubles a month, and when he made donations to the Bolsheviks he was able to enter the amount on his police expense account. The police on their side seem to have been quite adept at this double game; they once fined *Pravda* five hundred rubles for a seditious article written by Malinovsky.

Early in 1914, however, both the Okhrana and the Bolsheviks began to have doubts about their man. The Okhrana decided to end the connection. They ordered Malinovsky to resign from the Duma and gave him a round sum of six thousand rubles to start life afresh abroad. He made straight for Galicia, an unwise move, for the Bolsheviks at once started an investigation into his affairs. Lenin's influence, however, was enough to save Malinovsky's skin. (Though this did not prevent the Bolsheviks from executing him later on in Moscow.)

Such a story of purely personal adventure has perhaps just one importance: it reveals that now, on the eve of the First World War, when really vital days were approaching, the revolutionary stream was very far from being pure. It was contaminated throughout, and the occasional blindness of Lenin and the other leaders to what was really happening in their own ranks was no less than the blindness of the Czar to what was really happening in Russia at large. It is an odd spectacle of stubborn minds moving toward their own undoing; and in a wager as to whether the Czar or the Bolsheviks fostered the greater scoundrels in their entourage no detached observer would confidently risk a penny. It is certain at least that the blackness of Rasputin's character becomes a little less black when compared with the amorality of such men as Azev and Malinovsky.

Now, in any case, in the last days before the 1914 war there were forces at work which were stronger than either the Czar or Lenin could control. Again, as in 1905, it was the emotions and the feeling of the mass of the Russian people which were starting to take charge, and they did not act to the dictation of the leaders of either the left or the right; they acted out of the experience of their own lives and in response to the pervading idea that, in Trotsky's phrase, "the old order had become no longer endurable." The autocratic Czarist system had broken down. The attempt of the liberals in the Duma to find a remedy in democracy had been sabotaged. And so the Russian people turned to the only other available solution. Between January and July over a million workers went out on strike in the cities. In Baku open street fighting occurred between the oil workers, the Cossacks and the police.

These disturbances had very little to do with the revolutionary parties. Bolsheviks and Mensheviks alike had all but ruined their effectiveness by their internal disputes, and their leaders were more scattered than ever. Trotsky was in Vienna working as a journalist. Parvus, who also had escaped from Siberia, was in Constantinople. Plekhanov and his circle were still debating the theory of revolution in Switzerland. Gorky had abandoned his school on Capri and had come back to Petrograd. Many of the lesser figures like Stalin (who, incidentally, had had a hand in the Tiflis holdup and was later betrayed by Malinovsky) were prisoners of the Czar in Siberia, and were practically cut off from the world. Lenin and Krupskaya had moved from Cracow to the little Polish resort of Poronin in the Carpathian Mountains. Even the threatening war was a further cause for disagreement among the exiles, and some indeed did not believe that war would come at all.

"A war between Austria and Russia," Lenin had written in a letter to Gorky in 1913, "would be a very useful thing for the revolution, but it is not likely that Franz Joseph [the Austrian Emperor] and Nikolasha [the Czar] will give us that pleasure."

Plekhanov took an entirely different line: when the war actually did break out he became a devoted patriot and recruited among the Russian exiles for the French army. Trotsky thought that in their early stages wars were very bad for revolutions, and in this he was certainly right. Gorky was a pacifist. In Germany the German Socialist party backed the war; other revolutionaries split up into those who wanted a victory for the Allies and those who supported Germany and the Central Powers, and those who simply stood aside. Probably the actual opening of the hostilities—Germany declared war on Russia on August 1, 1914—took them by surprise.

Practically the first Lenin knew of it was when in his remote mountain retreat he found himself under arrest as an enemy alien living in Austrian territory. After three weeks in prison he was released by the good offices of an Austrian Socialist, and with Krupskaya he journeyed on to the safe haven of Switzerland, and from there for the next three years he watched the catastrophe unfold.

CHAPTER SEVEN

The War

<hr />

THE WAR was a mighty clarifier of the Russian scene. It had an effect such as some chemicals have when dropped into a muddy solution, and it was a change that happened almost overnight. In the last week of July, 1914, there was hardly an aspect of Russian life that did not appear to be caught up in a hopeless insoluble muddle. In Petrograd the workers were out on strike again and demonstrating against the government. The Duma was involved in a series of angry brawls against the Czarist ministers. Inside the Okhrana and the revolutionary parties the same futile intrigues continued as venomously as ever. The aristocracy had meandered into a listless ennui where nothing mattered, where gossip spent itself in an aimless inflation of little things, and even the excitement of mysticism as a substitute for religion was growing dim.

Rasputin was about to return to the palace, still loathed and feared by almost everybody but apparently secure from any harm. The Empress was ill, and on the rare occasions when she did appear in public she was so nervous and distraught it was painful to watch her. Poincaré, the French President, arrived on a state visit, and there was a spectacular round of banquets and parades, but it aroused no enthusiasm in Petrograd; in fact, the very reverse. The visit was thought to be the harbinger of war and there was a slump on the Petrograd stock exchange.

It was a warm summer—the short light milky nights hardly divided the evenings from the mornings—and people who were living in Petrograd then recall a certain heaviness in the air, a sense of apathetic dread.

Then on August 1, when war did come, this dismal atmosphere evaporated in a moment. Suddenly everyone discovers that he is possessed with an intense hatred of the Germans and a new emotional love for Russia and the Czar. The workers abandon their strikes at once, and their demonstrations now are all in favor of the government. The national flag comes out on the streets, and the churches are filled with vast congregations who can think of nothing but self-sacrifice and victory. This is no phenomenon confined to Petrograd. All over Russia the peasants and the workers respond willingly to the first army call-up; something over ninety per cent answer the summons, and the young sons of the nobility rush to take up their commissions in the army. On Sunday, August 2, Nicholas publicly takes the same oath that Alexander I had taken at the time of Napoleon's invasion: he swears that he will not make peace until the last foreign soldier has been expelled from Russian soil. According to Bernard Pares, "The vast multitude fell upon their knees and sang 'God Save the Tsar' as it had never been sung before."

Two days later the mob sacks the German Embassy in Petrograd, a huge lump of a building between the Cathedral of St. Isaac and the Mariinsky Palace with two bronze horses on the roof. These horses are hurled into the street and the crowds with flags and ikons go off to cheer their allies in the French and British embassies.

The government, meanwhile, outdoes itself in proclaiming patriotic decrees: the German-sounding name of St. Petersburg is changed to Petrograd. To prevent drunkenness the sale of vodka is banned, and nobody seems to mind. In the Duma all animosity is forgotten: the deputies come out with an almost unanimous vote in favor of the war. In Poland the people hear with shining eyes that as soon as the war is over they are to be given self-government at last. Now they too are all for the Russian Czar and the Polish revolutionary movement subsides to nothing.

The war works a wonderful change on the royal family as well. Just a few weeks before, at one of the official banquets for Poincaré,

Maurice Paléologue, the French Ambassador, found himself sitting opposite the Empress. "Her forty-two years," he wrote later, "have left her face and figure still pleasant to look upon. After the first course she entered into conversation with Poincaré who was on her right. Before long however her smile became set and the veins stood out on her cheeks. She bit her lips every minute. Her labored breathing made the network of diamonds sparkle on her bosom. Until the end of dinner, which was very long, the poor woman was obviously struggling with hysteria. Her features suddenly relaxed when the Czar rose to propose his toast."

All this is now altered. The Empress throws herself into hospital and Red Cross work, and although sometimes she has to go about in a wheel chair she looks years younger. The Czar too is transformed. His ministers no longer find him murmuring of his bad luck, or prepossessed with gloomy ideas of death. He is furious with the Kaiser. He is on fire to take personal command of his armies in the field, and is only with difficulty persuaded to appoint the Grand Duke Nicholas instead. With emotion he salutes the regiments as they go off to the front, and they answer him with cheers. Now finally after twenty bitter years Nicholas is at one with his people. It is not at all like the 1905 war with Japan, when half Russia was defeatist. Now nearly everybody not only wants to fight but is convinced that Russia will win. It is true that there are a few people in Petrograd at this moment—Rasputin is one, Count Witte is another —who stand aside from the delirium and look with misgivings into the future. Witte indeed makes the round of the ministries and the dinner parties protesting that it is madness for Russia to go to war, that win or lose war will bring on the revolution. This, he says, has always been the aftermath of wars. But few people listen. Witte is out of office and has no influence. In any case it is now too late; already the Germans are marching through Belgium and the Russians themselves are about to launch their own offensive on the eastern front.

There is something unassimilable about the spectacle of the Russian army at war, whether in the first or the second of the two great struggles of this century. The numbers involved are too vast; a flat anonymity descends upon those endless hordes of men, and where one can comprehend the suffering of a thousand, a million is too much. They vanish like ghosts into the awful icy wastes of Poland, and for anyone who was not there to see the carnage and who is not a student of military history it is difficult to distinguish one battle from another. A second million men follows the first and is swallowed up, and so the process goes mercilessly on until, in the end, one is left with a picture which is an arid generality, a list of figures, an enormous abstract. Too much is crowded onto this canvas, every face is lost in the mass; it is, quite simply, too inhuman and too big.

Then too, the First World War was in many ways more disastrous for Russia than the Second. In 1914 she was not nearly prepared. Even by the standards of the time the army was poorly commanded, antiquated in its methods, and it was administered by a Minister for War who was a military fossil. General Vladimir Sukhomlinov was an appointee of the Czar, and he is said to have boasted that he had not read a military manual for twenty-five years: he believed in the bayonet. Moreover he was a disappointed man; he had hoped for the command in the field himself and was consequently jealous of the Grand Duke. And as if all this were not enough Sukhomlinov was also politically corrupt: he doted on a much younger and pretty wife who had thousands to spend, and those thousands came from the sale of army contracts and possibly from the sale of information to the Germans as well.

"With his [Sukhomlinov's] sly look," Paléologue says, "his eyes always gleaming watchfully under the heavy folds of his eyelids, I know few men who inspire more distrust at first sight."

The War Minister had good reason to believe in the bayonet since all other weapons were in hopelessly short supply. In rifles, machine guns, artillery and ammunition there were deficiencies of every kind, and even the means of getting the soldiers up to the front were lacking; when the railways broke down horses were used and the men marched. For every one man employed on the lines of supply in France four were needed in Russia, and this discrepancy increased as the war went on.

The men certainly were available; some fifteen millions of them were called up in the end and they were very brave. Yet they were controlled by a discipline which surely must have debased the human spirit and have made it stubborn and unwilling. Enlisted men were forbidden to ride inside streetcars, eat in public restaurants except in buffets at railroad stations and similar places, receive books or newspapers without the permission of their officers, belong to any political organization, or attend lectures or theater performances without a special pass. Flogging was still used sometimes as a penalty. When a man was given an order he did not reply, "Yes, sir." He was required to say, "Glad to try, Your Excellency." Instead of saying "Yes" and "No" and "I don't know" to an officer he was bound to answer, "Just so," "In no wise," and "I cannot know." He could not know because he was not supposed to know, he was not educated to know; he was getting above his station in life if he did know. His role was that of the loyal dumb retainer. Officers were not wanted from the ranks; they were wanted from the educated classes who had been through the required military academies and who had the right approach and manner, the chief of these being the Grand Duke Nicholas himself.

The Grand Duke was a Romanov of the Romanovs, a grandson of Nicholas I, a ramrod of a man well over six feet tall. At the outbreak of war, when he was fifty-seven years of age, he held the post of military governor of Petrograd, and he had spent most of his life in the army. He was confident, he was energetic, he was liked by the soldiers; and the complexities of his job were quite beyond him. It was not until the last possible moment—the day after Russia went to war—that he was appointed Commander-in-Chief, and the plans he was ordered to carry out were not of his own making. Even these plans had to be scrapped before the month of August was over.

With a front of five hundred and fifty miles to control and the army not yet prepared for major action it was quite obvious that, at the outset, it would be wise for Russia to remain on the defensive. But there was no question of this; the Russians themselves wanted to use up the fuel of their enthusiasm by attacking at once, and almost from the first day the French were urging them forward. The German blitz on Belgium and France developed rapidly into a bewildering and frightening success, and something had to be done to relieve the pressure. Through their ambassador in Petrograd the French sent desperate appeals to the Czar and the Grand Duke to attack in the east.

It was a difficult situation; Russia certainly could not allow the French army to go under since the Germans would then be free to turn the full weight of their forces toward the east. Yet how far could the Grand Duke afford to jeopardize his own positions by fighting when he was not ready? He decided to go the whole way. Gallantly, hastily and mistakenly he went into the offensive when only a third of his soldiers were deployed. His first plan was to strike where he judged the enemy to be weakest: against the Austrians in southern Poland and Galicia. Then when the French appeals became more pressing—it looked as though Paris was about to fall—he opened up a second offensive against the Germans in the north, in East Prussia. Presently a third offensive was added to the other two—north from Warsaw. All this was dangerous enough; it was made ten times more dangerous by the fact that two soldiers of great talent, Hindenburg and Ludendorff, were soon to be in command of the German army.

These then were the circumstances in which the Battle of Tannenberg was fought at the end of August, 1914, and that disaster was followed in September by the Battle of the Masurian Lakes which resulted in the Russians being swept entirely out of German territory. In January, 1915, a second Battle of the Masurian Lakes was fought, and with this third defeat the Russian offensive in the north was broken: an offensive from which the army never recovered.

In the center and the south there was success for a time against the Austrians; both Lvov and Czernowitz fell to the Russians in September, 1914, and although Turkey entered the war against them in October the Grand Duke's armies held on fairly well into the new year. Then in 1915 the Germans overran most of Poland and took Warsaw. Lithuania and Courland were both lost in the north, and in the south the Russians surrendered almost all the Austrian territory they had gained. By the summer of 1915 the Grand Duke had fallen back some two hundred miles, and his losses were computed at nearly four millions—possibly the greatest slaughter the world had ever known. Now the boot was on the other foot—it was the Russians who were asking their allies for help—and the British and French responded by landing an army on the Gallipoli peninsula in Turkey. The object of this expedition was to break through to Constantinople and to join hands with the Russians in the Black Sea. But the French and British soldiers remained pinned down within a few miles of their landing places on the peninsula.

The Russians, like all the other powers, had gone to war believing that they would have victory within a few months, and they were even less able than the others to adjust themselves to a long struggle. Temperamentally the Russian soldier was a fatalist; his sudden wild enthusiasms were soon followed by a mood of equally extravagant despair; and in any case his government had not given him the means to carry on the battle with much hope of success. By late 1914 ammunition both for artillery and for small arms had almost given out. The ration of rifles on some sectors was about one for every ten men, and conditions in the forward areas were chaotic. Refugees from Poland cluttered the roads, the railways were quite unable to cope with the extra traffic over these immense distances, and often, in many thousands, the wounded were simply left to die. Spy mania, an infallible sign of disappointment and defeat in war, seized upon Russians everywhere, and it was encouraged by the Grand Duke. Since some Russian Jews were believed to have co-operated with the Germans, then, according to his reckoning, all Jews were suspect. He rooted them out of Poland in whole communities, and turned them loose to wander back into Russia as best they could. Nearly a million Jews were on the move, and many of them were starving and dying of exposure.

It was apparent now that the Kaiser had acted very wisely in precipitating the war in 1914. His military experts had estimated that the French and Russian armies if left in peace would have reached their maximum strength by 1917. To have waited therefore would have been fatal; relatively German power was declining with every year that went by. "Now or never," the Kaiser had written on the margin of one of his official papers in 1914; and now in 1915 his policy was abundantly justified, at any rate as far as the Russian front was concerned. The Russians were in full retreat.

In Petrograd and Moscow there was as yet no panic, but the exuberance with which the people had first gone to war had been replaced by a steadily mounting resentment against the government. In February, 1915, when the Duma met for a short session the deputies had very much cooled toward the Czar; in August when they met again many of them were openly hostile. It was not only that they believed that the war was being mismanaged—that was clear enough for anyone to see—it was a general suspicion that the court and a section of the government had become defeatist, if not actually disloyal. There were at this time about two million Germans or people of German extraction living in Russia, and many of them held high positions in government or semigovernmental undertakings. They controlled banks and large businesses. Germany after all was Russia's nearest western neighbor of any size, and in Petrograd many people spoke German and thought in German terms. A number of marriages had been contracted between the German and the Russian nobility, notably the marriage of the Czar himself. And now it was thought that an influential clique of these people were not only acting as spies but actually hatching plans for surrender.

Moscow was often a jump ahead of Petrograd in expressing the true feelings of the masses (Petrograd, according to an old Russian saying, was the head of Russia and Moscow the heart), and in June there had been an hysterical outburst there. It was the ancient hunt for the scapegoat, the same blind hatred that had been turned against the Jews, and people went mad for a time. For three days on end German shops, banks and factories were looted and set on fire. Anyone with a German name was hunted down and if possible lynched. It was one of the most ferocious pogroms ever carried out in Russia and it was the clearest of all possible warnings that a crisis was on the way. Next time the mob would strike at the Czar and the government itself.

The truth was, of course, that twelve months of war had put an impossible strain on the bureaucracy and its outdated system of administration. No clear relationship had been worked out between the army fighting at the front and the ordinary civilian economy of the country. The Grand Duke acted virtually as a dictator in the military areas, and although he was entirely dependent on the civilian factories and workshops in the rear he and his staff often sabotaged their efforts by making erratic and impossible demands. Contradictory orders flowed out from headquarters, from the Foreign Office and from the Ministries of War and of the Interior, and the bureaucracy hardly knew what it had to do or whom it was to obey. The Allies, France and Britain, were unseen and very far away, and inevitably the cry went round Petrograd that they were doing nothing, that "the British and French were prepared to fight to the last Russian soldier." All the average Russian knew was that every other family had a son or husband dead or wounded, that the medical services had all but broken down, that prices were rising and that life was getting harder every day.

Meanwhile these hardships—and the criticism of the Czar that went with them—were working an electric change in the Empress. The outbreak of the war had already roused her, and now in this disastrous summer of 1915 she was in a blaze of patriotic and religious energy. There is something almost of the avenging prophetess about her pronouncements, and the fact that they were made in the artless language of a well-brought-up Victorian schoolgirl perhaps made them all the more effective. Her thesis was very simple. Russia must be saved. Nicholas alone can save her, and only Rasputin can show him the way. As for the scheming politicians of the Duma, they must be crushed, humiliated, hounded out of office: their criticism of Nicholas and Rasputin might have been tolerated with contempt before, now it is simple heresy. And if Nicholas will not act she must take a hand in dealing with the traitors herself.

Trotsky manages to instill a marvelous amount of bile into his portrait of the Empress at this time, but it is worth quoting for it does not exaggerate the dislike which she was now attracting to herself in Petrograd.

"In order to justify her new situation," he writes, "this German woman adopted with a kind of cold fury all the traditions and nuances of Russian medievalism, the most meager and crude of all medievalisms, in that very period when the people were making mighty efforts to free themselves from it. This Hessian princess was literally possessed by the demon of autocracy. Having risen from her rural corner to the heights of Byzantine despotism, she would not for anything take a step down."

On June 27 she wrote to Nicholas while he was at the front: "Be more autocratic, my very own sweetheart." In July she inveighs against "that horrid Rodzianko" (the president of the Duma) who wants to call the deputies together to debate the war. "Oh! please don't, it is not their business . . . they must be kept away. . . . Russia, thank God, is not a constitutional country."

In particular she reserves her real enmity for those who dared to attack Rasputin, and there was about this time a bitter denunciation of him in the Petrograd press. The minister who allowed the article to pass through the censorship soon found himself dismissed from office and an unfortunate assistant who had produced from the police files an account of Rasputin's latest debaucheries went the same way.

In July she had discovered still another enemy—the Commander-in-Chief himself. It was not the Grand Duke's failure on the battle-field that aroused the Empress: it was his opposition to Rasputin. When Rasputin had wished to come to the front to bless the soldiers the Grand Duke had permitted himself to reply, "Come and I'll hang you." And now the Empress declared that the Grand Duke must be removed. He was becoming too popular, she declared; he was even planning to displace the Czar; Nicholas himself must take command.

Day after day in endless letters to Nicholas she kept advising him, cajoling him, imploring him to listen to the words of "Our Friend," Rasputin, the embodiment of the soul of Russia. Nicholas was not altogether acquiescent. Against the Empress's and Rasputin's opposition he got rid of Sukhomlinov and put in his place General Polivanov, an abler and certainly a more honest man. Three other reactionary and inefficient ministers were also ejected, and five defense councils were set up to put the country's war economy onto a proper footing. They comprised the men the Empress hated most, representatives of the Duma, the zemstvos and the newly-formed war industries committees, and soon a better supply of arms and equipment began to flow toward the front. The medical services improved and the vast business of organizing transport and war production began to take on at least a little coherence.

None of this was done very gladly or willingly—Sukhomlinov's corruption had to become an open scandal before he was taken off to prison—and having gone so far Nicholas presently began to draw back. He was particularly sensitive about the Grand Duke's growing popularity, and from the beginning of the war he had never ceased to want the command himself. It was absurd of course—rather as if George V of England or later Woodrow Wilson of the United States had chosen to lead their armies in the field—and Nicholas's ministers did all they could to dissuade him. They pointed out that it was im-

possible for him to do two jobs at the same time, to be both a fighting soldier and a statesman, and that with the army in retreat his
name would become directly identified with failure. There was another danger, and although the ministers may not have dared to
bring it to Nicholas's attention, it was on everybody's mind: once the
Czar had gone to the front then there was nothing to stop the
Empress and Rasputin from taking charge of the government.

Through August, 1915, Nicholas hesitated, pulled one way by the
Empress and the other by his ministers. Then in early September
he appeared unexpectedly in Petrograd with his wife and they remained for a long time in no less than three separate churches kneel-
ing in prayer before the ikons. The next day, on September 4, he left
for the front. He set up a new commander-in-chief's headquarters at
Mogilev on the Dnieper, and the Grand Duke was packed off to a
command in the Caucasus. The only reassuring aspect about the
change was that Nicholas proposed to be more or less of a figure-
head: the actual control of the army was given to General Mikhail
Alexeiev, an uninspired man but still a professional soldier of some
ability. In Petrograd, where old Goremykin was still in charge of the
government, people waited to see what the Empress and Rasputin
were going to do.

They did not wait long. On September 16, twelve days after the
Czar's departure, the Duma was prorogued, and there began now
that series of government dismissals and reshuffles, of intrigues and
underhand dealings, that were to bring Russia to the very edge of the
revolution. "After the middle of 1915," Michael Florinsky writes in
The End of the Russian Empire, "the fairly honourable and efficient
group who formed the top of the bureaucratic pyramid degenerated
into a rapidly changing succession of the appointees of Rasputin. It
was an amazing, extravagant and pitiful spectacle, and one without
parallel in the history of civilized nations." Before the end twenty-one
different ministers were dismissed.

The *Starets's* methods had a certain barbaric simplicity. He took
a steam bath at night, and then having drunk several bottles of
Madeira wine he was ready to bring his mind to bear on politics.
If there was some specific problem before him he wrote a note about
it on a piece of paper. (Earlier, before he could write, he used a
notched stick for this purpose.) The paper was then placed under his

pillow. In the morning he rose and announced his decision with the words "My will has prevailed," and the decision was then communicated to the Empress. At once she sat down and wrote to the Czar asking for his approval.

Early in 1916 they had Goremykin out—he had been subservient enough but now he was altogether too old to carry through Rasputin's designs—and he was replaced as president of the council of ministers by a more active lackey, a provincial governor and a former master of ceremonies at the court named Boris Stürmer. Stürmer, aged sixty-eight, looked like Santa Claus, and had a reputation for corruption and disloyalty which vied even with that of Sukhomlinov. "It is impossible to speak of Stürmer's political programme," Florinsky says, "because he had none, and his position as an appointee of Rasputin and the Empress excluded the very possibility of his having one." Polivanov, the new Minister of War, a liberal and a good hater of Rasputin, was next on the list. "Get rid of Polivanov," the Empress wrote to the Czar on January 22, 1916. On March 17 she wrote again, "Remember about Polivanov." And on March 25, "Lovey, don't dawdle." That same day Polivanov was dismissed, and the Empress was grateful. "O! the relief. Now I shall sleep well." Next came Sazonov, the Foreign Minister, a brother-in-law of Stolypin. He was a cultivated man of Western ideas, and a close friend of the French and British ambassadors. They protested to the Czar, but they were unable to save him. Stürmer became Foreign Minister as well as Premier.

The only other important post which Rasputin now needed to fill was that of Minister of the Interior, and for this office he found a candidate whom one can only describe as grotesque. Alexander Protopopov was as improbable as his name, a sleek, good-looking man in the kind of way a tailor's dummy is good-looking. He had a smooth and ingratiating manner. Recently, as a vice-president of the Duma, he had led a delegation to England, and at Stockholm on his way back he had made contact with the Germans. How far he explored the possibility of making peace in Stockholm is not known, but such a policy quite possibly would have had Stürmer's support; Stürmer himself was a man of German extraction. The other distinguishing marks about Protopopov were that he was something of a mystic and a dabbler in the occult, and he was afflicted with a chronic disease, probably advanced syphilis. He was ill and half mad. The Empress was in raptures about him.

On September 20, 1916, she wrote to Nicholas: "Gregory [Rasputin] earnestly begs you to name Protopopov," and two days later, "Please take Protopopov as Minister of the Interior. As he is one of the Duma it will make a great effect and shut their mouths." Even Nicholas had jibbed a little at first. "Our Friend's opinions of people," he replied, "are sometimes very strange." However, he soon gave in; the new minister was installed on October 3, 1916. Protopopov was beside himself with childish excitement at his promotion. When one of the deputies of the Duma told him that the appointment was a public scandal and that he ought to resign he exclaimed, "How can you ask me to resign? All my life it was my dream to be a vice-governor, and here I am a minister."

Rasputin was now completely in charge of the government. He had left them all aghast, even the most sycophantic, the most skeptical and the most indignant. It seemed that there was nothing they could do: he was virtually the ruler of Russia. He moved in the grand manner through Petrograd, holding court in his rooms, distributing jobs to the husbands of wives who slept with him and turning out of office the husbands whose wives refused him. The high offices of the Church itself were filled with charlatans and political priests he had chosen. No man who opposed him was safe. As for the Empress, her chief worry was that Nicholas would weaken now that autocracy was coming back into its own again. "Don't yield. Be the boss. Obey your firm little wife and our Friend. Believe in us."

Nicholas in many ways had been enjoying life at the front. He had hated "the poisoned air of Petrograd," and ambassadors and ministers arriving at his headquarters found him looking well and confident. The new command had not worked too badly on the whole. After the summer retreat of 1915 the Germans had had no choice but to remain on the defensive; in France the desperate struggle in the trenches was apparently without end, and the Kaiser was in no position to undertake large operations in the east. In June, 1916, a new Russian offensive was launched in the south, and it penetrated the Austrian front to a depth of twenty-five miles. This was Russia's greatest victory of the war, and just possibly it might have been exploited had not Rumania entered the struggle in August. Rumania as a neutral had an advantage for the Russians in anchoring their lines in the south. As an ally—and it was largely at France's and Russia's insistence that she came in on the side of the Allies—she was a terrible liability. The Germans quickly overran their new and puny enemy, and the Rumanian army, streaming back into Russia, precipitated a general retreat. It was the onset of winter that saved the situation. The Russians settled down in the protection of their frozen trenches and without much hope began their long wait for the spring.

And now in October, 1916, Nicholas was being persecuted with messages telling of treachery behind the lines in Petrograd. The combination of the new defeats at the front and Rasputin's activities in the capital had been too much; from the extreme right to the revolutionary left every party was beginning to combine in opposition to the government. Petrograd was tied up with a new succession of strikes, and it was an ominous sign that the soldiers who had been brought in to restore order had refused to fire on the workers. The Cossacks had to be let loose in the streets before the city was quiet again, and it did not help matters that Stürmer caused 150 of the mutinous soldiers to be shot before a firing squad. Meanwhile, a Russian brigade which had been sent to France rebelled against its officers at Marseilles. The colonel was murdered, and French troops had to be called in to arrest and shoot the mutineers.

Among the liberals in Petrograd the saying "Through Victory to the Revolution" was being replaced by a slogan of a very different kind: "Through Revolution to Victory." And in the drawing rooms of the monarchists and even of the relatives of the royal family there was open discussion of the possibility of deposing Nicholas in favor of his son, with one of the Grand Dukes acting as regent. The Duma was the chief center of this agitation, and it was due to meet again. But the Empress was still confident. "It will be a rotten Duma," she predicted, "but one must not fear; if too vile one closes it"; and of the Duma's president she wrote, "How I wish I could hang Rodzianko."

On November 14, 1916, the deputies gathered at the Tauride Palace, and at once there was a storm against the government. It rose to its height when Milyukov, the leader of the Cadets, a man in favor of constitutional monarchy and by no means a revolutionary, made a direct attack on Rasputin, the Empress and Stürmer. Stürmer he accused outright of being in German pay, and as he enumerated one by one his charges against the government he kept repeating the phrase, "Is this folly or treason?" It came as near to sedition as any liberal had yet dared.

There was another important speech at this session which was almost as violent, and it was all the more effective since it came from Vladimir Purishkevich, a representative of the extreme reactionary right. Purishkevich directed his main attack against the *Starets*, and in the public gallery, listening to the speech, absorbing every word of it, was a young man named Prince Felix Yusupov, a relation of the Czar. He had a plan for murdering Rasputin.

By the end of November the Duma's opposition had become too serious to be ignored any longer, and Nicholas made another of his tactical retreats. Stürmer was dismissed, and Alexander Trepov, the Transport Minister, an anti-Rasputin man, was put in his place. Nicholas also decided that Protopopov had to go; he was too minor, too nondescript; he was making a farce of the government. "Only, I beg," Nicholas wrote to his wife, "do not drag our friend into this. The responsibility is with me. . . ." The Empress replied with a series of hysterical messages, and when these seemed to be having no effect she went to headquarters and persuaded Nicholas to change his mind: Protopopov was saved.

At this period the Empress's letters rise almost to a pitch of frenzy. ". . . take no big steps without warning me," she writes to Nicholas late in December, 1916. " . . . Russia loves to feel the whip. . . . How I wish I could pour my will into your veins. . . . I have had no sleep, but listen to me, which means Our Friend. I suffer over you as over a tender, soft-hearted child. Pardon, believe and understand." She had a plan now for deporting the leaders of the political parties to Siberia, and she writes again, "Be the Emperor, be Peter the Great, John the Terrible, Emperor Paul—crush them all under you." And she concludes, "We have been placed by God on the throne, and we must keep it firm and give it over to our son untouched. I kiss you, caress you, love you, long for you, can't sleep without you, bless you."

Trepov, the new Prime Minister, had taken on his impossible job with extreme reluctance—more than once he tried to withdraw but Nicholas refused to accept his resignation—and he saw that he would have to come to some sort of a deal with Rasputin. He hit upon the idea of buying him off: the *Starets* was to have the then equivalent of $95,000 cash down, a house and living expenses, provided that he kept out of politics. As an extra inducement—and one can hardly imagine anything more cynical—Rasputin was to be free to do what he liked with the clergy.

It was a clumsy bribe and Rasputin laughed at it.

So now in the last week of December, 1916, in the depths of one of the hardest of Russian winters, when people's minds turned naturally to melancholy and despair, the situation had become like nothing so much as one of the horrendous historical tragedies playing at the opera house. It was an extreme of confusion and hopelessness. The news from the front was that the soldiers were deserting in thousands every day, and few now believed in victory any more. Behind the lines it was an unequal struggle for the average citizen to get enough food to eat or even merely to keep the cold at bay. As a leader the Czar seemed to have collapsed; he floated in a limbo somewhere between the front line and the capital, controlling neither the army nor the politics, and in his place there was a parliament and a bureaucracy that hated one another, an Empress who hated almost everybody, and a mad priest who behaved like a devil in the name of God. Not even the most doom-stricken of the Slav legends had been able to achieve quite such a complicated and suicidal atmosphere as this. Just one thing was lacking: some act of high dramatic violence. And this presently was supplied by the murder of Rasputin.

The murder, says Trotsky, "was carried out in the manner of a moving picture scenario designed for people of bad taste." This may be true enough, and yet, however often the story is told, it has a certain ghoulish fascination, and it is not without importance in understanding the revolution that the revolutionaries themselves had no part in it. The conspirators were all patricians or avid monarchists. Prince Yusupov, who had been educated at Oxford University in England, was a son of one of the richest and most influential of the noble families and the husband of the Princess Irina, the Czar's niece. The Grand Duke Dmitri Pavlovich was a cousin of the Czar and a possible heir presumptive. Basil Maklakov and Purishkevich were right-wing members of the Duma. A Dr. Stanislas Lazovert, who also played a small and grisly part, was a fashionable army doctor. Others were involved too—indeed, the plot seems to have been noised about Petrograd in the most reckless way for days beforehand—but they were not Marxists or terrorists: they were the solid aristocracy of the capital. They did what they did, not against the Czar, but for him. Some of them hoped that after the murder the Empress would be taken to a mental home, and that Nicholas would resume his rightful place at the head of the nation.

A number of people, including two of the conspirators themselves, have described the actual murder, and none of them entirely agree as to the details. However, if we follow Bernard Pares, who made a synthesis of all the contemporary accounts, we probably come somewhere near the truth.

By the night of December 29, Pares says, all the plans had been made. A cellar in Yusupov's house had been carefully prepared: it was furnished with a bearskin rug on the floor, armchairs, a labyrinth cupboard full of mirrors on which stood a crucifix. Chocolate and almond cakes were laid out—some of them injected with cyanide of potassium—and there was also poisoned wine available. A stairway led to the room above where the conspirators were assembled, and for some reason they kept playing over and over again a record of "Yankee Doodle" on the gramophone. Toward midnight Yusupov went alone by appointment to pick up Rasputin at his apartment, and he found him "smelling of cheap soap, in a white silk blouse and black velvet trousers."

The *Starets* seems to have had some premonition of evil, but he had accepted an invitation to take supper at Yusupov's house as he was eager to meet Princess Irina, who was a pretty woman. The two men, Yusupov very nervous, set off together, and on reaching the house went straight to the cellar. At first Rasputin refused to drink or eat anything, but eventually he took two of the poisoned cakes and then asked for Madeira. Yusupov dropped an unpoisoned glass which was in his hand and gave Rasputin another glass with cyanide of potassium in it. The *Starets* now began to drink freely without showing any effect other than to glance at his host with a look of hatred. "My head reeled," Yusupov wrote later. Presently Rasputin demanded tea, and asked Yusupov to play on the guitar for him. Rasputin, says Pares, "sat listening with drooping head and called

for one [song] after another, but though the murderer sang on,
the murdered man did not collapse. Meanwhile the rest of the party
sat on upstairs, anxiously waiting for something to happen, and listening to the interminable 'Yankee Doodle.' "

From time to time Yusupov slipped upstairs to his friends to tell
them what was happening and in desperation to ask them what else
he should do. By two-thirty in the morning the strain had become
unbearable, and Dr. Lazovert on going outside for some fresh air
had fallen down in a faint. There was a feverish conference: the
Grand Duke Dmitri wanted to call off the whole affair: Purishkevich
was all for going on. In the end Yusupov went back to the cellar with
Purishkevich's revolver behind his back. Rasputin did not appear to
be very well; he was sitting drooping at a table and breathing
heavily. However, another glass of wine revived him and he suggested a visit to one of the gypsy establishments, "with God in
thought," he said, "but with mankind in the flesh." Yusupov, who
all this time was in deadly fear of Rasputin's supernatural powers,
now asked the Starets to get up and say a prayer before the crucifix.
His object, he said later, was to "subdue the devil" in his victim
before he shot him; and in fact he did shoot, aiming for the heart,
just at this moment. With a roar Rasputin fell backward onto the
bearskin rug.

At once the other conspirators came running down into the cellar
and the confusion was redoubled when someone inadvertently
rubbed against the electric switch and turned off the light. There
was a rapid examination of the body; it appeared to be lifeless, and
they retired upstairs again. After a short time Yusupov decided to
return to the cellar to have another look at the dead man. He shook
the limp body and was horrified to see that one eye was twitching.
At the same moment Rasputin rose up from the floor, grasped Yusupov by the shoulders, tore off an epaulette and then fell back again.
In panic Yusupov rushed upstairs and Rasputin on all fours came
clambering up behind him. There was a locked outer door in the
upper room, but Rasputin burst through it into the snow-covered
courtyard, "roaring with fury." Purishkevich ran after him, fired two
shots from his revolver which missed, and then, biting his hand in
despair, twice fired again. This time Rasputin fell, and Purishkevich,
standing over him, kicked him on the head.

Now they were all demoralized. Purishkevich ran through the house to the front door and declared to the two soldiers standing on guard there, "I have killed Grishka Rasputin, the enemy of Russia and the Czar." The two soldiers came back with him to the courtyard to help drag the dead man into the house. Meanwhile Yusupov had been violently sick, and he now threw himself on the body, battering at it with a steel press. Yet still there were signs of life; one eye was still open. The soldiers dragged Yusupov away and in a state of collapse he was handed over to his servants.

The plan now was to dispose of the body in the river. Still warm, according to Purishkevich, it was bound and wrapped in a blue curtain, and they drove rapidly to one of the bridges across to the islands of the Neva, and here at last it was bundled quickly into the freezing water below. In their haste the conspirators had forgotten the weights they had brought with them, and these together with Rasputin's fur coat and one of his snowboots were also hurled into the river. It was not until they reached home that they discovered that the other boot and the blue curtain, stained with blood, were still lying in the car, and these were burned.

On the following day, Saturday, December 30, the news was all over Petrograd, but it was not until January 1 that Rasputin's boot was found washed up on the ice, and divers went down to recover the body. According to one account, Rasputin had freed himself from the rope which had been tied round him, and the post-mortem was said to have revealed that the lungs were full of water, which would suggest that he was not entirely dead when he was thrown into the river.

But dead he now was; his body lay at the Chesmé Chapel on the road out to Tsarskoe Selo, and the Empress kneeled beside it in prayer. On New Year's Day, 1917, Nicholas came hurrying back from the front to comfort her. And now, when the news of these events reached Berlin, the Kaiser saw a great hope for getting Russia out of the war. Rasputin, it is true, had opposed the war, but it seemed likely that the political disturbance created by his death might prove even more valuable to the German cause.

CHAPTER EIGHT

The German Revolutionary Net

In THE DEBACLE of Germany at the end of the Second World War there occurred an event which is of major importance to historians: the archives of the Foreign Office in Berlin were saved from destruction, and these have now been made available to students. A vast mass of documents is involved, and its particular interest is the new light it throws on the workings of German diplomacy through the early years of this century. From week to week one can follow the shifting aims and ambitions of the German government through the dispatches of its ambassadors abroad and the instructions sent to them by the Wilhelmstrasse; one can learn also a very great deal about the planning methods of the Germans and the sources of their information. This is, in fact, the secret political history of a great power at the climax of its strength as it was seen at the time by the statesmen, the generals and the diplomats who were in control.

Naturally the most critical period is that which begins with the outbreak of the First World War in the summer of 1914 and leads on to the Russian revolution in 1917—the years when Germany very nearly accomplished the mastery of the world. The documents reveal very fully just what Germany's stake was in the revolution: how she planned for it, helped to finance it and attempted to control it through a network of agents and Russian revolutionaries.

There is of course nothing new in the principle of belligerents or even would-be belligerents promoting revolution in one another's countries. In the eighteenth century France, Spain and Holland came to the aid of the Americans in their revolt against England. A few years later it was the British who gave secret support to the insurgents in the French Revolution. We have already noticed the attempts of the Japanese to undermine the Czarist government from within during the Russo-Japanese war in 1905.

In all this it was not the principle of this political warfare that was altering, it was the technique. In former centuries one bribed or supported dissident aristocrats or political parties inside the enemy's territory; now in the twentieth century the appeal is made on a much broader basis to the whole mass of the enemy people through the aid of the radio and the printing press, and treason is injected if possible into every part of the enemy's government by a staff of agents well supplied with money. Already in the nineteenth century Bismarck had anticipated this modern strategy by setting aside state money (he called it the "reptile fund"), to bribe the press, and Clausewitz even earlier had turned his cold eye onto Russia. "Such a country," he said, "can only be subdued by its own weaknesses and by the effects of internal dissension."

Yet the fomenting of revolutions is a dangerous undertaking which is liable to backfire if not carefully handled, and it was particularly dangerous in Russia in 1914. Kings who undermine other kings by encouraging treason jeopardize the whole principle of monarchy—a point that the German Kaiser had carefully to consider. Moreover, the new revolutionary technique was then very new. The people who engaged in it had to feel their way, and matters that appear self-evident now were not at all so then. Thus the number of agents employed had to be small and as far as possible the minor links in the chain had to be kept in ignorance of their employers, or even their close superiors. Bases had to be established on neutral territories around Russia, and it was clearly undesirable for the German diplomats to be too obviously involved: agents or "cut-outs" had to be engaged to make contact with the revolutionaries inside and outside Russia.

Equally clearly secrecy was essential, and written communications had to be used as little as possible. As time went on it also became apparent that it was unwise for Germany to put all her eggs into one basket; she had to support a number of different Russian revolutionary parties lest any of them should become too strong and difficult to manage; and it was usually advantageous to keep these different parties in ignorance of one another's connections with the Germans. Always too there was the imminent danger of the double-cross, of the agent absconding with the money and taking a hostile line, of false information being deliberately passed, of the party leaders quarreling among themselves and giving the game away. A welter of practical difficulties existed; how were the agents in neutral or hostile territories to explain away the fact that they had suddenly come into the possession of money? How were you to get the cash (never checks) to them and in the right currency? How to transport the weapons and the seditious propaganda into Russia?

With the outbreak of the war in August, 1914, most of the German contacts inside Russia abruptly dried up. The ambassador and his staff were extradited, German agents also left the country or were arrested, others of Russian birth no longer wished to pass information to Germany since this was treason in time of war and punishable by death. Consequently the whole net inside Russia had to be built up again from the bottom.

It is clear from the Wilhelmstrasse records that Germany had made no long-range plans for creating revolution in Russia. Under Bismarck her policy in general had been pro-Russian. She had encouraged the Czar in the war against Japan in 1905, and it was not until 1909, when Theobald von Bethmann-Hollweg took over the chancellorship, that Germany began to switch to an anti-Russian line. The change had become particularly marked by 1913 when it was recognized in Berlin that war was probably unavoidable, but even as late as the summer of the following year the Kaiser still hoped that he could confine the hostilities to a struggle between Austria and Serbia, or at any rate between the Central Powers and Serbia and France, and that Russia would keep out. When that illusion vanished in July, 1914, the Germans turned their attention at last to the question of creating revolution behind the enemy's lines —not just revolution in Russia but revolution on a world-wide scale.

In the early days of August it was decided that trouble should be fomented in British India and Egypt as well as in the Caucasus, the Ukraine, Poland and Finland. The emphasis was to be—and how familiar the phrase has since become—on "the liberation of oppressed peoples." Gradually through the autumn of 1914 the program began to focus with special intensity on Russia.

It was a policy which, to some extent, was based on despair or at any rate a strong secret pessimism, for we find in the German files for November, 1914, an astonishing admission by Bethmann-Hollweg that he did not believe that Germany could win the war so long as the British-French-Russian alliance remained intact. In this he was supported by von Falkenhayn, one of the highest generals in the supreme command. Consequently revolution in Russia became a major German objective quite early in the war.

Five key German embassies in neutral countries were involved in the plans: that of Baron Hellmuth von Lucius in Stockholm, of Count Ulrich von Brockdorff-Rantzau in Copenhagen, of Baron Gisbert von Romberg in Bern, Baron von dem Bussche-Haddenhousen in Bucharest, and Baron von Wangenheim in Constantinople. Among them these five men covered all the routes into European Russia, and it is very largely through their correspondence in the Wilhelmstrasse files that we can watch the German plan unfold. The tactics were two-sided: to promote independence movements in the Caucasus, the Ukraine, Poland and Finland, and to strike at the heart of Russia herself through the Russian revolutionaries.

It was in the Ukraine that most headway was made at first. Already by July, 1914, the Austrians had sent in arms in the hope of raising a mutiny in the Black Sea fleet and of softening up the line of their advance into Russia in August. This was a halfhearted affair, partly because the Austrians did not want to spend much money and partly because their attack never developed; the incredible fact was that a member of their planning staff, a Colonel Alfred Redl, had sold their plans to the Russians, and so it was the Russians, not the Austrians, who advanced. Nevertheless, the Kaiser put his authority behind the revolution in the Ukraine. On August 8, 1914, he gave orders that it should be financed with large funds, and later he instructed von Wangenheim, his ambassador in Constantinople, to promote the movement "ruthlessly and mercilessly." Turkey, though still neutral, was strongly pro-German, and consequently Constantinople seemed a most favorable base for the forwarding of agents, money and weapons into southern Russia. Soon with the aid of German and Austrian money a "Bund for the liberation of the Ukraine" was set up, and it served as a useful cover for the distribution of funds not only inside Russia but in Europe as well. It was the first of a series of such organizations, which though apparently international in character were secretly controlled from Berlin. We now know that the driving force behind the Ukrainian Bund was Marian Melenevsky, alias Bassok, a Ukrainian Social Democrat and formerly a friend of Trotsky's. However, he was soon overshadowed by a much more important agent who had been living in Constantinople since 1910.

On January 8, 1915, Wangenheim reported to Berlin that Alexander Helphand had presented himself for an interview at the German Embassy. This was Parvus, Trotsky's partner in the 1905 Soviet in Petrograd, the Germanized Russian revolutionary who had such a talent for finance. Parvus had been sent to Siberia after 1905, but he had escaped and had put the last few years to remarkable personal advantage in the Balkans. He had become a financial adviser to the government of the Young Turks, who were now leading their country into war on the German side, he had been an agent for German business firms in the Balkans, he had reportedly engaged in the Russian grain trade and possibly in oil transactions as well; and now he was rich. He was also as eager as ever to raise rebellion in Russia. Wangenheim found that Parvus had some arresting ideas as to how Germany might bring about that rebellion, and in January, 1915, Parvus was summoned to Berlin.

He arrived in the German capital on March 6, 1915, and was received by Dr. Kurt Riezler, a confidential adviser to the chancellor, Bethmann-Hollweg. We know something of their discussion for, as a result of it, Parvus wrote out an eighteen-page report on his proposals, entitled "Preparations for a Political Mass Strike in Russia," and this is in the Wilhelmstrasse archives. It is an important document—indeed it became the blueprint for the German strategy for the Russian revolution—and in compiling it Parvus drew upon his experiences of the 1905 rising as well as his intimate knowledge of the politics of the Russian revolutionaries. His was an agile and comprehensive mind.

Having made the obvious proposals, the promotion of national minority parties inside Russia, press campaigns, and so on, Parvus got down to practical cases. Petrograd, he said, must be made the headquarters of the revolutionary movement, and political agitation must especially concentrate on three large factories, the Obukhov, Putilov and Baltic works. Street maps of Petrograd would have to be printed and smuggled into Russia along with arms and ammunition, so that when the moment came the workers could hold the key points of the city. A railway strike must be organized so as to cut the lines running from Moscow and Petrograd to Warsaw; and at the same time the southwestern railroad net should be disrupted. The leadership of the rising, he advised, should be confided to the Social Democratic party, and arrangements should be made to finance it from Germany. He proposed that a conference should be held in Switzerland or some other neutral country with the object of bringing together the Bolsheviks, the Mensheviks and all the other anti-Czarist Russian exiles. As for the Social Revolutionary party inside Russia, it could be reached through Russian agents, chiefly schoolmasters in the provinces. He proposed means for raising a mutiny in the Black Sea fleet, for firing the Baku oil wells, for promoting strikes in the mines in the Donets Basin. Further, he recommended that an expedition should be sent to liberate Siberia so that the political exiles there could be released. In the United States, meanwhile, the Jewish people were to be stirred up against Russia, and in Finland revolutionary bases were to be established on the Russian border. Finally he envisaged the abdication of the Czar and the setting up in Petrograd of a provisional government which would be ready to make peace.

In short, though he was overoptimistic (he thought that the strikes could be started within three months) Parvus very nearly anticipated what actually was to happen, and it did not take the Germans long to realize that they were dealing with a most useful and energetic man. Parvus was given a German passport and granted leave to travel about and work out his plans. A day later the German treasury was asked to make a grant of two million marks for propaganda in Russia.

An aura of money hangs over Parvus. Since he himself was rich and quite unscrupulous he was in a position to ask confidently for sums which the other revolutionaries would never have dreamed of, and the Germans were impressed. At all events, at the end of March,

1915, he personally received one million marks, which was just half the German revolutionary budget for Russia at that time. He spent money as he made it—handsomely, rapidly and with an air of professional indifference. Probably we will never know just how much passed through his hands or whence it came or how much went into his own pocket and how much into the revolutionary net, but it is established that when the war was over he temporarily took up residence in Switzerland; and there he declared to the taxation authorities a personal fortune of thirty million Swiss francs.

Now, however, in the spring of 1915, Parvus was in the early days of those dealings, and he proceeded carefully. He first returned to the Balkans to wind up his affairs, and then in May made for Switzerland, where he put up at the fashionable Hotel Baur au Lac in Zurich. He already had a practical plan, and the Germans approved it. This called for the setting up of a "scientific institute," the ostensible object of which was to translate and republish socialist literature. Its real, or rather major, purpose was to provide a foreign headquarters for the Russian revolution. Copenhagen in neutral Denmark was chosen as the place for this venture, since the Danes had a pro-German government as well as a strong socialist movement of their own, and fairly easy access to Russia. Also Rantzau, the German Minister there, was an enthusiast for the revolutionary strategy.

In Switzerland Parvus recruited his staff from among the revolutionary exiles, promising them high rates of pay and all facilities and expenses for their journey across Germany to Denmark. In June, 1915, the organization began work.

Parvus of course was by no means the Germans' only resource. There was by now much else going on besides. A special bureau for the Russian revolution had been set up in the Wilhelmstrasse, and it worked closely with both the German High Command and the Foreign Office. All over Europe German embassies were promoting subversive activities, recruiting agents and reporting upon affairs in Russia. And yet the work was not advancing particularly well. The Russian masses were proving to be much less revolutionary than had been supposed. The war had made them unexpectedly patriotic, and the very bitterness of the struggle had hardened them against the Germans. In those countries on the periphery of Russia which we would now call satellites—Poland, Finland and the Baltic States— the nationalistic parties had not shown any great eagerness to rush into premature risings at Germany's request. Germany, they foresaw, was not bound to win the war, and if the risings failed they could expect terrible reprisals from the Russians. They preferred to wait.

The Germans were also discovering, as Karl Marx had done so long ago, that once you start dealing with the Russians "all hell breaks loose." The revolutionary exiles were very difficult to handle. They had a mania for disputation; the parties were split and split again, and their leaders lived in a state of indignant and contemptuous rivalry. All this made it an arduous business trying to find reliable agents. Many of the older revolutionaries were hopelessly out of touch, and out of date, and the new ones were unpredictable and erratic.

However, in September, 1914, a man named Alexander Keskuela had turned up in Switzerland, and he proved himself to be every bit as useful and as well-informed as Parvus was. Keskuela was a socialist politician whose main object in life was to secure the liberation of his native country Estonia from Russia: to achieve this he was ready for anything. He hated Russia—this was the basis of his collaboration with the Germans—and moreover he had a cast of mind which made an appeal to the higher officials in the German Foreign Office, men like von Jagow, the Secretary of State, and Alfred Zimmermann, an undersecretary who was closely concerned with the revolutionary strategy. Keskuela spoke fluent German, and he was an intellectual with a subtle and experienced mind. Romberg, the German Minister in Bern, was so impressed with him that he sent him off to Sweden to inquire into the prospects there. From Sweden Keskuela wrote a number of letters to Romberg which have been preserved. He was not greatly enthusiastic about the chances of revolution inside Russia itself, and thought the Germans might do better to concentrate their support on the minority movements. Later he suggested a conference of non-Russian revolutionaries, with the idea of setting up a central control for the revolutionary efforts of the Poles and other peoples under Russian rule.

One of Keskuela's letters from Stockholm is of special interest. He reported, quite accurately, that several Bolshevik deputies in the Duma had been arrested in Petrograd, and he went on: "These were people of the orientation of Mr. Lenin (Bern)—but if one is skillful, it should be possible to make more of this than the persons concerned themselves desire." Or in other words, it might be useful to enlist Lenin and his friends in the German cause even against their will. This letter, dated November 30, 1914, is the first clear-cut reference to Lenin in the German files.*

Keskuela was well entertained in Berlin on his way back to Switzerland; he met von Jagow and other senior officials in the Foreign Office (one of whom, Baron Rudolf von Nadolny, was destined to become German Ambassador in Moscow during the early days of the Hitler regime), and he was given facilities for visiting a camp for prominent—and promising—Russian prisoners of war. The end of February, 1915, found him back in Switzerland, and soon after this he entered upon the work which gives him a particular importance in the Russian revolution; he became the channel through which the Germans dealt with Lenin. The first meeting of which we know took place at the end of March, 1915.

Lenin's position at this time was one of extreme hostility to the socialist parties throughout Europe. In England, France, Austria and Germany as well as Russia they had all taken a patriotic line, and had voted to support their capitalist governments in the war. They did this with immense misgivings. "I know one had to vote for it," said Viktor Adler, the leader of Austrian socialism, "but I do not know how I brought it over my lips."

The German socialists' line of argument was briefly this: socialism in Germany was more advanced than in any other country, and a German defeat would mean the end of it. The real enemy of social-ism was Czarism. Therefore the correct course to pursue was to defeat Russia and set up a socialist republic there in place of the Czar. When this had been done the German socialists would be in a much stronger position to proceed with their own revolution

* Another reference by an unknown but extremely competent hand does crop up in the files about this time. It occurs in a report on the possibility of creating strikes in Russia, and it says: "An attempt should be made to get into touch with representatives of the bolsheviks, [such as] Lenin, through private per-sons. . . ." The anonymous writer suggests that money should be given to Lenin and that every worker in Petrograd should be promised 1½ marks for every day he was on strike.

against the Kaiser; indeed, they might then be so strong that no revolution in Germany might be necessary.

This argument, which was so convenient for the German socialists, made no appeal at all to most of the Russian socialists. They thought that a German victory would simply mean a continuation of the Czar's reign, and that German militarism would probably lead to the suppression of socialism all over Europe. Germany, they contended, was an imperialist aggressor, and Russia must defend herself against her. When Russia had won the war it would be time enough to raise the rebellion against the Czar.

Lenin disagreed with both these arguments. He denounced "defensism"—the defending of one's country—as treason to socialism. The socialists in every country, he said, must rise against their belligerent capitalistic governments. The imperialist war, in short, should be converted into a series of civil wars and in the resulting chaos socialism would triumph everywhere.

As a practical program there were certain disadvantages here: wars do not end with a general and simultaneous collapse of all the contestants. One side or the other is bound to win, and as we noticed before, revolutions do not as a rule occur in victorious countries. If the German socialists had followed Lenin's prescription and had brought about a revolution in Germany, or only sabotaged the war effort, a German defeat might have occurred within the first two years of the war; the German socialists were quite strong enough and sufficiently well organized to have accomplished this. The inevitable result would then have been that the Russian troops would have occupied Berlin, and that the eastern half of Germany, not to mention the Slav areas of Austria-Hungary, would have fallen under Russian domination. In these circumstances a Russian revolution in all likelihood would never have taken place. The Czarist regime would have obtained a new lease of life, and if it had been overthrown at all would have been succeeded by a government that was strongly militarist and middle-class.

Both Marx and Engels had foreseen these things very clearly. In the many wars that were fought during their lifetime in the nineteenth century they always took sides. They did not think that socialism would come at a single thunderclap, but that it would progress gradually from the most developed states to the most backward. In practice this meant that they supported Germany because socialism was strongest there, and they constantly advocated the defeat of Czarist Russia. In other words, they took the line the German socialists took in 1914, but they added a rider: it was possible, they argued, that the German government might become too strong and threaten socialism. In that case it was the duty of the socialists to turn against it.

All these conflicting views were of course bound to undergo changes when the experience of the awful slaughter of 1914, 1915 and 1916 put them to the test. By 1916 the majority of the Russian socialists both at home and abroad had in fact altered their position. Some now declared that the Czar was incapable of defending Russia, while others feared that the Czar would make a separate peace with Germany so that he could devote all his remaining strength to suppressing the growing revolutionary movement at home. Therefore they no longer wished to postpone the revolution: they wanted it to take place at once, though in a mild form, so that they could take over the duty of defending Russia. Still others, aware that war weariness had begun to take a fatal hold on the Russian masses, clamored for an early peace. Naturally there were many cross-currents in these broad arguments, but it is probably true to say that many Russian socialists started out in 1914 as "defensist" patriots and by 1917 had become defeatist revolutionaries.

Lenin also changed, and quite early in the war. At first he was disappointed and disgusted at the sudden outburst of patriotism everywhere, at the way in which in one country after another, Germany, France, England and Russia, the socialists voted war credits to their governments. However, he soon began to advance a new line. He did not abandon entirely his ideas on world revolution, but he agreed that the defeat of Russia would be "the lesser evil"—lesser, that is, than the defeat of Germany.* It was halfway

* The full quotation was: "It is impossible from the point of view of the international proletariat to say which would be the lesser evil for socialism, an Austro-German defeat or a Franco-Russo-English defeat. But for us Russian Social Democrats there can be no doubt that from the point of view of the working classes and of the toiling masses of all Russian peoples, the lesser evil would be the defeat of the Czarist monarchy. We cannot ignore the fact that

toward saying that he supported a German victory, and it was enough to make the agent Keskuela seek out Lenin in Bern in the spring of 1915. Keskuela's handwritten notes of the meeting are unreadable, but it seems that he found Lenin somewhat unwilling. Lenin refused to make his organization available to the Germans. Indeed, he was reluctant to take any positive action at all; he simply stated his new line—defeat of Russia first and then the world revolution—and left it, as it were, hanging in the air. Yet some sort of an understanding was reached between the two men, and almost certainly money was involved.

Prior to this the Bolsheviks in Switzerland had had about six thousand dollars from the Bund for the Liberation of the Ukraine, and with that money Lenin had got out his new paper *Social Democrat*. Now, from the spring of 1915 to the summer of 1916—the period when he was in touch with Keskuela—Lenin was in funds again. Keskuela, we know, had a sum which was the equivalent of between fifty and sixty thousand dollars from the Germans, so he was well able to finance the Bolshevik publications as long as they took an anti-Russian defeatist line. The main printing job for these publications was done on the presses of the German Admiralty, under an arrangement by which the magazines were first produced in small editions and on cheap paper in Switzerland. Copies were then taken to Germany and reproduced photographically on thin paper by the Admiralty. The finished product finally found its way up to the front line or was smuggled by roundabout routes into Russia.

Another result of Keskuela's contact with Lenin and other Bolsheviks was that in May, 1915, he presented a report on them to the German Foreign Office. It is a sensible and closely reasoned document. He begins by pointing out that while the oppressed minorities in the Russian empire might be able to come out openly in support of Germany, the Russian revolutionaries could only do so in secret, if they were to escape the odium that attaches to all traitors in time of war. Also there was a fundamental disagreement between the

---

this or that issue of the military operations will facilitate or render more difficult our work of liberation in Russia. And we say: yes, we hope for the defeat of Russia because it will facilitate the internal victory of Russia—the abolition of her slavery, her liberation from the chains of czarism."

two groups: the minorities were all for decentralization, the splitting up of Russia after the war; the revolutionaries, on the other hand, wanted centralization, the concentration of as much power as possible in their own hands.

Keskuela described Lenin as a good organizer and ruthlessly energetic, but his following, he said, was limited to city workers in Russia while the Mensheviks had broader support. Since so many of the Menshevik leaders were Jews they received a good deal of money from Jewish sources. The catch about the Mensheviks, however, was that all of them with the exception of a small "internationalist group" in their ranks were patriotic and therefore opposed to a German victory.

The report went on to say that there was another drawback about the Social Democrats in general from Germany's point of view; both Bolsheviks and Mensheviks now (in 1915) believed the revolution in Russia to be inevitable. But they wanted to delay the revolution until the end of the war so that they would get control over a united country; a premature revolution, they thought, might lead to the dismembering of Russia. This explained Lenin's "do nothing" attitude: he did not want the revolution to be "used" by the Germans. And so neither he nor the rest of the Social Democrats were absolutely to be trusted.

Keskuela wound up his report by advising the Wilhelmstrasse to adopt a three-point program: outright support for the national minority groups, the building-up of an independent revolutionary movement inside Russia (thus short-circuiting the reluctant exiles in Switzerland), and finally a concerted effort to bring the exiles round to the German way of thinking.

There is evidence in the German files that Keskuela continued his meetings with Lenin in Switzerland through the summer of 1915, obviously with the last of his three points in view. At the end of September, 1915, he came to the German Legation in Bern with a most important document which was at once sent on to the German Chancellor in Berlin. This was nothing less than Lenin's proposals for making peace with Germany in the event of the Bolsheviks obtaining power in Russia. Lenin's seven conditions were these:

Russia to be proclaimed a republic.

The large estates in Russia to be expropriated.

The eight-hour day to become law.

Autonomy for the minorities.

No indemnities to be paid or territory ceded to the Germans (though he had no objection to buffer states being created between Germany and Russia).

The Russian army to evacuate Turkey.

Russia to launch an attack on India.

The last two points are extraordinary, and they reveal just how far Lenin was prepared to go at this time in making a deal with Germany. In effect they meant that Bolshevik Russia would be prepared to give Germany a free hand in the Middle East, and would become an ally of Germany in an attack on the British empire.

Whether or not Lenin ever intended to fulfill these conditions is something we will never know, but the willingness to negotiate with the Germans is certainly revealed, and the unearthing of this document throws a new light on the armistice terms between Russia and Germany which were eventually agreed upon at Brest-Litovsk in 1918.

The other event of importance which occurred about this time—the late summer of 1915—was the long-awaited international conference of left-wing socialists which was held at Zimmerwald outside Bern. It was attended by extreme socialists of many different races and ways of thinking, and it produced a manifesto which was a kind of counter-blast to the patriotism with which the center and right-wing socialists had supported the war. It called on the working class everywhere, in belligerent and neutral states alike, "to recover itself and to fight for peace," and for "the sacred aims of socialism." It envisaged a peace without indemnities or annexations, and it insisted on the liberation of "oppressed nations" and the right of self-determination. However, it did not propose a practical policy.

Lenin put his name to this document, but he did not like it: within a few weeks he joined with a group of his immediate supporters—Zinoviev, Radek, a Swiss delegate named Fritz Platten and others—in issuing a declaration saying that they were not satisfied. The manifesto, they thought, was too anemic: it did not oppose "opportunism," and it "made no clear pronouncement as to the methods of fighting against the war." They proposed a number of such methods: the refusal to vote for war credits, denunciation of the war in both the legal and the illegal press, the organization of street demonstrations against governments, fraternization in the trenches, economic strikes. In brief: "Civil war, not civil peace—that is the slogan."

On the face of it this was a considerable backsliding on Lenin's part from his "new line" which aimed at an early defeat of Russia as "the lesser evil." On the other hand, it hardly committed him to anything very definite since he was quite unable to put these ideas into practice; and the declaration was certainly useful in establishing his reputation as a pure and incorruptible socialist—a point that was forever on his mind.

It is impossible to regard Lenin as a driving force through these years. He hangs back, he hesitates, he advances a little only to retreat into his shell again, and he is suspicious and reluctant about nearly every approach that is made to him. At the start of the war he took money from the Bund for the Liberation of the Ukraine, but he soon grew chary of that organization; he seems to have thought that it was leading him into the Menshevik camp and he broke his connection with it. Parvus came to see him in Switzerland, and in Parvus at once he scented a rival. Parvus had the money, he had the energy, and he was every bit as ruthless as Lenin was himself; it was quite possible that Parvus could reach over Lenin's head and get control of the party organization both in Europe and in Petrograd. Yet at first Lenin did not openly break with Parvus; he listened to his plans and then privately arranged to keep an eye on Parvus's activities in Copenhagen. One of Lenin's most trusted followers, the Polish Marxist Ganetsky, was dispatched to Denmark with instructions to join Parvus's scientific institute and to report upon it; and it was not until the end of 1915 that Lenin publicly attacked his rival in print.

This incident was a typical revolutionary affair. The Germans had noted a growing reluctance toward the war among their own socialists; the socialists were even saying that since defeat of Russia was now certain, it was time to begin sabotaging the German war effort along the lines suggested at the Zimmerwald conference. Parvus, the Russian revolutionary who for the time being was more German than the Germans, offered to correct this deviation. He published an article in his magazine, *Die Glocke (The Bell)*, saying that the German General Staff were now the strongest ally of the revolutionary parties since they alone could accomplish the downfall of the Czar. Lenin pounced upon this in his issue of *Social Democrat* on November 20, 1915, but with surprising leniency; no doubt he still wanted to keep contact with Parvus.

It was the same with his relations with Keskuela. Having at first regarded Keskuela as, possibly, an *agent provocateur*, Lenin accepted him as his go-between with the Germans, took money from him, and confided his peace plans to him; but by the summer of 1916 the relationship had been broken.

It was the old loneliness and ineffectiveness of the outsider, and the war had made Lenin triply an outsider since he had no country of his own, no patriotism and still no political following of any consequence. We find him in the summer of 1916 wandering aimlessly about. He involves himself in the small affairs of the Swiss socialist movement, he writes a book on imperialism, and the war very largely passes him by. From July 1 to mid-September he took a holiday in the mountain villages with Krupskaya, and on their return to Zurich they had very little money.

"Ilyich," Krupskaya says, "searched everywhere for some way of earning money—he wrote about it to Granat, to Gorky, to relatives, and once even developed a fantastic plan to publish a pedagogical encyclopedia." Eventually she herself got a job in a refugee bureau which brought in a small income.

Parvus meanwhile was in a blaze of activity in Copenhagen. His scientific institute, beginning at first with eight people working in Denmark and ten agents traveling inside Russia, had spread out into all kinds of subsidiary activities. A weapons depot was set up in Denmark and a regular service of couriers was organized to get them into Russia. *The Bell* appeared twice weekly, and there were other publishing ventures as well. A spy network was operating, and it was bringing in a regular flow of information from Russia. All this needed money, and Parvus indicated to Berlin through Rantzau, the German Minister in Copenhagen, that he estimated that it would require twenty million rubles to get a revolution started in earnest. Some of this at least the Germans were willing to give—there is a record of one million rubles being handed over to Parvus at the end of December, 1915, in addition to the other large sums he had previously received—but the problem was to find enough money in Russian notes, and to get this money safely to the revolutionary groups in Russia.

Parvus tackled this matter with his usual flair; he entered into business with Russia. All through this period the Russian borders with Finland were very loosely controlled, and the Russian regulations for trading with the enemy had many loopholes. During December, 1915, and the following January the Russian Ministry of Commerce and Industry excepted a long list of commodities from their Trading with the Enemy Act, and specifically they allowed the importation into Russia of many German metals, including copper, iron, steel, aluminum, nickel, tin and lead. Parvus entered into this trade on a large scale, and even expanded the range to include electrical goods and such medicines as Salvarsan, which under false labels and by other means were shipped to Petrograd. A part at least of the rubles he collected were left in Russia and distributed to the revolutionary cells by his agents there.

At the same time a nice killing was made in Denmark. During the early part of the war Denmark got most of her coal from Britain, but as the U-boat campaign developed prices went up and Parvus was able to undercut the British with German coal. Subsequently he added to his income by withholding this coal from the market until scarcity prices prevailed: then he cashed in.

In all these dealings Rantzau, the German Minister in Copenhagen, was an active supporter. He liked Parvus and respected his intelligence, and he advised Berlin that as long as Parvus could be controlled he should be trusted and used. It was not altogether acceptable advice—there was a group in the Wilhelmstrasse which included von Jagow, the Secretary of State, who had their doubts about Parvus—but Rantzau persisted. His correspondence with the German Foreign Office indicates that he and Parvus were often together, at this time.

Meanwhile the other devices in Parvus's grand strategy for the revolution were developing. His idea of sending an expedition into Siberia was of course altogether too visionary, but contacts were made with the Social Revolutionary party which was still closer to the peasants than any other party, since it covered the provincial districts deep inside Russia. Chernov and Bobrov, the two leaders of the left wing of the Social Revolutionaries, were in exile abroad, and it was probably with their assistance that agents were sent with funds into central Russia. Everywhere, in fact, the German net was now spreading fast, and money in large quantities was flowing into Russia.

The fomenting of revolution inside the minority states was also going ahead. A League of Russian Nationalities was formed in Lausanne in Switzerland, and since its German origins were kept well to the background it drew support from people in all neutral countries who saw in Russia nothing but the tyranny of the Czar, the oppression of small states and the persecution of the Jews. In February, 1916, the American Jewish Relief Committee held a mass meeting in New York to collect money for Jewish refugees, and at this and other meetings the large sum of six and a half million dollars was raised during the early years of the war. About one-third of this money went to Russia. The Jewish Committee in America of course was not a German-sponsored organization—it was a purely philanthropic body—but there is no doubt that some of the money found its way to the Russian revolutionaries.

There were setbacks from time to time. In November, 1916, for instance, the Germans made a clumsy effort to rouse the Poles against Russia by announcing the establishment of an independent "Kingdom of Poland." This elicited no enthusiasm at all among the Poles. With the retreat of the Grand Duke Nicholas's armies their country was now under German occupation, and they saw the menace of German militarism rather clearer than anyone else. Moreover, it was becoming apparent by this time that things were really moving to a crisis inside Russia itself.

Through the last half of 1916 the Germans were getting a steady flow of information from Russia and some of them were encouraged by it. They knew about the strikes in Petrograd, about the increasing hostility to the Czar in the Duma, and about the tense condition of the Russian army. Parvus's agents were reporting these things with surprising speed and accuracy, and Parvus himself had great hopes that on January 22, 1917, the twelfth anniversary of Bloody Sunday, a major explosion would occur.

There was one sobering note, and it crops up more than once in the German files: agents also reported to Berlin that if revolution did come it would not be the Russian socialists who would form a new government, it would be the liberal parties; and the liberals were determined to continue with the war. This was confirmed by Keskuela, who had a meeting with Milyukov in Stockholm in September, 1916. He reported that the Cadet leader was anti-Czarist, but as regards the war and the defense of Russia he was even more patriotic than the Czar.

The Germans were in a difficult position. Having for two years or more raised this monster, the projected Russian revolution, and having spent millions of marks, they were no longer sure that they wanted it any more. If it was not going to put Russia out of the war, nor even seriously weaken her, then surely it was much better politics to explore the possibilities of making a separate and an immediate peace with the Czar. Could he not be blackmailed into coming to terms? The Germans had only to guarantee that they would not make unreasonable demands—that once the armistice was signed the Czar would be given a free hand to put down the unrest inside Russia—and at one stroke they would accomplish everything which up to now the revolutionary strategy had failed to do.

It was not an impossible proposition. There was a pro-German party in Petrograd. Protopopov had already put out feelers to the Germans when he had passed through Stockholm in 1916, and now Protopopov was a close adviser of the Empress. He was backed by Stürmer and others in the Czarist court who were known to be anti-British. Rasputin too was believed to be an opponent of the war. Surely then Nicholas himself was not beyond reach if the right approach was made to him.

These views began to take root in the Wilhelmstrasse in the summer of 1916, and the Foreign Office files reveal how from week to week they began to prevail. The contact with Lenin is broken. Keskuela, who is interested solely in a Russian revolution, receives less attention; and it is decided that no reference to the Protopopov-Stürmer group should be made in the German press. There is a general slowing down in the revolutionary strategy, or rather it is left to run along of its own accord, while at the highest and most secret level in Berlin plans for negotiating with the Czar began.

Sometime in the summer of 1916 the Kaiser instructed Bethmann-Hollweg to make an attempt to reach Nicholas through nonofficial intermediaries and Jews. The next important reference in the German files is dated October 3. On that day Bethmann-Hollweg informed the Kaiser that he had accepted the offer of the Swedish Foreign Minister, Wallenberg, to let him work for a separate peace with Russia, and that Wallenberg would be able to negotiate through General Brändström, the Swedish Ambassador in Petrograd, and other channels. Simultaneously with all this, other unofficial contacts were set in motion through the agency of newspapermen, bankers, merchants, politicians and members of the international aristocracy. A definite peace plan was under way.

This, then, was the condition of German political strategy at the end of 1916: one party in the Wilhelmstrasse is beginning to insist that the revolutionizing policy has run its course and that it now ought to be abandoned in favor of making a direct approach to the Czar. The other party still clings to the original idea that the revolutionary plan is the right one: that once the Czar is deposed such chaos will result that Russia will no longer be able to carry on the war. Yet neither side can produce any solid backing for their views. There is no real confidence that Nicholas is approachable any more than there is any proof that once the revolution is accomplished such men as Lenin could be trusted to seize the power and conclude a separate peace. Where, in fact, in this half-world of bribery and twisted loyalties can anyone be trusted?

It was in these confusing circumstances that in the first days of 1917 news reached Berlin that Rasputin was dead, and German planners and Russian revolutionaries alike waited in an equal ignorance to see what the aftermath was going to be.

CHAPTER NINE

The Rising, March, 1917

THE MURDER of Rasputin was a nine days' wonder all over Russia, and yet it accomplished very little. The Empress did not collapse; she merely went, day after day, in a trance of mystical grief, to pray for hours beside the *Starets*'s tomb; and her determination to destroy her enemies was as strong as ever. The murderers were not tried and hanged; they were too closely connected with the royal family for that. The public regarded them as heroes, even saints, and people burnt candles for them in the churches. In the end they were banished: Yusupov to his country estate in the south, the Grand Duke Dmitri to Kasvin in Persia, and Purishkevich to the front. We hear very little of them any more.

No demonstrations occurred, and the government did not fall. The *Starets*, having no philosophy and no real following anywhere, vanished from the scene in the same way as he had come in, as a kind of joker, a wild card in the game, and he was a supreme example of the truth that the evil men do lives after them. He had undermined the morality of the political life of Petrograd, and shaken people's loyalty everywhere; and when, after a few days, it was seen that there was to be no change—that Nicholas and the Empress meant to continue precisely as they had done before—a mood of utter despondency began to spread. Few now could see any hope of winning the war or of bringing Nicholas to his senses, and it became common talk around Petrograd that revolution was now inevitable; and with revolution starvation, chaos, the end of Russia. The Russians indulged in this pessimism in a way that only people with suicidal tendencies can hope to understand. It was virtue to despair; defeat and tragedy, it was felt, were the inevitable price of their own guilt, and what they foresaw now was an enormous atonement: the suicide of Russia itself. But since one cannot wallow forever in self-pity, these feelings were soon replaced—perhaps overlaid is the better word—by a more normal sense of exasperation, of anger against the Czar. There were so many plots against Nicholas and his wife in January, 1917, that it is impossible to keep track of them all. The Empress was to be arrested on her next visit to headquarters. The Czar was to be waylaid in his train. The whole of the royal family was to be kidnaped. These plots were not the inventions of terrorists or of Lenin's Bolsheviks; they were discussed by the most responsible men in the Duma, even the monarchist party itself. In the most blue-blooded of drawing rooms in Petrograd, and in the presence of the Czar's own relatives, disloyal toasts were drunk and plans for Nicholas's abdication were openly debated.

But it was argument without action. The very hopelessness of the situation seemed to numb people's energy, and to make matters even worse an appalling wave of cold weather settled on the country. In January, 1917, temperatures went down to more than forty degrees below zero, and the railway network upon which the cities utterly depended for their food and the army for its supplies was frozen to a standstill. The desire for food, warmth and peace dominated the mind of the ordinary man, and you had only to join a bread queue to realize that the Russian worker, with his docility, his famous capacity for enduring terrible hardships, was approaching one of his periodic outbursts of semimadness, when he could think of nothing but to smash and burn and destroy. This—not the Germans—was the danger which the "official" classes really feared and tried desperately to impress upon the Czar.

But Nicholas now was less approachable than ever. Rasputin's death seemed to have left him in a kind of fatalistic and resentful daze. He shut himself up in Tsarskoe Selo with his family as though he were besieged by enemies, and there was not much charm or gentleness left in him any more. Every attempt to argue with him drove him further back into hostility and suspicion; he was now the prophet Job and the autocrat combined. When the Grand Dukes, his own uncles and brothers, wrote to him earnestly warning him that revolution was becoming inevitable unless he set up a popular government, he replied with some such phrase as, "I allow no one to give me advice"; and he repeated flatly his conviction that it was his duty to preserve the autocracy to the end. On January 12 the British Ambassador, Buchanan, went to Nicholas to express the anxiety that the Allies, Britain and France, were feeling about the situation. He was received standing up, and it was during this interview that Nicholas made the celebrated remark, "Do you mean that *I* am to regain the confidence of my people, Ambassador, or that they are to regain *my* confidence?"

Others who saw Nicholas through these days say that they were given audience in a room which was screened at one end by a curtain; and they had the uncomfortable feeling that the Empress was sitting behind that curtain listening to every word that was said.

Early in January Trepov managed to get his resignation from the premiership accepted, and a career bureaucrat, Prince Nicholas Golitsyn, was put in his place. There seems to have been no reason whatever for this appointment unless it was that the Prince was ill, weak and extremely old, and therefore compliant. He was horrified when Nicholas appointed him but knew no way of refusing, and in any case the real Prime Minister of Russia now was Protopopov. The hatred and rage against Protopopov in the Duma was so great that he was shouted down whenever he appeared there, but he had other resources: each night he was said to hold séances in which he communicated with Rasputin, and the results of these mysteries were given by telephone to the Empress on the following morning. Protopopov also saw to it that the Empress should continue with her delusions by arranging that each day fictitious telegrams and letters should be sent telling her how splendid, how fine, how courageous she was, and how deeply the Czar was loved.

At the end of January an important delegation from the Allies arrived in Petrograd; it was led by Lord Milner of England, Doumergue of France and Scialoia of Italy, and its object was to co-ordinate plans with Russia and if possible stiffen the Russian front. A tremendous round of banquets and meetings was held and nothing was achieved, nothing except that it was made still more apparent that Russia was drifting into a crisis that nobody seemed able to prevent or even define. At the front the leading generals, Alexeiev, Brusilov and Russky were as gloomy as any of the politicians, and they too were surreptitiously discussing means of getting rid of the Czar. Brusilov was even quoted as saying, "If I must choose between the Czar and Russia I shall march for Russia."

During January at least three separate centers of agitation against the Czar began to take shape in Petrograd. There was the Union of Nobles, an organization of the aristocracy which was plotting for a palace revolution. There were the political parties of the extreme left, chiefly the Social Democrats, forever eating away underground, like white ants, inside the factories and the armed services. And there was the Duma itself. Through all three groups the Okhrana coiled itself like some parasitical creeper that flourishes best where it can generate rottenness and decay.

Both in the Duma and in the Social Democratic party there had been a tendency for the conflicting factions to coalesce through the war years, and this tendency gathered force after Rasputin's death. In the Duma all the more liberal and left-wing deputies, except the socialists, had grouped themselves into a single party known as the Progressive Bloc. They numbered 240 out of a total of 402 deputies, and their principal leaders were Rodzianko, the president of the Duma, Milyukov, the chief of the Cadets, Guchkov,* a monarchist who had fallen out with the Czar over Rasputin, and Prince Lvov, who, though not a member of the Duma, had had an admirable record as the chairman of the zemstvo councils in Moscow. Alexander Kerensky skirmished around the outskirts of this group.

In a similar way an organization known as the Mezhrayonka had grown up inside the Social Democratic party, and its object was to bring together the Mensheviks and the Bolsheviks. Its members had intellectual leanings—Trotsky was to become one of its leaders— but it was becoming increasingly active and influential at this time. Maxim Gorky, though not actually a leader of the Mezhrayonka, was perhaps the best representative of its feelings and aims.

* Guchkov, a former President of the Duma and a wealthy capitalist, was a fantastic figure, a kind of Russian D'Annunzio. He had traveled the Great Wall of China, had fought against the British in the Boer War in South Africa, and with Greek guerrillas in Macedonia, and had engaged in many duels. At this time he was a leader in the plot for a palace revolution.

By the end of January both the Progressive Bloc and the Mezhrayonka were working for a change of government in their own separate ways. On February 8 there was an incident that affected both groups: eight members of a workers' delegation to the War Industries Committee* were put under arrest for expressing pacifist views. While the Progressive Bloc was certainly not pacifist it resented arbitrary government action just as much as the Mezhrayonka and the Social Democrats did; and all were united in their common loathing of Protopopov and in their determination to remove the Czar.

On February 27 the Duma was due to reassemble, and from all sides there were plans to mark the day with an attack upon the government. Leaflets appeared in the industrial districts urging the workers to rise against the government, and although the Bolsheviks and Mensheviks tried to sabotage one another's plans a demonstration did take place. Inside the Duma Kerensky made a violent speech in which he declared that Russia was exhausted, and that the moment had come for "liquidating" the war.

There followed a further rapprochement between the socialist parties inside and outside the Duma; under Gorky's chairmanship a combined meeting was held of left-wing deputies, Bolsheviks, Mensheviks, the Mezhrayonka and the Social Revolutionaries. A bureau was set up to co-ordinate their actions.

Yet still there was nothing here that really amounted to revolution. Revolution was in the air, but no one yet seemed to be able to give it any practical expression. It hovered over Petrograd like a threatening thunderstorm, but still it did not strike, and no one party or group of parties had the power to make it strike.

On the day of the Duma opening Rodzianko, the president, had written urgently to Nicholas saying that revolution was imminent. There was no reply. After two depressing months at Tsarskoe Selo Nicholas was preparing to return to his military headquarters at Mogilev, 450 miles south of Petrograd, and he was looking forward to the peace and quietness there. "I shall take up dominoes again in my spare time," he said.

* The War Industries Committee was a universal non-party organization—it included representatives of the workers—which had been set up by the government with the object of increasing and controlling war production. It was one of the few successful branches of the government machine.

A dozen speculations can be made about Nicholas's behavior at this time. Had he been informed by Protopopov and the Okhrana that they proposed to provoke risings in Petrograd so that they could crush the revolutionary parties there once and for all? Was he warned that there was to be an attempt at a *coup d'état*—perhaps even an attempt on his own and the Empress's life—by Guchkov and his friends?

There has never been any clear proof of any of these suppositions. One is simply left with the conclusion that Nicholas departed from Petrograd at this critical moment without knowing that a crisis was at hand—or perhaps the better way of putting it is to say that he did not choose to know. Yet there had been warnings that the storm was about to burst. On March 1, 1917, bread rationing was introduced and there was a run on the bakeries. This was followed by strikes in the metal works and women's demonstrations. But it was the sort of thing that had happened so often before and there was no general alarm in Petrograd, no real upsetting of the city's life. The first week of March slipped away uneasily but uneventfully, and no really effective precautions were taken beyond the dispatch of a small force of seamen to the capital and a certain tightening-up of discipline in the police.

Nicholas at all events saw no reason to delay his departure any longer, and on March 8 he left: and on that day the Russian revolution began.

Looking back now on the events of March, 1917, reading the accounts of the people who were there, looking at the old photographs, one finds oneself immediately struck by the absence of spectacle, the ordinariness of it all. There ought to be some thunderclap, some highly charged act of drama that announces that a new age has begun; but nothing of the sort occurs. All civilian street fighting looks very much the same, no matter where it happens. There is no pattern to the scene, none of the panoply, the bugles and the uniforms, with which men normally go to war; and at any given moment it is difficult to say just who is fighting whom. There before you lie the familiar streets, the cobblestones, the tramlines running up the center, the shops, the office where every day you go to work and the restaurant where you eat; and it is an unreal and inexplicable thing that now there should be dead bodies slumped in the gutters and on the open roadway.

According to the eyewitnesses who were there at the time, it was like this in Petrograd. The revolution insinuated itself, as it were, into the city, and for a few days people did not believe what was happening before their eyes. They thought at first that the sounds of machine-gun shots must be the soldiers at firing practice in their barracks, that the youths who rushed by in lorries, yelling at the top of their voices, must simply have been out of their wits, and that the sudden spells of quiet—the absence of traffic—were nothing out of the ordinary. The everyday things of life went on and got mixed up in the oddest way with the fighting. A milkman's van was seen trundling down the Nevsky Prospekt at the very moment when the police were getting ready to fire; and when the firing did start groups of women typists could be seen looking down from the upper windows as though some kind of parade was going on, a ceremony for some visiting celebrity. Soon, of course, everyone realized the gravity of the situation, but that did not altogether halt the city's normal life. The social round in the palaces along the Neva, for instance, went on almost as before. We have Paléologue's word for it that as late as March 8 his dinner guests at the French Embassy were still debating just which of the three reigning prima ballerinas at the Mariinsky Theatre—Pavlova, Karsavina or Kshesinskaya— was to be preferred. On March 9 Buchanan, the British Ambassador, reported to London: "Some disorders occurred today but nothing serious."

There was another aspect to these March days in Petrograd which also made them seem unnatural and unreal: it was difficult to know who had started the rising or just what force there was behind it. If the revolutionary leaders were engineering things in the back-ground they certainly did not appear in the streets. The mob was in the streets, and the truth was that this March rising, like so many other lesser risings in the past, was not directly provoked by the revolutionary leaders, least of all by Lenin and the Bolshevik exiles. In the beginning it was a movement of the people themselves. You could not call it spontaneous; for weeks and months, even for years, an outburst had been expected, and many different revolutionary groups were ready to take advantage of it once it had happened. But quite plainly, at the start, it was a boiling over of mass discontent. The workers were fed up with the war. They had no bread, they were cold, and they were furious with the bureaucrats who were supposed to control their lives.

For the first few days many of the demonstrators did not know where they were going to go or what they were supposed to do: they simply wanted to protest. But then, as more and more men poured into the streets, the crowds took confidence from their own numbers and they found with astonishment and exhilaration how very much they were not alone: not just a reckless few, but a host of comrades in a fighting mood. And so they accepted the leaders who appeared as they went along, and in the absence of personal enemies they attacked symbols. The policeman in his uniform was a symbol. So was the rich man in his car. So was the Winter Palace. And so the law courts, the police stations, the jails, the Fortress of St. Peter and St. Paul, the arsenal. All these were symbols of the corrupt and hated authority and they were attacked.

There were many workers, of course, who hung back. They may have been secretly satisfied that some sort of demonstration against the government was being made at last, but they were not genuinely revolutionary and in their hearts they were afraid: they wanted others to make the rebellion for them and their main concern was to avoid being hurt.

But it was the attitude of the soldiers which counted most. There had been, as we have seen, many mutinies in the armed forces before this, and at times they had been accompanied by civilian strikes and demonstrations. Yet soldiers and workers had never really combined together in one united protest against the authorities, and in the end military detachments like the Cossacks and the Imperial Guards had always been willing to fire on the crowd. Now, however, it was different.

The Petrograd garrison at this time numbered something over 160,000 men with the addition of 3,500 police, and they were armed with rifles, machine guns, armored cars and even artillery. It seemed to be a formidable force with which to control a city of little more than two million people, and so it was, provided you could count on the soldiers' loyalty. But it so happened that many of these men were replacements—workers in their thirties and forties who had been recruited from the very industrial areas where the trouble was most acute. For a long time socialist agitators had been quietly active among them. Others again were non-Russians—Estonians and the like—and they too in the midst of this depressing war had been very ready to listen to seditious propaganda. As for the Cossacks, who were the immemorial bulwark of all the Czars against riots, they were mostly young and inexperienced countrymen and they had not been trained in street fighting.

So from the first there was a definite sympathy between the garrison in Petrograd and the striking workers from the factories. They did not immediately throw in their lot together, there were many hesitations and backslidings, but after the first few days of rioting, the bulk of the soldiers did go over to the workers' side, and then you got—to borrow a phrase from the nuclear physics—a critical mass, an explosive strong enough to blow the Romanovs out of existence. It was the soldiers who really made the revolution.

Yet it was still an unpremeditated explosion, and there was no real sense to it so long as the crowd itself was running wild; the sense came later when the politicians finally emerged and struggled with one another for control of the new situation which the workers and the soldiers and the Dark People had so haphazardly created. This political struggle was the real drama of the revolution, not the street fighting. Until the middle of March no one in Petrograd could guess what sort of a new government would emerge, or whose ideas were going to prevail.

There remains one other point of importance. The workers and the soldiers by themselves could never have made the revolution succeed. They needed money, leaders and political organization; and these they got from the many underground organizations that were interested in bringing down the Czar. The proletariat may have ignited the revolution, but others made it work, and used it for their own ends.

And so what we have to consider here in these next few days in Petrograd is a loose and disjointed imbroglio, a confused cracking, as it were, of the normal surface of life, an experiment; and it is a spectacle that is acted out in the most dismal of conditions, in freezing cold, in the dreary streets of a wartime city, and at a time of year when night still fell in the early afternoon. You might perhaps characterize the whole affair as a sudden fire burning at night on the ice.

On March 3 a branch of the Putilov works in the Moscow-Narva district had come out on strike as a protest against the dismissal of some of the men. There was a meeting of the strikers, and a delegation was sent off to the management to demand that the dismissed men should be reinstated. The management refused. Up to this point it was a purely industrial dispute and a small one at that. But now the atmosphere changed; the workers remembered other grievances and injured pride began to take a hand. They went back to the management with a demand for higher wages, and when this was refused other branches of the works were drawn in. They staged an "Italian strike"—a sit-down strike. The management's answer to this was to impose a general lockout on all employees at the works, a total of about thirty thousand men. Deputations of workers at once went off to other factories on the Vyborg side asking for their support.

And now a new and unusual factor entered the situation. March 8 had been chosen as "Women's Day." In the main this was to be a demonstration for better conditions by the working women of the capital, and plans for it had been maturing for a very long time. Even as far back as the prewar years socialists everywhere had been striving to draw women into the workers' movements, and women in fact had become an important part of striking technique. Their presence in a street demonstration was not only a gesture of solidarity: it also deterred the police from breaking up the processions too roughly, especially if there were children there as well.

On the evening of March 7 a women's meeting was held in the Lesnoy textile factory to make final plans for the following day, and it was decided to adopt two slogans: "Down with the autocracy" and "Down with the war." The meeting was addressed by a certain V. N. Kayurov, who was the organizer of one of the Bolshevik cells in the Vyborg district, not a great man in the Bolshevik party but a very important one at this particular moment when all the leaders were in exile. Kayurov advised the women against taking any provocative action. Probably he gave this advice because premature and isolated demonstrations usually came to nothing and were easily handled by the police. But it was not advice the women wanted to hear. On the following morning most of the textile factories which were staffed with women came out on strike, and they soon joined hands with the men who had been locked out of the Putilov works. A major political upheaval was on the way.

Kayurov was quick enough to see that if he could not block the movement the sooner he got to the head of it the better, and with two other organizers—a Menshevik and a Social Revolutionary— he formed a strike committee. All male and female workers were ordered into the streets, and columns of strikers marched from factory to factory gathering adherents on the way. Their cry was "Give us bread," and a number of bakeries were looted. In the course of the afternoon of March 8 two attempts were made by the demonstrators to cross the Neva into the main part of the city, and the police came out and drove them back. Later a third attempt was made, and this time a column which was chiefly made up of women succeeded in breaking through to the Nevsky Prospekt. They marched as far as the Kazan Cathedral, rhythmically singing "Give us bread" as they went along. Again the bakeries were looted.

March 9 was largely a repetition of the previous day except that this time the strikers came across the Neva in much greater strength —it was not yet so late in the winter that they could not walk across the ice on the river—and the police were unable to hold them back from the center of the city. Up to this point practically no firearms had been used by the police, and the workers themselves had resorted to nothing worse than lumps of ice, heavy sticks and occasionally cobblestones. The authorities indeed had been handling things rather gently; the soldiers were still confined to their barracks and the Cossacks had not even been issued with their whips, the weapons with which they habitually broke up disorderly gatherings.

Now, however, on the night of March 9 a genuine alarm begins. Everyone suddenly begins to act. Having been overtaken by events, we find the left-wing political leaders beginning to come forward for the first time. The Mezhrayonka were the first in the field; they issued a strike order halting all streetcars—always a very effective way of spreading disorder—and they followed this up on the night of

March 9 with a call for a three-day general strike. On what authority these orders were given no one could say, yet the Mezhrayonka was very confident at this time, and its roots went even deeper and more deviously into the revolutionary movement than those of the Okhrana. It was the most active of the left-wing groups in Petrograd, it had most influence with the women workers (who had really launched the whole movement in the first place), and we now know from the Wilhelmstrasse files that the Germans had been seeking contact with such organizations. The Mezhrayonka was late in openly attempting to direct affairs, but it well might have been very active in secret before this. It was the same with the Bolsheviks. Having opposed the rising in the beginning, or at any rate having stood aside from it, they were now filled with eagerness to get their share of the glory. A few hours after the Mezhrayonka acted they too came out with an appeal to the masses: "Everybody into the streets . . . the time has come for open combat."

The government on its side was also beginning to realize that this was no ordinary demonstration. Quite apart from the size and the vehemence of the mob, there was at least one ominous sign that a fundamental break with the past was occurring: the Cossacks had not charged upon the crowds as they had been ordered to do. They had ridden through singly or in groups of one or two, and at some places they had actually fraternized with the demonstrators. On the night of March 9 messages went flying forth to Nicholas at his headquarters at Mogilev. His ministers told him that the situation had become serious and that they must resign. They begged the Czar to return to Petrograd, and to enter into negotiations for the formation of a popular government. Late on March 10 Nicholas replied to this agitation by issuing a strangely complacent command to General Khabalov, the Military Governor of Petrograd: "I order that the disorders in the capital shall be stopped tomorrow." One wonders just how far the Okhrana was involved in this; had they been deliberately going slow in repressing the rising in order to lure the workers to a showdown? Were they now advising the Czar that the time had come to act?

In point of fact it was more than time; the situation was getting out of hand, and in the face of the three hundred thousand workers who were now raging through the streets General Khabalov's efforts to restore order were feeble in the extreme. On Saturday, March 10, he forbade assemblies and public meetings. He arrested a hundred-odd left-wing politicians, including several members of the Bolshevik Central Committee. And he ordered the workers back to work within three days; not immediately, it must be noticed, not on the following Monday, which surely would have been the normal time for them to go back, but on Tuesday, March 13, which was the very day on which the general strike called by the Mezhrayonka was to end. General Khabalov was playing it safe.

Early on Sunday, March 11, huge crowds were out in the streets again. They came swarming across from the Vyborg side carrying red banners and crying, "Down with the German woman," which could only mean one person, the Empress, and once more they made for the Nevsky Prospekt and the center of the city. This time they were met by soldiers, and although the soldiers were not altogether unfriendly confused skirmishes began. Shortly before noon there was an incident in front of the Nicholas Station, where the crowds were repeatedly breaking through the soldiers' ranks: a company of the Volinsk Regiment was ordered to open fire. They fired but they aimed their rifles at the sky. It was the first sign of defection in the garrison, but it was premature. In the afternoon another serious clash took place in Znamenskaya Square and this time the soldiers shot directly into the mob. Some sixty people were killed and as many wounded.

By now the crowd was running amok. Everywhere police stations were being attacked, looted and burned, and those police who were not lucky enough to be able to change into civilian clothes were being hunted down through the back streets. The law courts were stormed and rioters ran through the building hurling documents out onto the frozen canal below. Others attacked the jails and released the prisoners—murderers, thieves, political detainees, it did not matter whom. When night fell many fires were burning throughout the city, and there was yet another incident in the army: a company of the Pavlovsky Regiment mutinied and killed its colonel, and although the soldiers were eventually disarmed it was becoming clear that no officer could be absolutely certain of the loyalty of his men.

We are coming very close to the real crisis of the rising now.

Messages were flowing in spate between the city, Mogilev and the front line. General Ivanov, a former commander of the southwestern front, was ordered by Nicholas to proceed at once to Petrograd and subdue the city. He was promised four regiments of front-line soldiers. In Petrograd itself the Czar's ministers held one frantic meeting after another, and some were already creeping away into hiding. Rodzianko telegraphed Nicholas for the last time and ended his message, "May the blame not fall on the wearer of the Crown." Nicholas is said to have put the telegram aside with the remark, "Some more rubbish from that fat Rodzianko," and he gave orders for the Duma to be disbanded. But there was no question now of suppressing the men in the Duma; they refused to be suppressed. Like the revolutionaries they were being forced to take action; and the effective center of this force was the army.

The soldiers had been shocked, confused and made resentful by the events of the day. In the Volinsk Regiment in particular there was a sense of revulsion and horror at what they had done: to shoot at armed Germans was one thing but to murder their own people was another. The officers, and there were only two of them to each fifteen hundred men, were for the most part elderly and disgruntled reservists, and some of them shared in this feeling as well. A long debate continued in the barracks through the night of March 11, and out of it there emerged one of those many key figures in the Russian revolution who rise out of nowhere, who hold the stage for a moment with an air of natural and convinced command, and who then vanish almost without a trace. In this case it was a Sergeant Timofeyef Kirpichnikov. On the morning of Monday, March 12, Kirpichnikov led the Volinsk Regiment out of its barracks to fight for the revolution. In marching order and with the band playing the soldiers proceeded to the quarters of the Preobrazhensky and the Litovsky regiments, who had also been subjected to a good deal of subversive propaganda, and these men too came out against the Czar. A snowballing movement had begun, and it was the end of the imperial army in Petrograd. There was a short sharp fight with a detachment from the Moscow Regiment which obeyed its officers for a time, but one after another the other regiments in the city gladly joined the mutiny: the Oranienbaum machine-gun regiment, the Semenovsky, and finally the Ismailovsky. The Cossacks

The Winter Palace in Petrograd (St. Petersburg).

Alexander Palace.

A royal group at Coburg: Queen Victoria center front, Kaiser Wilhelm seated at her right, the Czar and Czarina standing behind them in second row.

Royal cousins, Nicholas II (left) and the Prince of Wales, later George V.

Czarina Alexandra Feodorovna about 1909.

Lenin as a boy of 15.

Lenin in 1897.

Leo Tolstoy (left) and Maxim Gorky in 1900

Czarist secret police ''mug shots'' of Leon
Trotsky at the age of 25.

John Reed.

The Russian royal family about 1914. The children: (back row left to right) Maria, Tatiana and Olga; (seated, front) the Czarevich Alexis and Anastasia.

Georgi Plekhanov, Social Democratic party leader for twenty years, mostly outside Russia.

J. M. Sverdlov, chairman of the Congress of Soviets Executive Committee, who played an outstanding part in the October revolution.

Alexis Rykov, an early Bolshevik, later one of the leaders of the Soviet Council of the People's Commissars.

Victor Chernov, leader of Social Revolutionary party.

Rasputin.

Kerensky, Prime Minister of Russia after the "July Days" crisis.

Underwood & Underwood

Kerensky (front center) watching the funeral procession of Cossacks killed defending the government, Petrograd, 1917.

Demonstration in Petrograd during the "July Days."

Sovfoto

The last photo of the Czar a few days
before he was executed at Ekaterinburg
in 1918.

The Empress of Russia in her wheel
chair at Tsarskoe Selo in 1917.

The children of the Czar during their confinement at Tsarskoe Selo in 1917,
only a few months before their murder. (Left to right) Olga, the Czarevich,
Anastasia and Tatiana.

Leon Trotsky in 1919.

Lenin and Stalin in 1922.

were still neutral, but soon news came from the outlying suburbs that other units had also risen "for the people."

March 12 was a day of continuous upheaval. Many of the soldiers went off to join the mobs that were attacking the police stations and looting through the streets. They sacked the Okhrana building, they stormed the arsenal and distributed the arms they found, and they broke into the Fortress of St. Peter and St. Paul itself. The police force now had disintegrated, and many of its minor minions had disguised themselves as soldiers by borrowing army greatcoats. General Khabalov's actions, meanwhile, were descending through tragedy to farce. Late at night he got out an order proclaiming martial law in the city, but no glue could be found to post up the announcement. A remnant of loyal troops numbering between fifteen hundred and two thousand men still adhered to the general, and he retired first to the Winter Palace and then to the Admiralty.

But it was the Duma which had now become the real center of events, and all through this day there was a continuous stream of people pressing on toward the Tauride Palace. They thrust themselves into the building, shouting, arguing, waving red banners and singing the "Marseillaise." They were triumphant, they were beside themselves with excitement, and they were beset with something else as well: an urgent and perhaps instinctive feeling that someone must be found to take charge of the situation. This feeling was very strong among the soldiers who by their mutiny had put themselves outside the law. They had the habit of obeying commands, and now they needed new leaders to replace those whom they had deposed. They came swarming into the courtyard of the Tauride Palace calling for the deputies, demanding that someone in authority should come out and speak to them.

The deputies themselves had spent the first four days of the revolution in a state of great uncertainty, and it was only now on March 12, under the extreme pressure of the mob outside, that they forced themselves to admit that the Czar's government had collapsed and that there was no alternative but to take over the power themselves. The responsibility for taking this step clearly fell on Rodzianko, Milyukov, Guchkov and other leaders of the Progressive Bloc, since they controlled the majority of the deputies, but they were not yet willing to act alone. They wanted support from the socialists as well. They sounded out Kerensky, and found that he was willing to join them, but Nicholas Chkheidze, the leader of the Mensheviks, was not. Others stood vacillating on the sidelines. In the end a group of moderates led by the Cadets formed an Emergency Committee of the Duma, and in the next few days, in a confused and erratic way, this body began to act as the new government of Russia. On March 12, of course, nobody quite knew where events were leading them, and the Emergency Committee aimed at no more than restoring order. But from hour to hour Milyukov and his friends found that power dropped into their hands or was actually thrust upon them, even though it was power that was challenged and weakened at every step of the way by the socialists.

The socialists too were very busy at this moment. They were constructing an emergency committee of their own, and this was essentially a re-creation of the Soviet which had appeared in Petrograd twelve years before in the rising of 1905. This new Soviet was by no means a ready-made organization that emerged suddenly from the underground into the open, and its origins can hardly be fixed upon any one man or any single party. Yet it was not spontaneous. Like the rising itself it was the result of an intricate network of influences and pressures that came from all the socialist parties, from the mutinous garrison and from the insistence of the crowd itself. The structure of the organization was there: it existed in the strike committees in the factories, in the socialist party cells, and in the group of socialist deputies in the Duma; and of course there was the experience of 1905 to draw upon. Yet the actual formation of this Soviet was a haphazard and hastily contrived affair. A few men gravitated together in the midst of the swirling mass in the Tauride Palace on March 12 at the very time that the Emergency Committee of the Duma was forming in another part of the building, and they grouped themselves into a sort of *ad hoc* committee of the left. N. D. Sokolov, the socialist deputy, was one of these men. Sukhanov was another. And they were soon joined by other Social Democrats and Social Revolutionaries. They decided to call a meeting in the Tauride Palace that same evening, and messages were sent out by telephone and by hand to the factories, to the barracks and to various socialist groups and individuals asking them to appoint representatives. The meeting took place at 9 P.M. that night, and it was attended by some fifty workers and twenty soldiers.

It was the most undisciplined of gatherings: everyone wanted to talk at once, to interject, to argue, to bring news and offer advice. And yet it did have a certain coherence; it was a kind of mixed strike committee and workers' parliament, and at least the leaders there had some notion of what they were doing. They formed an Executive Committee of the Soviet (henceforth to be known to the movement as the Ex Com), and they succeeded in establishing two commissions, one dealing with food and the other with military affairs. Nobody appointed the Ex Com's members; they elected themselves and they went on co-opting others until their numbers rose from a score to nearly a hundred. Chkheidze was the chairman, and among the members were Kerensky (who at first had his foot in both the Duma and the Soviet camps), Sokolov, Sukhanov, Skobelev, Steklov (who subsequently became editor of *Izvestiya*), and later Shlyapnikov, Molotov, Zalutski and other Bolsheviks who emerged either from hiding or from prison. Predominantly, however the Ex Com was a left-wing Menshevik group, and it continued so until the bitter end in November.

One wonders how the Mensheviks could have been so tolerant of the Bolsheviks, who were ultimately destined to destroy them all —Ex Com, Duma and everyone else—but one must remember that this was March, not October, everything was in flux, the real leaders were still absent, and there was a great feeling of brotherhood and elation in the air. Even if at this early stage the Mensheviks did distrust the Bolsheviks they still felt them to be an intrinsic part of the left wing.

So now on the night of March 12 there were two rival groups in the Tauride Palace to whom the striking workers and the soldiers could come for leadership: the Emergency Committee of the Duma and the Executive Committee of the Soviet. Outwardly the Duma Committee had the advantage in the struggle for power, since the Duma was a name in the world and the Ex Com was not. Important sections of the community—the civil service, the shopkeepers and the merchants, the army generals and even sections of the army rank and file—were only willing to come over to the revolution provided that the Duma was in control. Moreover, it was the old issue of 1905 all over again: the Mensheviks, that is to say the Ex

Com, were unwilling to take over the responsibility of power because they believed that a period of bourgeois government had to
precede the socialist revolution.

Yet there was much hostility between the two groups, and neither
trusted the other. The Duma Committee feared that the Soviet might
soon grow strong enough to turn them out of office. It feared that the
Soviet might encourage the workers and soldiers to abandon all
discipline and tear away the last shreds of orderly government. It
feared Marxism like the very devil, and the Ex Com was Marxist
almost to a man.

The Ex Com on its side suspected that the Duma Committee
would betray the revolution, that it would make a deal with Nicholas,
that it would force the country to go on with the war indefinitely,
that it would forget all about the wages of the workers and the eight-
hour day.

And so from the start each side maneuvered against the other.
The Duma Committee, which had control of the treasury, refused a
demand of ten million rubles from the Ex Com (though they paid
the money later on). The Ex Com, for its part, started issuing
proclamations and orders to the army and the workers over the head
of the Duma, and it greatly strengthened its own hand by passing
a resolution that 10 per cent of the workers should be armed and
formed into a militia which would replace the unfortunate Czarist
police. Already Red guards complete with machine guns and red
cockades in their hats were appearing on the streets. The Ex Com
also used another weapon which became time-honored practice in
international politics later on—the veto. It neither destroyed nor
genuinely supported the Duma Committee; it merely allowed the
Duma Committee to assume the outward form of power, to initiate
laws, and then it vetoed such of these laws as it did not like.

Yet neither side at this critical moment could do without the
other. There was chaos in the streets of Petrograd, and it was
spreading fast throughout the country. More important still, there
was a great fear in both camps that the revolution would fail, that
Nicholas would rally forces for a counter-revolution and return to
Petrograd to crush them all. The Duma were just as much in rebellion against the Czar at this moment as the Soviet and its Ex Com
were.

On Tuesday, March 13, there was, at least, a somewhat calmer atmosphere in the streets. A few soldiers still hung doubtfully about outside their barracks, others had deserted, others again stood in groups voting by a show of hands whether or not they should mutiny, but in general it could be said that there were no longer any loyal detachments left in the city.* A group of army officers was still holding out in the Astoria Hotel, but General Khabalov in the Admiralty had collapsed: the insurgents in St. Peter and St. Paul fortress sent him a message that they would turn their artillery onto the building unless it was evacuated in twenty minutes. The defenders left at once. The District Court was on fire and all the key points of the city had fallen. Even Kshesinskaya's house—the prima ballerina was an obvious symbol of wealth and Czardom—had been broken into. The next day there was tremendous news from Tsarskoe Selo where the Empress and her family were immured: General Ivanov had at last arrived there with his pitiful force—one battalion had been substituted for the four divisions he had been promised— only to find that the Empress's garrison had mutinied. General Ivanov telegraphed the Czar that there was no chance whatever of his advancing on Petrograd, and that it was not even possible for the Empress to be moved to a place of greater safety since her five children had come down with measles and she was nursing them.

Now at last Nicholas brought himself to face the situation. He announced that he would return to Petrograd and would consider proposals for a new government, possibly with Rodzianko at its head. With two trains he set out for the capital from Mogilev. But he was already too late: the railway workers soon got word of his

* According to the data subsequently produced by the military commission of the Duma Committee, the mutiny in the army developed as follows:

Date	Time	No. of Mutineers
March 11	Afternoon	600
March 12	Morning	10,200
	Mid-day	25,700
	Evening	66,700
March 13	Morning	72,700
	Mid-day	112,000
	Evening	127,000
March 14	Morning	144,700
	Mid-day	170,000

approach and blocked the line. Nicholas was forced then to double back to General Russky's headquarters at Pskov on the northern front, and it was there in his railroad car, isolated from his family and from almost all of his subjects, that he lived out the last few hours of his reign.

It is one of the ironies of the revolution that this isolation of Nicholas was not caused by the Ex Com, but by the Duma Committee, who would still have saved the monarchy had it been able to do so. The Duma Committee had appointed as its commissar of communications a right-wing deputy named Alexander Bublikov, and at 2 P.M. on March 13 Bublikov took it on himself to telegraph all railroad stations saying that the Duma had now taken power (which incidentally was not true as yet). He called on the railway workers for their support, and ordered them to block all troop movements within a radius of 250 versts of Petrograd. This was the first news that many of the outlying districts had of what was taking place in the capital, and its effect was electric.

The railroad workers responded at once, and it was directly as a result of Bublikov's message that Nicholas's train was diverted to Pskov. The incident had another importance. The impression was given in Bublikov's message that the revolution was an accomplished fact, and no mention was made in it of the part the Ex Com and the Soviet were playing in Petrograd. When the generals at the front received the news they presumed that the Duma and the Duma alone was in power. And to the Duma they were willing to submit.

Already Alexeiev, the virtual Commander-in-Chief, and Russky on the northern front had been sounded out by Rodzianko, and they had indicated that they would favor Nicholas's abdication.

We have now reached March 14. In the streets of Petrograd things were somewhat quieter, but the Tauride Palace was in a state of headlong commotion. Here, in circumstances of the utmost confusion, with impromptu meetings going on in every part of the building, the Emergency Committee of the Duma and the Ex Com were hammering out their rival programs. Kerensky was acting as a go-between, and it is Kerensky that eyewitnesses seem particularly to remember in these days. He was in a fury of activity, and neither the lack of sleep nor the surrounding tumult could hold him. Pale-faced, impassioned, his eyes blazing, he rushed from place to place, now arguing with the Duma Committee, now with the members of the Ex Com, now pausing to harangue the crowd outside. The mob greeted him with cheers: he appeared to be the very embodiment of the revolution at this moment.

The Soviet was now beginning to spread itself over a whole wing of the palace (leaving the Duma Committee to conduct its own affairs in the other wing). Soldiers roamed everywhere. They slept on the floor. They came tramping through the slush in the courtyards and cooked their food in the drafty corridors. They came wandering into the room where the Ex Com was trying to work. Delegates from the factories and the regiments kept arriving in scores, all of them seeking instructions, and hardly five minutes would go by before some messenger would burst in upon the Ex Com demanding an audience "on an emergency." Some of these emergencies were bizarre. A mob of students had decided to hunt down and arrest the former Czarist ministers, and now they came marching their prisoners into the palace: old Stürmer, who had altogether gone to pieces, the wretched Protopopov, who had been routed out of a tailor's shop where he had gone into hiding, and others again who had simply given themselves up in mortal fear of their lives. What to do with them? It was decided to lock them in the Duma council chamber along with the other political prisoners who had been rounded up in the city. There at least they would be safe from lynching by the crowds that thronged the courtyards and the streets outside.

The Ex Com remained in session through the day and night, making decisions with the breakneck and imperious speed that seems to be peculiar to revolutions at their height. The bank workers telephoned: should they reopen the banks? The railway workers wanted to know if they were to provide a special train for the Grand Duke Michael. What was to be done about the huge numbers of soldiers who were prowling the streets, unable or unwilling to return to their barracks, and liable to become a menace? Who was to find food and housing for them? Who was to command the Red Guards and so dispose them that they could defend the city if a Czarist force arrived? Civil governors were needed to control the various parts of the city.

These matters, one might have thought, should have been settled by the Duma Committee. But the delegates and the messengers did not go to the Duma, they came directly to the Ex Com, and the Ex Com, though overwhelmed, had no alternative but to assume responsibility. Meanwhile the Soviet itself was in session in one of the halls of the palace, and there were so many delegates—some two thousand of them—that the chairs had to be taken away to make more room. In a tightly-packed mass, their greatcoats reeking and steaming, the delegates gathered round the platform which was no more than a large table that had been set up at one end of the room; and here Chkheidze, the president, stood and did what he could to keep the meeting in order. Sukhanov gives a picture of the scene:*

Standing on stools, their rifles in their hands, agitated and stuttering, straining all their powers to give a concentrated account of the messages that had been given to them, with their thoughts concentrated on the narrative itself, in unaccustomed and fantastic surroundings, without thinking and perhaps quite unaware of the whole significance of the facts they were reporting, in simple rugged language that infinitely strengthened the effect of the absence of emphasis—one after another the soldiers' delegates told of what had been happening in their companies. Their stories were artless, and repeated each other almost word for word. The audience listened as children listen to a wonderful enthralling fairy-tale they know by heart, holding their breaths, with craning necks and unseeing eyes. . . . "We had a meeting . . . we've been told to say . . . that we refuse to serve against the people any more, we're going to join with our brother workers . . . we would lay down our lives for that." It was then and there proposed, and approved with storms of applause, to fuse together the revolutionary army and the proletariat of the capital, and create a united organisation to be called from then on the "Soviet of Workers and Sailors Deputies."

In short, it was wildly exciting: every minute brought fresh news, a fresh sensation. But it was still a long way from meaning that the revolution had succeeded. Somehow a provisional government had to be formed, and the Ex Com had to work out just what its relations with that government were going to be.

* These and other quotations from Sukhanov which follow are taken from *The Russian Revolution, 1917* by N. N. Sukhanov, edited and translated by Joel Carmichael, Oxford University Press, 1955.

By the early morning of March 15 Milyukov was ready with a list of ministers. Prince Lvov was to be Prime Minister, Milyukov himself Minister for Foreign Affairs, Guchkov, Minister for War, Tereshchenko (a multimillionaire of liberal views aged only thirty-two) Minister for Finance. Kerensky, after some anxiety about how his friends in the Ex Com were going to like it, had accepted the Ministry of Justice.

It remained now for a policy to be decided upon, and a series of meetings began between the new ministers and the Ex Com. There was a fairly large area of agreement. Both sides were decided that the Provisional Government should eventually be replaced by a constituent assembly elected upon a universal and secret vote. Both agreed that Nicholas must abdicate. They had no serious quarrel over such matters as the freedom of the press and equal rights for minority races in the Russian empire.*

But the Ex Com wanted a good deal more. It wanted not only the abdication of Nicholas but the abolition of the monarchy as well. It wanted an entire reorganization of the army, and it wanted the Petrograd garrison (that is to say the mutinous part of the army) to remain in the city. This last question—the control of the army— was the real issue between the two sides, and already the Ex Com had stolen a march on the Provisional Government in this matter. It had issued its famous Order Number One.

Order No. 1 had a nebulous beginning in the meeting of the Soviet in the Tauride Palace in the early afternoon of March 14. The meeting had debated the military situation and many soldiers had vented their grievances against their officers. Finally a resolution had been passed: it recommended that the soldiers should keep their arms, that they should form committees and elect delegates to the Soviet, and that they should carry out only those orders which were issued by the Soviet. It was also decided that the soldiers should only obey their officers while on duty; outside the service they should be considered as the equals of officers and should enjoy all the rights of free citizens.

When these proposals reached Guchkov and other members of the Provisional Government they were naturally rejected. Guchkov

* The population of Russia at this time was 173 millions. It included 200 different peoples and languages.

was particularly adamant about still another demand: that the soldiers should elect their own officers.

But this did not deter the Soviet. They appointed a committee to draw up a direct order to the army. Nine soldiers and a sailor served on this committee, but the actual drafting of Order No. 1 that emerged was the work of Sokolov, the near-Bolshevik member of the Ex Com. It went some way beyond the original resolution of the Soviet; all military units were included, the navy as well as the army, and it stated that in all political matters the men were under the command of the Soviet and of their own committees. They would obey the orders of the Emergency Committee of the Duma only if they were not in contradiction with those of the Soviet. Further, the soldiers' committees were to control all weapons and were not to deliver weapons to officers. Salutes were abolished off duty, and there was even a provision by which officers must be polite to their men and not use the customary "thou."

This order, with no other authority than that of the Soviet, was broadcast over the Tsarskoe Selo radio station on the night of March 15 and published in *Izvestiya* on the following day. It was a foreshadowing of the shape of things to come, and it hardly meant less, in the long run, than the breakup of the army and the ending of Russia's part in the war. As yet of course no one knew how far the order was going to be obeyed at the front, but here in Petrograd the Provisional Government had no choice but to accept it as a *fait accompli*. They simply hoped that it would not take effect.

But upon one other matter Milyukov was prepared to fight the Ex Com to the last ditch: if Nicholas were to abdicate, the monarchy at least should be preserved. He drew up a formal document which provided that the succession should pass to the Czarevich Alexis, then twelve years old, with Nicholas's brother, the Grand Duke Michael, acting as regent. It was not through any great admiration for the Romanov family that Milyukov pressed this matter; privately he described the projected heir and regent as "a sick child and a thoroughly stupid man." It was simply that he did not believe that any government would survive, still less keep the pressure of the Soviet and the Ex Com at bay, unless it had the traditional weight of the monarchy behind it. He did not communicate the document containing these proposals to the Soviet leaders on the

other side of the Tauride Palace, but instead he entrusted it to
Guchkov, the Minister of War, and to Basil Shulgin, a right-wing
Duma deputy, with instructions that they should proceed at once
to Pskov and obtain Nicholas's signature to it. A train was com-
mandeered, and early on March 15 the two men set off. They
reached Pskov at ten that night. Nicholas himself, meanwhile, had
accepted the fact that he must go. Those who were with him at
headquarters at this time all comment on his extraordinary impassiv-
ity and calmness. He looked exhausted but he slept and ate in the
normal way, and even when one after another his generals told him
they could no longer give him their support his composure remained
unaltered; he was both gentle and dignified. The descent from
autocracy to nothingness was accomplished at a single move, and
except for one heart's cry written into his diary that night—"All
around nothing but treachery, cowardice and deceit"—it elicited
nothing from him, no recriminations, no anger at all or surprise,
merely an air of fatalistic resignation. It was most impressive.

Nicholas, however, had one change to make in the Milyukov
proposals. Directly he understood the abdication was inevitable he
sent for his doctor and asked him to say truly whether or not his
son's illness could ever be cured. The answer was no. Upon this
Nicholas decided that the boy should stay with him in the family,
and that the crown should go directly to the Grand Duke Michael.

Late at night on March 15, he received Guchkov and Shulgin in
his drawing room aboard his train, and he listened very patiently
while they explained the situation at length. He read the document
they had brought, and without difficulty carried his point that the
Grand Duke and not his son should succeed. Going into another
car he himself altered the wording to this effect, and before midnight the document was signed. It began with an appeal to the
armed forces to carry on the fight against the enemy, and went on,
"In agreement with the Imperial Duma, we have thought it good
to abdicate from the throne of the Russian State, and to lay down
the supreme power. Not wishing to part with our dear son, we hand
over our inheritance to our brother, the Grand Duke Michael Alexandrovich, and give him our blessing to mount the throne of the
Russian State." The document ended, "May the Lord God help
Russia!"

It was sincere, this last exhortation, not merely a ceremonial phrase, and the two Duma deputies found themselves very much moved when they came to say good-by. Shulgin related later that he burst out with "Your Majesty, if you had done all this earlier, even as late as the last summoning of the Duma, perhaps all that . . ." He was unable to finish. "The Czar," Shulgin goes on, "looked at me in a curiously simple way: 'Do you think it might have been avoided?' "

Early the following morning, March 16, the two deputies got back to Petrograd to find the streets much quieter but the Duma building still in an uproar. The feeling against the Romanovs had hardened considerably while they were away; the Ex Com now made it clear that they were no longer content with Nicholas's abdication, they wanted the end of the whole dynasty and the formation of a republic. The crowd had got wind of Guchkov's and Shulgin's mission to the Czar, and they were met on their arrival at the station in Petrograd by a mob of railway workers who demanded an account of what had been done. Shulgin with emotion and perhaps some pride announced the accession of the Grand Duke. But he had altogether misunderstood the feelings of his audience: they were not at all content to have another Romanov on the throne, and they refused to allow Guchkov and Shulgin to leave the station.

Milyukov now got through to the two deputies on the telephone and told them to say no more about the abdication document, but to bring it at once to Prince Putiatin's house on the Millionnaya, where the Provisional Government were negotiating with the Grand Duke Michael. Eventually, Guchkov and Shulgin extricated themselves and made their way to the rendezvous. Here in a drawing room a distracted group was assembled: the Grand Duke himself, a thin and pale figure sitting in an armchair, Milyukov, Rodzianko, Lvov, Kerensky and one or two others, all of them quite worn out. Milyukov and Guchkov put up a last desperate struggle to save the monarchy. Rodzianko and Lvov urged the Grand Duke against accepting. Kerensky was in a rage against the very thought of the monarchy continuing. The Grand Duke listened quietly and then very sensibly said he wished to withdraw into the next room while he considered. He returned in five minutes and announced that he would accept the throne only if it were offered to him by a constituent assembly. Pending the election of such an assembly he would abdicate.

"Monseigneur," Kerensky cried out, "you are the noblest of men."

Within a few minutes a second instrument of abdication was typed out and signed and now for the first time in more than three centuries Russia found herself without a Czar. In his place she had two exhausted and mutually suspicious groups of politicians struggling for power in the Tauride Palace, a mob in the streets, and no certainty in the future anywhere. Dark heavy clouds had begun to roll over Petrograd from the Gulf of Finland, and snow fell so thickly along the Neva it was impossible to see the icy course of the river, even from twenty paces away.

CHAPTER TEN

The Soviet Versus
the Provisional Government

THE BREAK," Sukhanov wrote, "had been accomplished with a sort of fabulous ease." Very little physical damage had been done, and the total number of serious casualties could hardly have been much over a thousand; and now an enormous red flag floated over the Winter Palace, which had been the ultimate stronghold of the Czars since the time of Peter the Great.

Yet clearly nothing had been decided. On March 16 the only definite indication of the way ahead was a statement put out over the signatures of both the Provisional Government and the Petrograd Soviet. It revealed that an agreement had been patched up between them during the night; the Romanovs were to go, at any rate for the time being, and the Provisional Government was to rule in their place until such time as a constituent assembly could be elected by the people. It was to carry out a revolutionary program: an amnesty for political prisoners, freedom of speech, equal rights for all citizens whether of foreign nationality or not, and the defense of the country against the common enemy in the west.

It was a good bland statement of aims, and it concealed a welter of differences inside and outside the Tauride Palace. The Provisional

Government—which is to say the liberals—which is to say Milyukov —had only a secondary interest in questions of citizen rights. Their first object was to restore order, to get the Dark People under control, and after that they were all for going on with the war. The "honour of Russia" counted very much with them; they were determined not to make a separate peace with Germany but to continue the fight with their allies, and they hoped that as a reward Constantinople would be given to Russia when victory was won.

With the Ex Com, on the other hand, domestic issues came first, the eight-hour day, the improvement of the condition of the working classes, and they were by no means eager to go on with a war which to them seemed both senseless and hopeless. They wanted peace, and they did not care two straws about Constantinople. Yet they were unwilling to risk the unpopularity of making a definite declaration against the war. It sounded at this stage too much like treason, and they knew that all the educated classes—the bureaucracy and even a large section of the army—were against them. And so they hedged over the question of the war. They adopted what they called a "defensist" policy, by which they meant they were neither defeatist nor belligerent: they were simply ready to defend the country and no more while arrangements for a negotiated peace were made.

It seemed valid tactics for the time being; the Ex Com could control any move the Provisional Government made in a reactionary direction, and later, when the war was over and the country had had a period of bourgeois government, it would be time enough to turn the liberals out of office and convert Russia to Marxian socialism.

Then, outside these two political groups, outside the Tauride Palace, there remained the illiterate mass of the Russian people themselves, the real material of the revolution, and in a confused and irresponsible way they were very much further to the left. They wanted peace and they wanted it immediately. They had never even heard of Constantinople. They wanted the land and they wanted food. These differences, Florinsky points out, were "fundamental, insoluble, fatal." There was no real hope of compromise.

Yet compromise there had to be in Petrograd, at all events until they discovered just what backing the revolution had throughout Russia. The news was not long in arriving, and it was both encouraging and alarming. Moscow rose and formed a Soviet of its own, and presently most of the other cities followed suit. The army too declared for the revolution and acknowledged the new government. So did the foreign minority states inside the Russian empire. All this was satisfactory, but in each case there were serious reservations. By the mere act of rising against the Czarist officials the provincial cities did nothing to solve the vital problem of the food shortage in the capital: they made it worse. Meanwhile, Soviet Order No. 1 was being interpreted at the front by some of the soldiers as an invitation to do pretty much what they liked: and what they liked was not war but peace. At places along the line they fraternized with the Germans and the Austrians, and all sorts of optimistic rumors flew about: it was said that the Kaiser had abdicated, that the German workers and soldiers had risen in a glorious revolution of their own, that soon the war would be over. These delusions led on to something which was even more demoralizing: desertion began in the Russian lines. Now that the revolution had come the moujik-soldier was seized with the idea that he must get home and enjoy the benefits of it; he must get back to his village and share in the free distribution of land while there was still time. Within a few weeks of the March rising about a million soldiers had deserted and were making their way home in trains, in carts, and on foot, and there was no authority capable of holding them back.

In the navy the Provisional Government did not even get political support. The Kronstadt base, with a population of fifty-five thousand, mutinied against its officers, and having butchered some held about two hundred of the rest as hostages whom they forced into the heaviest and most degrading work. And now they were running a semi-independent camp of their own. At first they refused to recognize even the Soviet in Petrograd.

As for the minority states, they accepted the Provisional Government's statements about equal rights with the greatest enthusiasm. One after another Finland, Estonia, Lithuania, the Ukraine, the Caucasus and Siberia demanded independence or autonomy; they too had had enough of war, especially a Russian war, and now they were proposing to break up the Russian empire.

In the official Bolshevik accounts of these March days in Petrograd an impression of inevitability is given; each event is said to have happened because it had to happen and in just that way: an irresistible historical process was at work. This hardly squares with the recollections of more impartial observers who were there at the time. They make it clear that from day to day nobody really knew what was coming next, and that if the Ex Com had chanced to take a different decision over some such question as Order No. 1, or if the German fleet had attacked while the sailors at Kronstadt were in revolt, or if the Allies had somehow intervened, then everything would have been changed, and the revolution might there and then have ended. In other words, there was nothing inevitable about these days; at every moment a dozen alternatives presented themselves, and often it was only by chance that one of these alternatives was adopted. It was the exhilarating sense of freedom that really dominated things in Petrograd in March.

But, as Florinsky says, the revolution as yet "had no organisation, no leaders, and in the beginning, it would seem, even no definite purpose. Like a snowball rolling down the slope of a steep hill it grew in size and gathered strength on its way." They had escaped from Czardom and that for the moment was all they really knew. Probably the best assessment of the situation is that attributed to an unknown Siberian peasant: "We feel," he said, "that we have escaped from a dark cave into the bright daylight. And here we stand not knowing where to go or what to do."

Now more than ever it was the dead weight of ignorance in Russia that was pressing on the few responsible men at the top who were trying to establish a government. It was so great an ignorance that (to quote one of the Duma's reports) "an educated man felt his energy drain away" when confronted by it. Since few of the people could either read or write with fluency the crowds were particularly susceptible to any orator who happened to appear at some street corner, some army barracks or factory workshop. Newspapers were treated with great reverence. And since there were orators galore of many different hues, and the Ex Com's paper *Izvestiya* said one thing, the Bolsheviks' *Pravda* (which reappeared in March) another and Maxim Gorky's *Novaya Zhizn* still something else it was all very confusing. *Izvestiya* meant "News," *Pravda* "Truth," and *Novaya Zhizn* "New Life," and all of them professed to be inspired with the true Marxian light, even though they changed their editorial views from time to time. Then, on top of this, there were other right-wing papers as well. One can hardly blame the workers and the soldiers for being puzzled and for being forever hungry for the truthful news of their new life. They took refuge in talk. A flood of talk engulfed Russia during March. All over Petrograd meetings were going on, and since opinions could never take the place of facts there was a spontaneous move from time to time toward the Tauride Palace. Great crowds gathered outside and threatened to break into the building unless Chkheidze or one of the other members of the Ex Com came out and told them what was going on.

Kerensky was a great favorite on these occasions. He had marvelous oratorical gifts; he would drop his voice to a thrilling whisper and then blaze out as though he had been suddenly swept by some inner emotional storm which he was quite unable to control. He looked terribly pale and exhausted, and although quite often he was helped, coughing and hardly conscious, from the platform, his nervous energy never deserted him. He dashed from place to place about the city, followed by a cloud of disciples, and to the "pharaohs"—the police agents—who had had the unfortunate job of shadowing him he had been known as "Speedy."

Sukhanov, like most of the revolutionary leaders, did not think much of Kerensky. "This noisy lawyer," he says, "was flying high." Even early in March when Kerensky "had been galloping along the broad highway of historical immortality for three days" thoughts of forming a government of his own had occurred to him. He had adopted an autocratic and slightly hysterical manner. One day, Sukhanov relates, there was a panic in the Tauride Palace. Two shots rang out and the cry went up, "The Cossacks."

Kerensky rushed to the window, leaped on the sill, and sticking his head out shouted in a hoarse, broken voice: "Stations everyone! Defend the Duma! Listen to me—I, Kerensky, am speaking to you, Kerensky is speaking to you! Defend your freedom and the revolution, defend the Duma! Stations everyone!" . . . It was clear that the shots were accidental—most probably from the inexperienced hands of some workers handling a rifle for the first time. It was ridiculous and a little embarrassing. I went over to Kerensky. "Everything's all right," I said in a low voice, but one quite audible in the silence that had supervened. "Why create a worse panic than the shots?" I hadn't reckoned on the result of this remark. Standing in the middle of the room, Kerensky broke into a rage and began bellowing at me, shakily picking his words, "I demand— that everyone—to do his duty—and not interfere—when I—give orders!" "Absolutely right," I heard someone remark approvingly.

There is a good deal of malice and probably jealousy too in such tales, and they cannot destroy the fact that in the midst of the surrounding confusion Kerensky did supply an element that was badly needed: a note of demagogic certainty, a voice to which the crowd would listen. Paléologue, the French Ambassador, was much struck with him. He wrote in his diary:

One alone among them [the members of the Provisional Government] appeared to be a man of action—the Minister for Justice, Kerensky. He is thirty-five, thin, of medium height, clean shaven; with his bristling hair, waxed complexion and half-closed eyes (through which he darted sharp and uneasy glances) he struck me all the more because he kept apart, standing behind all his colleagues. He is obviously the most original figure of the Provisional Government and seems bound to become its main spring.

For the moment, however, Milyukov was in command. And he was confronted with difficulties that seemed to make his task impossible. The Provisional Government had no legal status—it had elected itself —and it was responsible to no one, certainly not to the Soviet, which also had no rights in law. Of the apparently insoluble problem of the food and fuel shortage only one good thing could be said: the people were more willing to put up with it now that the revolution had come and spring was on the way. As for the army at the front, it was in a critical state and no one knew whether or not the Germans were preparing an offensive. If that happened very little effective help could be expected from the Allies, for they were obsessed at this time by the German U-boat campaign, and the railway to Murmansk, though recently completed, was barely functioning; it could not even transport the supplies of guns and ammunition which Britain and France had already delivered there.

It was a situation that was so black that almost anything that happened was likely to be a turn for the better, and in fact, in this last fortnight of March, when Russia was utterly exposed, events were turning in her favor. The German fleet did not sail on Kronstadt, and their land attack when it did come was a halfhearted affair. Somehow or other, perhaps because of the prodding of the Ex Com itself, the trams, the factories, the banks and the arsenals started up again, and the bureaucracy returned to work. And although the appeal of the Petrograd Soviet to all foreign workers and soldiers to rise against their capitalist bosses* ended without the whisper of an echo in the empty air, help came to Russia from another quarter; America, France, Britain and Italy promptly recognized the Provisional Government so that it had at least a standing in the eyes of the outside world. Much more important than this, America was not only about to come into the war herself, she also was prepared to back the Provisional Government with both supplies and money.

I could never have believed [wrote Paléologue shortly before this] that two great countries could know and think so little of each other as Russia and the United States. As types of humanity the Russian and the American are the very antithesis of each other. . . . The Russian's will is always passive and unstable: moral discipline is unknown to him, and he is never happy save in dreamland. The American has a positive and practical mind, a sense of duty and a passion for work. To Russian society the United States appears a selfish, prosaic and barbarous nation, without traditions or dignity, the natural home of democracy and the natural refuge of Jews and nihilists. In the eyes of the American Russia is simply the iniquities of Czarism, the atrocities of anti-Semitism and the ignorance and drunkenness of the moujiks.

While all this may be true, it must also be accepted that the Americans were in no two minds about the revolution: they were in favor of it. They gave it the most ardent support. On April 2, 1917, President Wilson in calling for a declaration of war against the Central Powers spoke of "The wonderful and heartening things that have been happening in the last few weeks in Russia"; and on the follow-

* This appeal was based on an original draft by Gorky. "Workers of all countries," it ran, in part, "stretching out to you a brotherly hand over mountains of brothers' corpses, over rivers of innocent blood and tears, over the smoking ruins of cities and villages, over the perishing treasures of culture, we call to you to restore and strengthen international unity. In this is the guarantee of our future victories and of the complete liberation of humanity. Proletarians of all lands unite."

ing day the Provisional Government was offered credits which in the end amounted to $325 million.

America was also the first of the Allies to recognize the Provisional Government, an action which was very largely due to David R. Francis, the United States Ambassador in Petrograd. Francis, a wealthy Missouri businessman in his late sixties, had arrived just twelve months before with his Negro valet Philip Jordan and had taken up residence on the Furshtatskaya, close to the Tauride Palace. He was a remarkable figure, more attuned to the world of O. Henry than the Czarist court (and indeed O. Henry mentions him as a gourmet). He had his portable cuspidor with a foot-operated lid, his cigars, his Ford touring car for summer and his sleigh and team of horses for winter; the horses had United States flags stuck in their bridles, and according to Norman Armour, the second secretary at the Embassy, "gave you the impression when you drove with him that you were in a merry-go-round." At the Ambassador's dinners (which were rare; he preferred poker) a hand-cranked phonograph played from behind a screen.* In short, it was a strange décor for an ambassador in Petrograd, and in 1916 it may have amused the Czarist court and fashionable society in the city. Now, however, things were very different. Francis was not afraid of the revolution, and in this, among the diplomatic corps, he was almost unique. He saw a possibility here of setting up a new democracy on American lines, and in pressing for every possible assistance for the Provisional Government he very accurately interpreted public and official feeling in America. He was in a position to do more for Russia than any of the Allies, and he cannot be blamed for not recognizing in March, 1917, the force and menace of the Bolsheviks, who were already mustering under the cover of this popular rising. No one in Petrograd had yet seen as far as that.

At the outbreak of the revolution on March 8 the Bolshevik party in Petrograd was a second-rate organization, and there was not one name of the first rank among its list of members. One young man there, however, was destined to make a reputation: Vyacheslav Skryabin, otherwise Molotov, the future Commissar for Foreign Affairs. Molotov was an intellectual from Kazan, and he was very

* See George F. Kennan's *Russia Leaves the War*, Princeton University Press, 1956.

much to the left. He was a defeatist: he wanted the immediate ending of the war, and he was opposed to all dealings with the Provisional Government. When *Pravda* reappeared in March (its first
issue free, its second selling 100,000 copies), Molotov was its editor,
and he lost no time in putting his extreme views into print; he also
expressed them in the Ex Com and the Soviet. It was the old hard
Leninist line, and the Soviet could afford to ignore it since the Bolsheviks were a small minority. Then on March 25 things began to
change: Kamenev* arrived back from exile in Siberia under the
terms of the amnesty issued by the Provisional Government, and he
was accompanied by Stalin, who had also spent the war years hunting and fishing on the edge of the Arctic Circle. They at once took
charge of the Bolshevik committee. Molotov was removed from the
editorship of *Pravda,* and the paper soon began to take a much more
conciliatory line. It was still left of the Mensheviks, but it was prepared at least to continue a defensive war against the Germans until
the revolution was consolidated. Kamenev seems to have been
chiefly responsible for this change—he was the only acknowledged
leader of the party on the spot—but there is no doubt that he was
supported by Stalin.

Stalin's position is a little difficult to disentangle, all the more so
since so much about his life has been distorted, suppressed and
exaggerated by Soviet historians. It seems clear, however, that we
must regard him at this time as no more than a promising member
of the party. He had brought himself to the favorable notice of
Lenin by his activities as a holdup man and terrorist in the Caucasus; he had served his apprenticeship in Siberia, and had attended
several conferences abroad; but his influence was still small, and
the suggestion that he was already one of Lenin's closest friends is
absurd.

Sukhanov has a cautiously derisive note about him: "The Bolshevik Party," he says, "in spite of the low level of its 'officers corps,'
had a whole series of most massive figures and able leaders among
its 'generals.' Stalin, however, during his modest activity in the

---

* Kamenev (Lev Borisovich Rosenfeld) though four years younger than
Stalin was senior to him in the party. He was married to Trotsky's sister.
Kamenev usually stood to the right wing of the Bolsheviks but was a waverer.
Sukhanov says of him, ". . . he jibbed against Lenin, jibbed at the October
Revolution . . . but—he always surrendered on all points."

Ex Com produced—and not only on me—the impression of a grey blur, looming up now and then dimly and not leaving any trace. There is really nothing more to be said about him." Nothing at any rate that Sukhanov could say since when he wrote this in 1919 he was living in Russia and Stalin was rapidly coming to the top. One cannot at all events quarrel with the phrase "grey blur" since that is precisely the impression Stalin gives in comparison to the sharp and commanding aspect of the other exiled revolutionary leaders who now began to arrive in the capital with every week that went by.

There was "Grandma" Breshko-Breshkovskaya, one of the leaders of the Social Revolutionary party, and a terrorist from the early days. She was given a tremendous ovation. There was Irakli Tseretelli, the Georgian Menshevik who soon began to emerge as a leader in both the Ex Com and the Soviet. There was Dan (Fyodor Ilyich Gurvich) who was a member of the Menshevik central committee. And finally there was Plekhanov, who came from Paris after thirty-six long years in Europe. With the possible exception of Dan, all these exiles in varying degrees were in favor of the "defensist" line and of co-operation with the Provisional Government. And now with Kamenev's arrival they appeared to have the support of the Bolsheviks as well.

There was one other voice that counted among the Petrograd socialists and that was Maxim Gorky's. He was the outstanding left-wing writer of the day, and he represented something which was more permanent than the day-to-day politics of the revolution and the excitement in the streets. He saw an extreme danger in the violence of the mob, and he knew better than any Bolshevik that neither this nor any other revolution could entirely sweep away the past. His manifesto written at the height of this crisis has a simple prophetic dignity.

Citizens [he wrote], the old masters have gone away and a great heritage is left behind. Now it belongs to the whole people. Citizens, take care of this heritage, take care of the palaces—they will become palaces of your national art; take care of the pictures, the statues, the buildings—they are the embodiment of the spiritual power of yourselves and of your forefathers. Art is the beauty which talented people were able to create even under despotic oppression and which bears witness to the power and beauty of the human soul. Citizens, do not touch one stone; preserve the monuments, the buildings, the old things, the documents—all this is your history, your pride. Remember that this is the soil from which will grow your new national art.[*]

Nobody at the time took much notice of this appeal—the Ex Com listened to it politely and without debate sent it off to the printers —but it had its effect later on when the hubbub died down, and in fact the palaces were saved. Nor was it only a few scattered intellectuals like Gorky who protested against physical destruction: there seems to have been an instinctive reaction of the same kind within the illiterate crowd itself, and there were some odd manifestations of this during these early days. At first half Petrograd had been in a frenzy to remove every trace of Czardom: Nicholas's portraits were torn out of their frames in the palaces, and everywhere, in the theaters and the public buildings, men hacked down the imperial emblems and coats of arms. But then there was a halt. The mob paused before the great rooms hung with tapestries and filled with beautiful furniture, and the first rush to loot soon expended itself. In most cases it only needed one responsible man to get up and remind the soldiers that they had not revolted in order to loot—that in any case these things now were everybody's property—and the wrecking stopped.

Perhaps the most picturesque instance of this concerned the Bolsheviks. They had taken roost in, of all places, the ballet dancer Kshesinskaya's house, an ornate pagoda-ish building on the banks of the Neva, and had set up their headquarters there. The dancer herself, a small agitated figure in black, brought the news to the Ex Com. All her world and all the wealth she had amassed since the far-off days when she had been a favorite of Nicholas and the Grand Dukes were centered in that house, and she pleaded now that something should be done to save her things. Yet on investigation it was found that the Bolsheviks had packed away the more valuable objects into the back rooms: they had bigger aims in view than Louis Quinze beds and rugs from Turkestan.[†]

It was a similar spirit that touched the public funeral of the men and women who had died in the rising. At first they were to be

---

[*] Joel Carmichael's translation of Sukhanov, *The Russian Revolution, 1917.*
[†] Later, of course, the Bolsheviks seized Kshesinskaya's property and she herself fled abroad to Paris, where she was still living in 1958.

buried before the Winter Palace as a gesture of defiance against the past regime, but since that would have ruined one of the finest squares in the city the site was changed to the more suitable Champ de Mars. The funeral on April 5 was an event that astonished and sobered them all. A million people—just one half of the Petrograd population—appeared on the streets, and in silence and in perfect order, an order that never could have been imposed by police, they filed past the common grave. At one-minute intervals the guns boomed out from the Fortress of St. Peter and St. Paul: there was no other sound. The coffins were painted red and no religious ceremonies were allowed. On the following day, however, a murmuring began through Petrograd. Up to a month ago few of these people had passed an ikon without crossing themselves, and now they felt a current of fear, a premonition that some terrible retribution would fall on them if they allowed their dead to be buried in this way. Priests were then sent to the Champ de Mars, and they blessed the grave.

With Nicholas and his family, however, it was another matter. The hostility remained, or rather it was the hostility of indifference, and perhaps there was here also an element of fear: the fear that somehow he might emerge again and punish them. And so they were determined to suppress him, and by that very act find some sort of a justification for what they had done. He reached Tsarskoe Selo on March 22 under open arrest—the guards were necessary for his own safety—and rejoined his family there. They were confined to a part of the palace and were allowed access only to a corner of the gardens. Sentries were placed to watch their every move, and at times the family was ordered about as though they were common convicts. Nicholas bore it very well. He remained courteous. He cut wood for fuel, he shoveled the snow off the paths outside, and the children planted vegetable gardens. At times the Empress burst out with an impassioned protest, but she managed to keep her sanity by reminding herself that this could be nothing but a penance ordained by God. Anna Vyrubova was sent off to the Fortress of St. Peter and St. Paul, but the other personal retainers of the royal family were allowed to remain in the palace. The official suite of court chamberlains and the like vanished very quickly of its own accord.

Late in March Buchanan, the British Ambassador, informed the

Provisional Government that King George V would offer his cousin asylum in England. Nicholas would have preferred to go to his estate at Livadia, in the Crimea, but he was warned that his life would be in danger there, and so preparations were made to send the family by train to Murmansk, where they were to embark on a British warship. Kerensky as Minister for Justice was to see them on their way. These plans had not advanced very far when the Ex Com got wind of them and there was an immediate outcry. The hunger for revenge had not quite spent itself, and "Citizen Romanov" was not going to escape them in this way; it was not inconceivable, they argued, that from England he might rally new forces and start a counter-revolution. The Ex Com sent out a message to all the main railroads ordering the workers to halt any imperial train that approached, and to place its passengers under arrest. At that the Provisional Government very quickly backed down, and Nicholas and his family were informed that they must remain at Tsarskoe Selo. A workers' delegation came out from Petrograd, and Nicholas was ordered to appear so that they could reassure themselves that he had not escaped.

It was also about this time that Rasputin's coffin was taken from the chapel at Tsarskoe Selo by a gang of soldiers. They pried the body out with sticks, soaked it in petrol and burnt it on a pyre of logs. A crowd of moujiks gathered, and with fascination stood all night watching the flames burning on the snow. From the *Starets* at least the Soviet had nothing to fear: the bishops he had appointed had long since fled to distant monasteries, and his followers in Petrograd, the Stürmers and the Protopopovs, were all in hiding or in prison.

By the second week in April, when the revolution had been in existence for a month, both the Ex Com and the Provisional Government were getting down to the basic issues, and none of them were as lucid or as easy to handle as they had first appeared to be. It was the lack of established principles of government that hampered them. In the matter of the freedom of the press, for instance, there was great debate. Before the revolution it had appeared to many, both socialists and liberals alike, that this was a self-evident virtue, a watchword of the revolution. But now right-wing groups, parties which still secretly supported the monarchy, were demanding

the right to publish their own newspapers. Could you allow them to
denounce the revolution at this critical moment? Were they to be
permitted to build up a following which might defeat the new
government? In the Ex Com the intellectuals wrestled with their
consciences over this problem for a long time, and in the end they
came to precisely the same decision that Nicholas and all the Czars
had come to long ago: censorship was necessary. Chkheidze jumped
from his seat and shouted furiously, "No, we are not going to per-
mit them. When a war is on we're not going to give the enemy any
weapons." The proposed right-wing paper was refused a license.
But on March 23 restrictions on the press were lifted.

The question of the eight-hour day was even more difficult. Since
Father Gapon's time and even earlier this had been a fundamental
demand of the workers, and even the employers were now willing
to accept it. Nothing it seemed could be easier to declare than that
the eight-hour day was law. But suddenly a new and formidable
opponent to the idea appeared: the soldiers. Why, they demanded,
should the worker sit safely in Petrograd and the other cities behind
the line working an eight-hour day when they at the front had to
expose themselves for twenty-four hours to the enemy? The army
needed the ammunition and the supplies; let the workers get on with
their jobs and take a fairer share of the burden of the war. Once
again the Ex Com had to shift its ground: it agreed that the factories
should work overtime.

The peasants presented still another problem. All over Russia
they were beginning to feel their power, and they were armed. They
claimed that this was their revolution—they, not a handful of industrial workers in the cities, were the bulk of the population. Why
should they accept the decrees of a workers' government in Petrograd?

But for the moment these and all other questions were absorbed
by the urgent problem of the war. Who was to have control of the
army? The Provisional Government who wanted it to fight on to
the end, or the Soviet who wanted it merely to defend itself while
Russia opened negotiations for peace? Even the army itself was
divided on this issue, for it soon became apparent that the deserters
and the revolutionary regiments by no means represented all the
soldiers, let alone the officers. In many regiments there was a great

determination to fight on now that they had something to fight for, a government of their own. It was a matter of pride not to give up, not to let all their heroic efforts of the last three years go for nothing. They had another argument: the Kaiser was quite capable of swallowing up the revolution. If you allowed the German armies to break through their first action might be to set up Nicholas on the throne again. General Kornilov, the newly appointed Military Governor of Petrograd, marched his loyal regiments through the streets—some of them, incidentally, the very regiments which had revolted against the Czar—and they demanded that the war should continue. In the Soviet it was becoming unsafe for a deputy to call for immediate peace; he was likely to be met with cries of "traitor" and be howled down. And yet hardly anybody really wanted the war. A deputation of socialist politicians arrived from France and Britain to urge the Russian workers and soldiers to go on with the struggle, and they were received coldly by the Ex Com. Even Plekhanov—Plekhanov who was the revered father of the revolution —was rebuffed when he urged the Soviet to stick to the Allies and continue with the fight. His speech fell flat. He was an old man now, and he was ill; he drifted away out of the public scene and nearly all his following was gone.

From right to left the argument swept back and forth all through these early days of April, and it was a matter of nice judgment to know whether a pacifist was a patriot or a traitor to his country, whether a belligerent was a reactionary Czarist or a true soldier of the revolution.

One man of importance was lacking from this agonizing debate, and that was Lenin. Lenin was in Switzerland, where he had been lingering all these years since the beginning of the war. And now in mid-April word was received in Petrograd that he was on his way back. He was crossing Europe in a German train, and was due to arrive at the Finland station in Petrograd on the night of April 16.

CHAPTER ELEVEN

Lenin's Return

TOWARD the end of Winston Churchill's *The World Crisis,* his monumental history of the First World War, this passage occurs:

In the middle of April [1917] the Germans took a sombre decision. Ludendorff refers to it with bated breath. Full allowance must be made for the desperate stakes to which the German leaders were already committed. They were in the mood which had opened unlimited submarine warfare with the certainty of bringing the United States into the war against them. Upon the western front they had from the beginning used the most terrible means of offense at their disposal. They had employed poison gas on the largest scale and had invented the "Flammenwerfer." Nevertheless it was with a sense of awe that they turned upon Russia the most grisly of all weapons. They transported Lenin in a sealed truck like a plague bacillus from Switzerland into Russia.

Behind this lively irony there lies a story which we can now put together in some detail from the Wilhelmstrasse records and other sources, and it is one of the most revealing chapters of the Russian revolution. The Germans had not expected the rising to happen so swiftly. Through January and February they knew that the atmosphere in Petrograd was becoming increasingly tense, but the Foreign Office in Berlin seems to have been more preoccupied with the possibility of coming to terms with the Czar than with the plans for destroying him by revolution. A letter to Nicholas containing the German peace proposals had actually been drafted, and Prince

Max of Baden had been entrusted with the negotiations, when the abdication occurred. Certainly in early March few of the German leaders had any notion of getting Lenin and his friends back into Russia, and of setting them up in place of the Czar. Lenin himself as recently as January 22 had given a lecture in the People's House at Zurich in which he said that "we of the older generation may not live to see the decisive battles of this coming revolution."

Lenin was approaching his forty-seventh birthday, and his life with Krupskaya in Zurich was as calm and uneventful as. only neutral Switzerland could make it: long walks around the lake, long hours in the public library, long peaceful days spent in writing innumerable pamphlets and letters to his friends. It was a routine that hardly varied from one week's end to another and it seemed to be leading nowhere. When the news of the early street battles in Petrograd did reach Zurich—and it took a week to arrive—Lenin could not bring himself to believe in it. On March 15, 1917, a Polish friend named M. G. Bronsky ran into his rooms with the first reports, and according to Krupskaya they all went down to the lake where "on the shore all the newspapers were hung up as soon as they came out." Lenin apparently read the accounts with great skepticism—one can picture him standing there in the placid landscape peering intently at the printed sheets—and it was not until a few days later when word of the Czar's abdication arrived that he was prepared to admit that something of importance had happened. Even then he had his reservations. He wrote a letter to Alexandra Kollontai° in Sweden saying that no great political change had taken place. It was a capitalist upheaval, he said: the bourgeoisie had simply taken over the power it already possessed. He rather hoped that Milyukov and the Cadets in the new Provisional Government would not legalize the Marxist parties since that would create the danger of the Menshevik and Bolshevik groups combining. There was certainly no thought of his returning to Russia in Lenin's mind at this moment; indeed, he raised with Kollontai the question of whether one of the Bolshevik Duma deputies who had been arrested might now find it possible to come out to Stockholm for a con-

---

° Kollontai was a woman follower who had been converted from Menshevism and was destined later to become Minister of Social Security and the first Soviet woman ambassador.

ference. Kollontai had been asking Lenin for "directives" to guide her and the party comrades in their political work. Lenin replied that this sounded "almost like irony"—the Bolsheviks were at a very low ebb; however, he agreed to send his latest articles to her in Scandinavia, and he added that he was afraid that "it will not be possible to get away early from this damned Switzerland." This was on March 17.

On March 18 he went to western Switzerland to make another political speech in which he made only a glancing reference to the revolution, and he seems to have been quite unaware that the Bolshevik committee in Petrograd at that moment was urgently trying to get into touch with him. They wanted him to return to Russia at once.

At last on March 19 he began to bestir himself. He wrote a letter to V. A. Karpinsky, the Bolshevik who ran the Russian library in Geneva: "I am carefully considering from every point of view what will be the best way of travelling. . . . Please procure in your name papers for traveling to France and England, and I will use them when passing through England and Holland to Russia. I can wear a wig. . . . You must then disappear from Geneva for at least two or three weeks (until you receive a telegram from me in Scandinavia). During that time you must be extremely careful and go into hiding somewhere in the mountains, where we shall of course pay for your board and lodging."

It was an absurd proposal and nothing came of it. By now, in any case, all the revolutionary exiles in Switzerland—and there were several hundreds of them—were caught up in a great current of excitement over the news from Russia, and were discussing plans by which they could all join forces and return together. A joint meeting was held on March 19, and it was attended by Zinoviev and the Bolsheviks, Martov and the Mensheviks, Bobrov and the Social Revolutionaries, and others like Lunacharsky, who drifted about from place to place in the revolutionary twilight. Martov suggested that they should all try and go home together by way of Germany. The Germans, he said, might be persuaded to let them pass if the Provisional Government in Petrograd guaranteed to release a number of German and Austrian prisoners-of-war. The best way to approach the Germans, Martov thought, would be through the neutral Swiss government, and the whole plan, of course, depended upon the Petrograd government giving its approval.

All agreed that this was an excellent idea, and it was decided that Robert Grimm, one of the leaders of the Swiss socialists, should be asked to sound out the Swiss government on the matter.

An interesting point arises here: all these Russian exiles were allies of the British and French, and technically enemies of the Germans. Yet it never seems to have occurred to them at this stage to approach the British or the French for passports to enable them to travel by the sea route; they appear to have assumed that as notorious Marxists and socialists their application would have been refused, or that they would have been arrested as soon as they crossed the border into France. In point of fact, both the British and the French were quite willing to forward any Russian who was asked for by the Provisional Government, and later on Chernov, the Social Revolutionary leader, did take this route. It was of course a fairly dangerous business to make any journey through the North Sea in the spring of 1917, and this aspect certainly had an effect on some of the exiles.

During the next two days the plan for the return via Germany was pushed forward. It would seem that Robert Grimm saw Hoffmann, the Swiss Minister for Foreign Affairs, and officially drew a blank; Hoffmann did not want to endanger Swiss neutrality by openly involving himself in the affair. However, he informed Romberg, the German Minister in Bern, of what was on foot and Romberg was very willing to help. On March 22 he cabled Berlin that "outstanding Russian revolutionaries desire to return to Russia via Germany since they are afraid to go via France on account of the submarine risk"; and he asked for instructions.

Berlin was at once interested, for by now it was becoming apparent from their intelligence reports that the abdication of the Czar had not turned matters to Germany's advantage; Milyukov and the Provisional Government were going to carry on with the war as before. The obvious course therefore was to bring down the Provisional Government, and replace it with another government which would make peace. Parvus was already urging this line in Copenhagen; Rantzau, the German Minister there, reported that he had had a meeting with him on March 22 to discuss the matter. The Foreign Office in Berlin were also eager to capitalize on the new situation in Petrograd while it was still fluid, and had already asked the treasury for a further five million marks for propaganda inside Russia. Simultaneously the question of providing a train for the Russian exiles was referred to Ludendorff and the Supreme Army Command. The Germans still had a good deal to ponder here. Could these revolutionaries really be trusted? Would they really work in Germany's interests once they were back in Russia?

Lenin at any rate soon made it clear what he was going to do, and his ideas were in flat contradiction to the line that his Bolshevik colleagues Kamenev and Stalin were taking in Petrograd at that moment. He was going to attack the Provisional Government tooth and nail, and he was going to sue for peace. Lenin had been using these days of waiting in getting out the first three of his "Letters from Afar," which were designed to be printed in *Pravda*, and he made it plain that he had meant what he said so long ago after the Zimmerwald conference: he was going to promote civil war in Russia. He asserted that there was a conspiracy between the Russian capitalists (represented by Milyukov and the Provisional Government) and the British and the French (represented by their two ambassadors in Petrograd, Buchanan and Paléologue). The first object of this conspiracy had been to prevent Nicholas and the Kaiser from signing a separate peace, and to bring about Nicholas's abdication. Marxists, he said, should have no illusions about these facts, which were being disguised by the Anglo-French press (Lenin's chief sources of information at this time were the London *Times*, the Paris *Le Temps*, and the *Neue Zuercher Zeitung*). He urged the proletariat to support the Soviet and bring down the Provisional Government. As a first step in this direction he recommended that the workers should be armed.

These ideas were followed up in a telegram which Lenin sent to a group of Bolsheviks who were on the point of leaving Norway for Petrograd. "Our tactics," he wrote, "absolute distrust, no support of new government, Kerensky particularly suspect; to arm proletariat only guarantee; immediate election Petrograd Duma; no rapprochement with other parties."

On March 24 events were turning in Lenin's favor. The Kaiser indicated that he wished the Russian socialists to know that he supported them in their opposition to the Provisional Government, and word also arrived from the Supreme Army Command that they had no objection to the revolutionaries traveling through Germany. They added on the following day that the exiles were to travel together and under escort.

In the fourth of his "Letters from Afar"—Lenin seems to have written them day after day at tremendous speed—he criticized Gorky, who, while advocating peace, had insisted that it must be peace in conformity with Russia's honor. Gorky, he said, should keep out of politics. What Russia wanted was an immediate peace program such as he had already outlined in his *Social Democrat* as far back as 1915, a peace in which she broke her engagements with her allies, and opened up armistice negotiations with all the belligerents. The government of Milyukov, he repeated, was simply the tool of Britain and France. "The German worker," Lenin went on, "now sees that the militant monarchy in Russia has been followed by a militant republic, a republic of capitalists who want to continue the imperialist war and who adhere to the robber treaties of the Czarist monarchy. Judge for yourself whether the German worker can have confidence in such a republic."

If the German authorities saw this pronouncement—and it is almost certain that they did—they can hardly have failed to warm toward Lenin. He was just the man they wanted. The German General Staff, at all events, was now particularly keen to press forward with the idea of repatriating the exiles, and on March 27 they sent an agent to Switzerland to make contact with Lenin. This man was Georg Sklarz, a close collaborator of Parvus's, and therefore not likely to be much welcomed by Lenin. However, he had full official backing from the Germans, and both the German legation in Bern and the consulate at Zurich were asked by the Foreign Office in Berlin to give him every assistance. Sklarz's instructions apparently were to smuggle Lenin and his chief lieutenant Zinoviev across Germany to the Swedish border, and he was supposed to do this without the Swiss authorities knowing anything about it.

We have no record of Sklarz's meeting with Lenin (who still all this time was with Krupskaya in Zurich), but the result of it emerges very clearly: Lenin did not accept the offer. He did not want to leave just yet, not, at any rate, until conditions had cleared somewhat in

Petrograd. Was there any guarantee that he would not be arrested on arrival as a traitor, especially if he came like this, almost alone, and as a result of a private deal with the Germans?

This question of the treason of dealing with the Germans was weighing very much on the minds of the other revolutionaries as well. Not all of them by any means were as eager as Lenin for peace at any price. After all, they were Russians as well as socialists; their own people had died by the million in defending Russia from the Germans, and it was a serious step to walk now into the enemy's camp, however correct (in the Marxist sense) their motives might be.

On March 29 about twenty of the party leaders met in conference, and we have an account of what took place from several sources. The exiles knew by now that the Germans were willing to provide a train for them, but they also knew from Robert Grimm that the Swiss government was unwilling to give the venture an official and respectable aura by treating with the Germans on their behalf. There remained, however, the other face-saving device: if the Provisional Government or even the Petrograd Soviet sanctioned their acceptance of the German offer, then they could still arrive in Russia with clean hands. But there was no word from Petrograd.

Lunacharsky, who was present at this meeting, says that with the exception of Lenin all the Bolsheviks there were opposed to taking the train. They argued that it would create a bad impression in Russia, and that the whole plan might be nothing more than a German ruse to discredit the socialist movement. Then Lenin got up, and started pacing about the room. When he spoke he astonished everybody. "When the revolution is in danger," he said, "we cannot pay attention to silly bourgeois prejudices. If the German capitalists are so stupid as to take us over to Russia, it's their own funeral. I accept the offer. I go."

According to Lunacharsky, this made a great impression, and some of the Bolsheviks began to take back their words. Finally they agreed to go. Others (including Lunacharsky himself) declared that they would wait and see.

Martov and Bobrov were adamant that they must first receive sanction from Petrograd before they would budge, and when Lenin and Zinoviev subsequently appealed to them by letter they still refused to change their views.

If Lenin did in fact take this stand at the meeting his subsequent actions reveal that he was very far from being easy in his own mind. At this time he was in correspondence with Ganetsky, his old follower whom he had posted in Copenhagen to keep an eye on Parvus. The Danes had recently expelled Ganetsky because of his illegal trade deals with Russia, and he was now in Oslo, where he was in telegraphic communication both with Petrograd and Switzerland. Through the last days in March he had been urging Lenin to return via Britain. Now on March 30 Lenin wrote him a long letter flatly rejecting the British plan and urging Ganetsky to do all he could to get Petrograd to give its blessing to the German train.

The German General Staff was now pressing still harder for action; in a message to the Foreign Office in Berlin they stressed the importance of getting Lenin and his friends (about forty in all, they thought) into Russia as quickly as possible, and they proposed that no special conditions or bureaucratic regulations should be imposed; men of military age, for instance, should be allowed to join the train.

Apparently as a result of this, Romberg in Bern got an imperative message from Berlin on April 2; he was told to expedite the arrangements, and there was an immediate flurry of activity. An intermediary was sent to Zurich to tell Lenin and Krupskaya to get ready at once, and upon this they packed hastily, settled their affairs and within two hours were aboard the train for Bern. Lenin evidently expected to set off for Germany there and then, for he sent a telegram to his sister Elizarova in Petrograd telling her to expect him on April 11. But as yet there was a great deal to be done.

Robert Grimm, the Swiss socialist, by now had had enough of acting as the go-between. He had seen Romberg at least four times, he had been warned off by Hoffmann, his own foreign minister, and he had not particularly relished the handling of so many fiercely disputing Russians. He knew too that he was loathed by Lenin; Lenin regarded Grimm as a reactionary, and he had once described his political views as "repulsive."

Grimm, however, bowed himself out with grace; he produced as his substitute Fritz Platten, another Swiss socialist leader of rather more left-wing views, and it was Platten who now began to round up the exiles and to sort out the sheep from the goats.

On April 3 he informed Romberg that between twenty and sixty were ready to go. They would accept the German conditions, he said, but they were anxious that their names should not be given and that they should travel in closed compartments with "extra-territorial rights." They also wanted a guarantee that the Germans at the last minute would not turn any of their number off the train. All this was acceptable to Berlin, and on April 4 a formal agreement about the journey was drawn up.

Yet again there were delays. The exiles were finding that it took time to wind up their affairs after so many years in Switzerland, and it was only now that it dawned upon them all that the permission of the Swedish government was needed before the party could enter Sweden. A message was sent off to the German minister in Stockholm to arrange this matter.

Lenin and his friends were still beset with misgivings about their reception in Petrograd, and on April 7 they engaged in a curiously naïve piece of whitewashing. They persuaded a group of French, German, Swiss, Polish and (subsequently) Scandinavian socialists to sign a declaration to the effect that as "Russian internationalists" they were against all imperialism, especially German imperialism, and were returning to Russia by this means solely because they were determined to work for revolution there—a revolution which would benefit the proletariat all over the world.

Yet another declaration was drawn up by the travelers themselves on the following day: they announced that they would support revolution in Germany as soon as they themselves had come to power in Russia. If the Germans got word of these documents—and again there is every evidence that they did—there is no indication that they were much disturbed. Either they regarded Germany as "revolution-proof" and did not take such threats seriously, or they were prepared to accept them at their face value, as simply a camouflage to make the adventure more palatable to the revolutionaries themselves and to their supporters in Russia. On April 8 we find Romberg reporting to Berlin that there was still a great deal of worrying going on about the party's reception in Petrograd, and it was important that while the train was passing through Germany no German should be allowed to speak to the travelers lest they incriminate themselves still further. Moreover, the trip, he urged, should be ignored by the German press.

On April 9 the party was at last ready to set off. They assembled in Bern and departed in a body for Zurich, where they lunched at the Hotel Zaehringer Hof. They then proceeded to the station and boarded the train, which left on time at 3:15 P.M. There were wild scenes on the platform before the train drew out, for by now the news of the departure had got out and a fiercely divided crowd had gathered. When the Bolsheviks waved revolutionary banners and sang the "Internationale" they were answered with cries of "Spies —German spies," and there were unpleasant references to their traveling at the Kaiser's expense. Platten, who was also going with the party, got into an argument that almost came to blows, and Lenin himself was involved in a scuffle. At lunch the party had voted that they would not take with them a certain Oscar Blum, whom they suspected of being an Okhrana agent. Blum, however, had managed to get aboard the train, and it was Lenin who grabbed him at the last moment and physically kicked him out.

So now they were off, thirty-two of them in all: nineteen Bolsheviks, six members of the Jewish Bund, three internationalist Mensheviks and four others, one of them a four-year-old boy. The most important were Lenin, Krupskaya, Zinoviev, Inessa Armand and Sokolnikov. Radek, who was an Austrian citizen, joined the train at the German border. It was also said that there was a British secret service agent on board, and that he was subsequently removed in Germany; but upon this point the German records are silent.

Platten in his account of the journey says they had food with them, a ten-day supply, and that some of it, mostly sugar and chocolate, was confiscated by the Swiss before they crossed into Germany. It is also related that Lenin disliked smoking and insisted that smokers should retire to the toilet, for which special tickets were issued. As for money, the party seems to have been fairly well provided: Platten had borrowed three thousand Swiss francs for them, and Lenin we know (from his letters) had another thousand of his own. There is also some evidence that he left money behind in Switzerland in case things went wrong and he was obliged to return.

The route they were to follow across Germany was by way of

Mannheim, Frankfurt and Berlin, and they were due to arrive at the port of Sassnitz on the Baltic on April 11. But once again there were delays; and these delays have never been satisfactorily explained. The train missed a connection at Frankfurt, and in Berlin they were shunted for some hours onto a siding (where, incidentally, several German socialists tried to greet them, but succeeded only in speaking to the little boy). Finally, after two days in Germany they arrived in Sassnitz late on April 12. The party then proceeded by boat to Malmoe in Sweden, and they continued at once to Stockholm, where numerous socialist colleagues were waiting to meet them. In Stockholm further funds were raised from the Swedish socialists to carry the party forward on the last stage of their journey. The Swedes were a little surprised to get a request for an additional thousand crowns for Lenin's personal use, but they paid up, and after a delay of a day or more the party continued on its way. A Swedish train took them to the Finnish border at the top of the Gulf of Bothnia, and the border itself was crossed on sledges. Here Platten turned back, and the rest went on by train southward through Finland to the Russian border. A few miles outside Petrograd the train was boarded by Lenin's sister and a group of supporters from the Bolshevik Central Committee. Lenin inquired keenly about what sort of a reception he could expect in Petrograd —according to Trotsky he quite expected to be taken directly to prison—and when he was reassured about this he rounded smartly on his old friend Kamenev who had come to greet him: "What's this you're writing in *Pravda?* We saw several numbers and gave it to you good and proper." It was the first rumble of the explosion that lay ahead.

In the evening of April 16 the train steamed into the Finland Station in Petrograd. Ten years had passed since Lenin had seen Russia.

Lenin's return had been contemplated with mixed feelings in Petrograd not only by the Provisional Government but by the Executive Committee of the Soviet itself; Tseretelli, the Menshevik leader, had been chosen by the Ex Com to represent them at Lenin's arrival, but he flatly refused to go, and Chkheidze, the president of the Ex Com, and one or two others, had reluctantly agreed to take his place. From Trotsky we learn that there were also forebodings inside the Bolshevik party itself. A conference had been held on the eve of Lenin's arrival, and Kamenev, Stalin and others were very well aware that the line they had been taking—a truce with the Mensheviks and temporary support of the Provisional Government— hardly squared with Lenin's recently expressed views. But Lenin was their intellectual leader, and any discredit he suffered was bound to reflect on themselves. There was already criticism of him in Petrograd for having taken the German train. They decided, there- fore, as a counterblast to this hostility, to put on the biggest possible show when the train arrived.

The matter was brilliantly organized. By the late afternoon on April 16 a vast crowd blocked the square in front of the Finland Station, and innumerable red banners were waving everywhere. Troops with military bands were drawn up near the side entrance through which Lenin was expected to emerge, and the ominous shapes of armored cars loomed in the square where there was scarcely room for the trams to pass by. A mounted searchlight kept moving its bright beam across the faces of the crowd onto the build- ings beyond. On the platform itself more soldiers were standing ready to present arms, and there were displayed more banners, more printed Bolshevik slogans and triumphal arches of red and gold. A band was posted at the point where Lenin's railway car was to come to a standstill, and a group of Bolsheviks stood waiting there with flowers in their hands. No, Lenin was not going to be arrested.

Chkheidze could scarcely make his way through the crowd to the place that had been prepared for him in the former waiting rooms of the Czar. The train was very late. They settled down into the boring vacuum of a long delay.

Lenin's arrival has become so much a part of Soviet folklore and has been so drummed-up by official writers and artists (Stalin of course well to the fore of the reception committee in all the paint- ings) that it will be well here to follow the account of it given by Sukhanov, who was at least a practiced and ironical observer. At long last, he says (and he was there with Chkheidze) the train arrived.

A thunderous Marseillaise boomed forth on the platform, and shouts of welcome rang out. We stayed in the imperial waiting rooms while the Bolshevik generals exchanged greetings. Then we heard them marching along the platform, under the triumphal arches, to the sound of the band, and between rows of welcoming troops and workers. The gloomy Chkheidze, and the rest of us after him, got up, went to the middle of the room and prepared for the meeting. And what a meeting it was, worthy of—more than my wretched pen.*

There were cries of "Please, comrades, make way," and in the midst of a throng of people Lenin came hurrying in.

He wore a round cap, his face looked frozen, and there was a magnificent bouquet in his hands. Running to the middle of the room, he stopped in front of Chkheidze as though colliding with a completely unexpected obstacle. . . .

Chkheidze got in first with his speech:

"Comrade Lenin, in the name of the Petrograd Soviet and of the whole revolution we welcome you to Russia. . . . But—we think that the principal task of the revolutionary democracy is now the defense of the revolution from any encroachments either from within or from without. We consider that what this goal requires is not disunion but the closing of the democratic ranks. We hope that you will pursue these goals together with us. . . ."

Lenin plainly knew exactly how to behave. He stood there as though nothing taking place had the slightest connection with him—looking about him, examining the persons round him and even the ceiling of the imperial waiting-room, adjusting his bouquet (rather out of tune with his whole appearance) and then, turning away from the Ex Com delegation altogether he made his "reply."

"Dear comrades, soldiers, sailors and workers. I am happy to greet in your persons the victorious Russian revolution, and greet you as the vanguard of the world-wide proletarian army . . . the piratical imperialist war is the beginning of civil war throughout Europe . . . world-wide socialism has already dawned . . . Germany is seething. . . . Any day now the whole of European capitalism may crash. The Russian revolution accomplished by you has prepared the way and opened a new epoch. Long live the world-wide socialist revolution."

Suddenly [Sukhanov goes on], before the eyes of all of us, completely

* This quotation and those on the following pages are from Joel Carmichael's translation of Sukhanov, *The Russian Revolution, 1917.*

swallowed up by the routine drudgery of the revolution, there was presented a bright, blinding, exotic beacon. . . . Lenin's voice, heard straight from the train, was a "voice from outside." There had broken in upon us in the revolution a note that was . . . novel, harsh and somewhat deafening.

The crowd now tried to break through the glass doors of the waiting room, roaring for their leader. Again the "Marseillaise" burst forth and under the searchlight Lenin was swept out and up onto one of the armored cars. Here again he briefly denounced "the shameful imperialist slaughter," and with Lenin on board and the searchlight still shining on him the car moved off over the Sampson Bridge followed by the band, the banners, the crowds and the soldiers. The procession was constantly interrupted at street corners to enable Lenin to make more speeches.

Eventually they arrived at Kshesinskaya's house, where the Bolshevik party was now solidly installed. Here too all the lights were shining and the balconies were hung with flags. From the second-floor balcony Lenin, now hoarse, addressed the crowd again. He still inveighed against the war, and according to Sukhanov a strange reaction began to overtake the soldiers who were standing about. They did not like what Lenin was saying. They wanted to defend Russia. He heard one of them say, "We ought to stick our bayonets into a fellow like that."

Bolshevik guards were carefully screening anyone who wanted to get into the house, but Sukhanov slipped in and under the resplendent ceilings made his way up to the apartments on the second floor. "In the dining room upstairs tea and snacks were being prepared. . . . Triumphant and contented, the Bolshevik élite were strolling about in anticipation of their first banquet with their leader, towards whom they displayed a really extraordinary piety."

Zinoviev had also arrived but no one took much notice of him. Lenin, however, greeted Sukhanov affably; coming back from his speech on the balcony he "smiled, screwing up his merry eyes and wagging his untidy head, took me into the dining room."

When dinner was over the inner group of the Bolsheviks moved downstairs with Lenin for the official party meeting, and speeches of welcome began afresh. Finally Lenin got up to reply. He opened with a bitter attack on the policy of the Petrograd Soviet and said that it was playing into the hands of the bourgeoisie. The Provisional Government, he said, must be destroyed and the workers, soldiers and peasants must themselves take control. Peasants were to seize the land at once. Armed workers were to run the factories. Capitalism was to be wiped out. There was to be no compromise of any kind between the Bolsheviks and any other party. As for Chkheidze and the other leaders of the Ex Com, they were nothing but "social-lackeys" and would have to be removed.

This outburst continued for two hours. It was, Sukhanov says, a "thunder-like speech which startled and amazed not only me, a heretic who had accidentally dropped in, but all the true believers. I am certain no one had expected anything of the sort. It seemed as though all the elements had risen from their abodes, and the spirit of universal destruction, knowing neither barriers nor doubts, neither human difficulties nor human calculations, was hovering round Kshesinskaya's reception-room above the heads of the be-witched disciples."

When it was all over the party members cheered willingly enough, but, says Sukhanov, there was a bemused look in their faces. None of them knew what to say. "Their eyes roved about unseeingly, showing complete confusion: the teacher had given the minds of his marxist disciples some work to do.

"I went out into the street. I felt as though I had been beaten about the head that night with flails . . . I breathed in with pleasure as much as I could of the fresh spring air. It was already quite light, the morning was just beginning."

CHAPTER TWELVE

The July Days

IN MID-APRIL, a full month after the revolution had taken place, Petrograd was still living at that pitch of nervous political excitement that usually precedes a *coup d'état*. There is almost the character of a minor Latin republic about the city during this time. Any chance happening—a crowd running down the street, an orator holding forth from a balcony, even a lurid rumor flying about the town—abruptly changes the public mood and threatens to overturn the government. Then all is suddenly calm again; the rumblings subside to nothing and an uneasy pause intervenes until the next eruption.

Lenin's appearance in Petrograd was just such an event. On the night of April 16 it had seemed that something really drastic was taking place. At the Finland Station and again at Kshesinskaya's palace he had stirred up the socialist camp as no one else could have done. His proposals had sounded reckless and extreme, and there had been murmurings against them, but it had been a dramatic experience to hear the guttural and insistent voice after so many years of exile. It breathed the true fire of revolution, and to the Bolsheviks at least it seemed to presage that great things would occur on the following day.

Yet nothing happened. By the midday hours of April 17, when the comrades gathered again at the Tauride Palace, a few hours' sleep and calm reflection had worked a wonderful change. What after all had Lenin done? He had come back to Russia in very dubious circumstances, having taken no share at all in the real heat of the day, having no practical knowledge of the conditions of the revolution, and he had lectured them as if they were a group of guilty schoolboys. Yet the fact was that the people of Petrograd had created the revolution and made it work while Lenin had loitered safely in Switzerland. It was time now for Lenin to keep quiet and learn something of the realities of the situation.

But Lenin did not keep quiet. He had spent the remaining hours of the night of April 16 in his sister's apartment, and on waking his first concern after a visit to his mother's grave was to proceed at once to the Tauride Palace with Zinoviev and there give an account of himself to the Ex Com, whom he had so violently abused on the previous evening. He knew that there was much suspicion about his having traveled in a German train and he wanted to give his own version of the matter before damaging rumors got about.

Lenin's argument—and he was supported by Zinoviev and other followers—was a simple disclaimer that he had had any subversive dealings with the Germans. He had taken the train, he said, because it was the only means of his returning to Russia, and the sole condition the Germans had imposed was that on his return he should use his influence to obtain the release of a number of German and Austrian prisoners of war. There had been no contact with any Germans while the sealed train had been traveling across Europe. In any case, Lenin concluded, the plan had not been his own—it was Martov's. This was not strictly true, and the fact that Martov had not been one of the travelers made it all the more untrue. Martov was still in Switzerland waiting for the sanction of the Provisional Government before he made the journey, and the Ex Com seems to have been very well aware of all this, for they listened to Lenin's explanations somewhat coolly and the only man who spoke up for him was a collaborator of Parvus. Without committing themselves to any comment the Ex Com decided that Lenin should be permitted to state his case in their official newspaper *Izvestiya*.

With this business out of the way, at any rate for the time being, Lenin next proceeded to a wider audience. The All-Russian Conference of Soviets had assembled in Petrograd, and it contained a strong Bolshevik element which was eager to hear him speak.

The Bolshevik and Menshevik delegates were treated to a lecture which subsequently became celebrated under the title of the "April Theses." In substance this address was a toned-down repetition of the arguments and proposals Lenin had advanced the night before, but it was more precise and practical. The Provisional Government, Lenin declared, must be replaced by a republic of the proletariat, and all power must be handed over to the Soviets. Capitalism was to be overthrown, and in its place there was to be one state bank, state control of all production and the nationalization of land. The police, army and bureaucracy were to be abolished, and every worker and peasant was to be armed and made eligible to hold office. At the front the soldiers were to be encouraged to fraternize with the Germans, and so pave the way for revolution not only in Germany but throughout the world.

Many of the delegates heard these views with open hostility. One man got up and declared that such a speech was "the ravings of a madman," and after a confused and angry debate the meeting closed with a flat rejection of Lenin and his whole program. Even Kamenev, formerly one of the strongest of Lenin's adherents, joined in the general opposition. On April 18 he published a criticism of the "April Theses" in *Pravda*, and when the text of the lecture was printed on the following day he returned to the attack a second time. Word soon got about Petrograd that Lenin had been disowned by the Bolsheviks, and there was much relief in the Ex Com and the Provisional Government.

Outwardly Lenin appears to have remained composed. Through the columns of *Pravda* and inside the inner group of the Bolshevik party he kept hammering away at his critics with the old persistence, and it is only from his private correspondence that one learns of his secret misgivings. On April 25 when he appeared to be drifting back into the revolutionary limbo where he had spent the last ten years he wrote to both Ganetsky in Stockholm and Karpinsky in Geneva, and there is a faint note of nostalgia for Switzerland—"that damned Switzerland," in his words. He complains that Russia is terribly cut off—the censorship blocks all letters. "The atmosphere here," he writes, "is one of frenzied persecution of us by the bourgeoisie . . . the bourgeoisie are attacking us frantically for having passed through Germany . . . there is a desperate chauvinist fever raging

among the Social Revolutionaries and the Social Democrats. . . .
We are being frantically attacked for being against unity." And he
asks for money. It is the voice of the outsider, of the man who has
returned home only to find his own people dull, boorish and provincial.

Yet there was one factor that was working in Lenin's favor, and
it was an important one. In a situation where every party and every
politician was being pushed first one way and then another Lenin
alone stuck to one uncompromising line of argument, and it was
closer to the feelings of the illiterate and irresponsible mass of the
Russian people than any other. His promise of shared wealth and
freedom to the underdog was bound to have tremendous force and
the masses were in the mood for continued rebellion against authority. He was out for destruction, for the looting of the last traces of
the Czarist past, and this appeared to the crowd to be a great deal
more attractive than the work of trying to build up law and order
again. In the face of this bold program the agitated efforts being
made by the Ex Com and by the Provisional Government to put a
brake on the revolution and to restore a solid routine were not very
impressive.

Then too Lenin's opponents aided him at every step of the way.
Their only hope lay in combining, but instead the Ex Com persistently sabotaged the Provisional Government, and the right-wing
socialists continued to fight with suicidal energy among themselves.

Matters boiled up to a crisis at the beginning of May, and the
creator of this crisis was Milyukov, the scholarly historian, the one
man who at all costs ought to have avoided it. He chose this dangerous moment to overplay his hand entirely. On May 1, in his
capacity as Foreign Minister, he sent off a note to the Allies saying
that Russia would fight on to the end, and that she would honor
the obligations she had contracted with them. In other words, nothing was to be changed; the secret treaties were still valid and this
was still a "capitalist" war. It was the last sort of declaration that
the socialist parties wanted, and there was an immediate outcry.
The Ex Com demanded an explanation, and once again the crowd
in the streets took charge. On May 3 the Finnish Regiment appeared
with their arms before the Mariinsky Palace, where the Provisional
Government had now set itself up, and threatened violence unless

Milyukov resigned. They were soon joined by a crowd of some twenty-five thousand people, and there were furious shouts against the cabinet ministers. Next day shooting broke out in the streets. Kornilov, the Military Governor, was forbidden to use force, and the uproar only subsided when it was learned that the Provisional Government had offered to water down the terms of the note and to agree to a policy of peace without annexations or indemnities. In disgust Kornilov resigned and went off to take up a command at the front.

It was now clear that the Cadets had insufficient support in the country, and that the Provisional Government would have to be converted into a coalition with the socialists, if it was going to have the ghost of a chance of success. The negotiations moved briskly and erratically forward through the second week of May. On May 12 Guchkov, the Minister for War, threw in his hand. He was in poor health, he hated the idea of the socialists entering the government, and his few weeks of trying to control the new revolutionary army had left him in despair. Next Milyukov himself was dropped; he declined the Ministry of Propaganda and never again managed to fight his way back through the revolutionary tide. The new government that emerged in the middle of May was on the whole a reasonable compromise. Lvov was again the Prime Minister, and he had with him a cabinet of ten liberals (or "capitalists" as Lenin preferred to call them), and six socialists approved of by the Ex Com. The most interesting appointments were those of the young liberal Tereshchenko, who replaced Milyukov at the Foreign Ministry, and Kerensky, who went to the Ministry of War. Lenin could have asked for nothing better than the creation of this coalition government. By joining it the other socialist parties cut the ground away from under their own feet. The Ex Com now was no longer an independent committee where the more militant mass leaders could let off steam against the authorities; it had a stake in the government, and to some extent it was responsible for the government's actions.

The Bolsheviks now became the center of the opposition, and they soon attracted to their ranks many people who could think of nothing but their hostility to the "capitalists" and the "bourgeoisie": the out-and-out pacifists, the people who believed that only through violence could they escape from the appalling squalor and poverty of their lives.

To these extremists Lenin's "April Theses" did not seem at all alarming. In a wilderness of argument his slogan "All Power to the Soviets" shone with a bright and simple clarity; in this drastic illness here was the panacea for the world. And the fact that nobody yet had put the Marxist experiment into practice made it all the more attractive to those who had long since committed themselves to violence.

Lenin seems to have been at his most forceful during these days. He wore down the opposition inside his party with a schoolmasterish air of rightness, going through each point over and over again until even Zinoviev and Kamenev, his strongest opponents, were at a loss for further argument. They appear to have found it impossible to get the better of him in debate. "Lenin," Gorky says, "was a man who prevented people from living their own lives as no one before him was able to do." By the middle of May he could fairly claim that he was again the undisputed leader of the party.

The Bolsheviks of course were still a long way from exerting a deciding influence on public affairs; they were outvoted by the other socialist parties and were reviled as disloyal and pro-German in all the moderate newspapers. But then neither the press nor the new coalition government was in a very good position to know much about the labyrinthine activities of the Bolshevik agitators. They worked like persistent burrowing insects in every corner of discontent, in the factories, in the armed forces and in the mines, from the Black Sea to the Baltic, and their dual object was to end the war with Germany forthwith and to promote the class struggle inside Russia. They encouraged the workers to turn against their own leaders in the Soviets.

In the middle of May Martov was eventually persuaded to accept the German offer of another train, and he turned up at the Finland Station with a large party of exiles who had remained with him in Switzerland. The bulk of them were non-Bolshevik, but it was not long before a number found themselves disgusted with the woolliness of the right-wing socialists, and they slid into the Leninist camp, often to become more Bolshevik than the old Bolsheviks themselves.

On May 17 Trotsky arrived. Earlier in the year he had sailed for

America, and he had set himself up in New York on 164th Street. Here for a month or two he had scraped out a living writing for various publications such as the revolutionary *Novy Mir—New World*—which circulated among Russian exiles and sympathizers in the United States. At the outbreak of the revolution money for him to return to Russia had been raised at a political rally in New York and he had left America on March 27. When the ship reached Halifax he was arrested by the British and taken ashore. Here he had been detained for four weeks until at the request of the Provisional Government the British had released him.

Trotsky was not yet officially a Bolshevik, and was unpopular in the socialist movement. Lunacharsky says of him, "Tremendous imperiousness and a kind of inability or unwillingness to be at all caressing or attentive to people, an absence of that charm which always surrounded Lenin, condemned Trotsky to a certain loneliness. . . ." However, like Lenin, Trotsky was a great "name" in the movement (and in some people's opinion a greater man), and he was made an "adviser" to the Ex Com. From this strategic perch —and he quickly began to take a leading part in the Ex Com's work —he moved steadily left toward Lenin throughout June, and in July he came the whole way. Trotsky was by far the most important convert Lenin had yet made—he was the ideal man of action to put life into that dry hard Leninist logic—and soon the two men were closer together than they had ever been in the early days of the century. It was the most ruthless and formidable combination that one could well imagine and there is a certain fascination in watching it grow in power from day to day.

Already in June the factories and the regiments were quietly returning more and more Bolsheviks as their delegates to the various socialist conferences. By the middle of the month Lenin felt strong enough to show his hand in the First All-Russian Congress of Soviets. Tseretelli, the leading Menshevik and the Minister for Posts and Telegraphs, made a speech in which he rejected the idea that the Soviets should seize power from the government. "There is," he said, "no political party in Russia which at the present time would say 'Give us power.'"

Lenin interjected, "There is."

There was an outburst of derisive laughter, but Lenin returned to the point when he himself got up to speak. "The citizen Minister of Posts and Telegraphs," he said, "has declared that there is no political party in Russia that would agree to take the entire power on itself. I answer: there is. No party can refuse to do this, all parties are contending and must contend for the power, and our party will not refuse it. It is ready at any moment to take over the government."

He went on to say that, on obtaining power, the first act of the Bolsheviks would be to arrest fifty or a hundred capitalists and hang them. After that they would denounce all capitalists, regardless of nationality, as enemies. Kerensky answered this: "You Bolsheviks recommend childish prescriptions—arrest, kill, destroy. What are you—socialists or police of the old regime?"

In an aggrieved voice Lenin called to the chairman: "You should call him to order."

It was a significant exchange. The Bolsheviks had now made it blindingly clear that they had no use for democracy or for free elections or indeed for the freedom of anybody or anything. As a minority—and they were very much in a minority—they were ready to take over the government and enforce their will on the majority, and with violence if need be. Lenin made no bones about this question of violence. He always insisted it was necessary in a revolution.

Barely a week later the party made another move. It announced that it would hold a demonstration in the streets. Already the placards had been prepared: "Down with the Ten Capitalist Ministers," "All Power to the Soviets," "Bread, Peace and Freedom." A fiery leading article urging the workers into the streets had been written for *Pravda* and was to appear on the front page on the following day.

There was a commotion in the Ex Com when the delegates heard this news. They went off to the Congress of Soviets and got a clear vote which denounced the intended demonstration and forbade it to take place.

Lenin and the Central Committee of the Bolsheviks hesitated. They themselves had no clear idea of the extent of their own following as yet, and it was a serious step to defy the Congress. Late at night the demonstration was called off and messengers were sent to *Pravda* to stop the presses. The paper appeared next morning with a blank space on its front page.

It was now decided by the Congress that a general, all-party demonstration should be held, and it was timed to take place on July 1. The official slogans were to call for a democratic republic, for "general peace," and for support for the coalition government. On the morning of July 1 some 300,000 people or more poured into the streets, and it was soon seen that the Bolsheviks were stronger than they themselves had ever dreamed. Most of the official slogans had been ignored, and in their place the soldiers and the workers carried the banners of the forbidden Bolshevik demonstration of the week before. One must date the first real acceleration of the Bolshevik cause from this moment. From now onward their actions had more and more the aspect of a conspiracy. No one quite knew what they were doing. Lenin disappeared—it was said that he was ill and had gone off to rest in Finland—and it was noticed that the other Bolshevik leaders were often missing from their places at the meetings of the Congress and the Ex Com. A vague uneasiness settled over the Tauride Palace, an atmosphere that was not unlike that which had preceded the rising in March. "Everywhere," Sukhanov writes, "in all corners, in the Soviet, in the Mariinsky Palace, in people's apartments, on the public squares and boulevards, in the barracks, in the factories, they were talking about some sort of manifestation to be expected, if not today, tomorrow. . . . Nobody knew exactly who was going to manifest what, or where, but the city felt itself to be on the verge of some sort of explosion."

The real source of this demoralization was of course the war itself and the loyalties—or rather the lack of loyalties—it involved. The city was bedeviled with intrigue and rumors of every kind, no politician could absolutely trust his colleagues, and even the black market helped to create an impression that there was nothing that could not be bought and sold.

After the March rising it was a fairly easy matter for German agents—mostly Russians in German pay—to make their way from Sweden to Petrograd, and Stockholm became a major center for German espionage and propaganda. There was a regular channel by which German money was paid from Stockholm into agents' accounts in the Russo-Asiatic Bank and the Siberian Bank in Petrograd, and little doubt exists that some of the Bolshevik funds arrived by this route. Lenin was closely watched by the Germans after his return to Russia, and his speeches were noted in Berlin with much approval.

Germany's policy remained the same after April: she wanted peace with Russia, peace almost at any price. By May an intensive peace program was under way, and agents were instructed to work for the overthrow of Milyukov and his replacement by a government that was more amenable to the Germans, if possible a government of Bolsheviks. In addition there were to be contacts on the front line, and both open and secret propositions for an armistice. As a sideline intermittent German support was given to a proposal for an international socialist conference in Stockholm; socialist leaders from all the belligerent countries were invited, and it was hoped that the meeting would lead to a softening-up of the Allies' resistance, especially in Russia.

A newspaperman and former collaborator of Witte's named Kolyshko was one of the most active German agents at this time. He arrived from Sweden in April with a draft peace plan which he was to canvass among the Russian socialist parties. He was also instructed to set up a pro-German newspaper in Petrograd, and a sum of three million rubles was made available to him for this purpose.

In May Robert Grimm, the Swiss socialist leader, arrived. He appears to have had secret backing from both the Germans and Hoffmann, the Swiss Foreign Minister, and the main object of his mission was to sound out the Russians on their terms for an armistice. By May 31 he was able to report to Hoffmann in Bern that he had made contact with the Marxist parties in Petrograd and Hoffmann let him know in a general and unofficial way just how far the Germans were willing to go in getting a separate peace with Russia. The terms were as follows: it was to be an "honorable" peace. The Germans would not try to restore the monarchy, nor would they interfere in Russian internal affairs. An agreement would be negotiated over the future of Poland and the Baltic States, and Germany would mediate between the Russians and the Turks over Constantinople. There was to be the usual exchange of prisoners of war, and no British troops were to be allowed on Russian soil. Financial support was to be given to Russia, and there was to be economic co-operation. (It seems possible that the Germans here were thinking of the Ukrainian wheat which they badly needed, and the huge arms dumps which the Americans and the other allies were building up in Vladivostok and Murmansk.) Finally, the Germans guaranteed not to launch an offensive while the negotiations were going on.

All in all, it was an offer which the Russians were going to look back upon with some regret in the days ahead.

These then were some of the secret dealings of the German propaganda program in May and June (and many others are revealed in the Berlin Foreign Office files). At the front meanwhile more obvious approaches were made. The Germans welcomed the efforts of the Russian soldiers to fraternize, but it was not quite the kind of fraternization the Russian Marxists had envisaged. Russian-speaking Germans were sent into the forward trenches to urge the moujiks to go home and grab the land from the nobles and wealthy proprietors while there was still time. The Russian soldiers on their side wanted to know when the Germans were going to revolt against *their* Czar, the Kaiser, but on that score they got no encouragement at all.

A curious incident—it was one of several such happenings—occurred on the Russian Fifth Army front toward the middle of May. Five German civilians appeared under a flag of truce and General Dragomirov, the Russian commander, questioned them in Russian. The Germans said that they had come by order of the German High Command, and that they wanted to discuss peace negotiations. Apart from this, however, they were rather vague about their mission—they seemed more anxious to pick up information than to give it—and it was not until June 4 that a more positive move was made. On that day a radio message purporting to come from the German Supreme Commander on the eastern front was picked up in Russia. He offered an immediate armistice.

These feelers met with strong opposition in Petrograd, and on the whole it was not surprising. Russia was not yet ready to give in. The Germans were quite wrong in thinking that if Milyukov was turned out of office there would be an immediate loosening-up of Russian resistance. With the creation of the new coalition government many of the more responsible socialist leaders began to feel that they had a definite stake in Russian policy at last. They were no longer fighting for the capitalists and the landowners, nor for the foreign allies, nor for such remote goals as Constantinople; they were fighting for themselves, for the revolution itself. They wanted peace, but they did not want it at the expense of seeing the revolution collapse.

By mid-June this new spirit of resistance was working strongly. The agent Kolyshko was arrested for espionage. Grimm's activities were declared subversive, and he too was arrested and sent back to Switzerland. Commanders at the front were forbidden to hold parleys with the enemy; and the German plans for an international socialist conference in Stockholm were outmaneuvered by the Allies.

But it was inside the socialist movement itself that this change was most marked. Through the last half of May and June a series of national congresses was being held in Petrograd, congresses of Mensheviks and Social Revolutionaries, of the peasants and the railwaymen, of the trades unions and the co-operatives, and the debates revealed an increasing desire to take up a tougher line against Germany.

On May 13 the Ex Com in Petrograd appealed to the soldiers to fight on, since they were no longer "fighting for the Czar, for Protopopov, Rasputin and the rich, but for Russian freedom and the revolution." On June 7 a congress of peasants in Petrograd passed a resolution that there should be no separate peace, and that the army should fight on with better discipline than it had shown before. Two days later the Petrograd Soviet issued a declaration rejecting the peace offer which had been sent over the radio by the German commander-in-chief. On June 10 the Kronstadt sailors were at last persuaded to accept the authority of the Provisional Government. On June 16 when the First All-Russian Congress of Soviets met in Petrograd under the presidency of Chkheidze, the delegates (248 Mensheviks, 285 Social Revolutionaries and 105 Bolsheviks) gave their approval for a new offensive against Germany and Austria. The Bolsheviks of course voted against the resolution, but they were shouted down, and Lenin in particular was met with jeers.

A great readjustment was taking place in the Russian army. Through the early days of the revolution the dazed moujik-infantrymen had been bombarded by subversive pamphlets and newspapers (notably the Bolshevik *Soldatskaya Pravda*) and Marxist orators were constantly arriving from Petrograd to harangue them with defeatist views. Life in the trenches became a perpetual mass meeting, and there were frequent cases of officers being insulted, imprisoned and even shot. But by June the first flush of irresponsible freedom was over, and a new sense of discipline was beginning to assert itself. A hundred and fifty high-ranking officers had been retired, and the generals that remained were making a genuine effort to support the Provisional Government. They even contrived to find ways around the famous Soviet Order Number One. Alexeiev, the Commander-in-Chief, had issued orders for the establishment of army committees on every front. They were made up of officers, soldiers and representatives of the Duma and the Soviets, and constituted a sort of military trades union. Capital punishment was abolished. These changes did not suddenly turn the soldier from a revolutionary lion into a loyal lamb; desertions still went on, officers were still defied, and several regiments which refused to take part in the coming offensive were disbanded. But at least a certain coherency was restored to the ranks, and the Germans on their side did not attack. Had the Provisional Government and the Russian High Command also been content to remain on the defensive this improvement no doubt would have continued. But they were not content. For the best of reasons and for the most patriotic of motives they were determined to embark upon the suicidal policy of attack.

At least half a dozen separate influences pushed the Russians into this disastrous decision. Basically there was a general feeling that an offensive, if successful, would improve morale and put the country in a better position for bargaining for peace. This was going to be the great opportunity for the new revolutionary soldiers to show what they could do. The Cadets and the right-wing parties were in favor—indeed, it was one of their conditions in agreeing to a coalition government that the offensive should go forward. Then there was the Allies' part in the affair, and it was no more sensible than the part they had played in forcing the unprepared Russian armies into action at the very beginning of the war. Earlier in the year the Allies had been promised that a Russian attack would be made in the spring, and now with a bland indifference to all the implications of the revolution they kept pressing the Provisional Government to redeem its promise. Albert Thomas, the French left-wing Minister for Munitions, visited Petrograd, and having bestowed a socialist's blessing on the new government urged it forward. The United States on May 29 extended a credit of $100 million to Russia and began shipping arms to Vladivostok. On June 13 the Root Mission arrived in Petrograd.

Senator Elihu Root, a Republican and a former Secretary of State and of War, was aged seventy-two at this time, and he was sent to Russia by President Wilson to arrange American co-operation with the new revolutionary government. A large party of well-known people accompanied the Senator, and they traveled from Vladivostok across Siberia in the Czar's former train. Root remained in Petrograd for close on a month, and was not much impressed by what he saw. The Russians, he said, "are sincerely, kindly, good people but confused and dazed." He summed up his attitude to the Provisional Government very trenchantly: "No fight, no loans." And that was the way it had to be.

Kerensky, the new Minister for War, was more than willing. He saw the offensive not only as the salvation of Russia but as a great personal adventure. At the end of May he gave orders for the preparation to begin, and soon afterward, dressed in a simple soldier's tunic, he set off on a tumultuous morale-raising tour of the front. It was not unsuccessful. General Brusilov, the most aggressive and successful of the Russian generals—and incidentally the most socialist-minded—was appointed Commander-in-Chief in place of Alexeiev, and a new breeze began to blow through the army for the first time since the previous year.

There remained one other factor in the situation: the great amorphous mass of the Russian people themselves. Up to this point the revolution had not improved their living conditions in the least, at any rate in the cities. The food shortage in the cities had grown worse, and prices had now risen to seven times above the prewar level. The bread ration had gone down to 1½ pounds for manual workers and one pound for others. In Petrograd many factories had closed down, and the unemployed men, mingling with the idle military garrison, formed a solid pacifist block. They believed that their leaders in the Ex Com and the Soviet had betrayed them by joining a belligerent coalition government. They wanted peace.

This then was the strange alignment of influences at the end of June: a German government and a nameless horde of Russians (nameless except for the small group of Bolshevik and left-wing socialists), who were united in wanting to end the war at once, and, opposed to them, a Russian government, backed by the right-wing socialists and a part at least of a Russian army that was ready and perhaps even eager to fight on.

On June 29 the artillery opened fire, and two days later the offensive began along a forty-mile front in Galicia. Thirty-one divisions were engaged, and they were supported by thirteen hundred guns. Through July 1 and 2 there was a fairly steady advance, but on July 3 the first impetus began to slow down, and there was indecisive fighting for the next two days. Then on July 6 General Kornilov, attacking from the south, resumed the advance again with initial success.

On July 16, with some of their best shock troops, the Germans came in for the counterattack. By late July the Russian army was in retreat, and the Kerensky offensive ended in a crushing Russian defeat.

The full seriousness of this disaster was not at once made known in Petrograd—the communiqués were extremely noncommittal—yet the feeling of disaster was in the air, and it was an additional strain that the highly-charged atmosphere of the capital was quite unable to bear. Once again it was the Cadet party that precipitated the crisis. On July 15 four of their ministers resigned from the government over the question of granting autonomy to the Ukraine. That was the ostensible reason for their going, but it seems certain that other less obvious influences were at work as well: the defeat of the army, perhaps even the general air of menace that was brooding over Petrograd. At all events, when the news of these resignations got around the town it was received as some kind of a signal or portent. There was a sudden snapping of the tension, a sudden mass urge for action and for violence. The July Days had begun.

The first impulse appears to have come from the First Machine-Gun Regiment, which was quartered in Petrograd in the huge club known as the House of the People. From the early days of the revolution the Bolsheviks had carefully cultivated this unit, for it was mutinous to the point of anarchy, and machine guns were the most effective of all weapons in street fighting. Trotsky, in his account of the rising, says that the Bolsheviks—or more particularly the military organization of the party—did all they could to hold the machine gunners back. Throughout July 16 he says speaker after speaker was sent over from Kshesinskaya's palace to urge them to remain calm, but the soldiers would not listen. They were determined to come out armed into the streets to demonstrate against the government, and in the afternoon delegates were sent to other disaffected regiments and factories on the Vyborg side inviting them to take part. Other messengers were sent to Kronstadt. At the Putilov works the bulk of the thirty thousand odd workers downed tools at once, and a confused mass meeting ended in their deciding to advance with the soldiers upon the center of the city. It needed very little time then before the normal life of the capital came to a standstill. While the machine gunners and other soldiers gathered at Kshesinskaya's palace, the bulk of the workers marched in a dense mass toward the Tauride Palace, breaking open liquor stores and tobacco shops along the way. One general war cry swept the mob: "Down with the Government—all power to the Soviets," but neither in this nor in the wild shooting that now began was there any real design; it was demonstrating for the sake of demonstrating, and no one seemed to have had any real authority or a plan.

Eventually late at night the disorder ceased, and in the pale half darkness the rioters went back to their homes. Kerensky had gone off to the front to collect loyal soldiers to defend the capital.

This, then, is Trotsky's account of the happenings on July 16 and it does not square with the known facts. The Bolshevik military organization was very far from taking the passive role that he claims for it. Its members—and they are reckoned at some twenty-six thousand men—were extremely active among the Vyborg factories and the military garrison prior to July 16. They may not have had the official backing of the Bolshevik leaders but they certainly had plans for organizing a rising—the Provisional Government, indeed, had prior warning from its intelligence service that those plans were being discussed in Kshesinskaya's house. Bolshevik agents were seen among both soldiers and factory workers. Arms were distributed. The Kronstadt sailors too were in a state of readiness that can hardly have been spontaneous.

The truth seems to be that the Central Committee of the Bolshevik party were perfectly well aware of all this but, in the beginning, they did not altogether like it: they felt that a rising at this stage might be premature. But then, as events developed from hour to hour on July 16, they realized that a great opportunity was opening out before them: A *coup d'état* that was timed to coincide with the German offensive at the front might have a very good chance of success. By nightfall the committee decided to switch: instead of opposing the rising they decided to get behind it and give it leadership. A proclamation against the rising which was to have appeared in *Pravda* on the following day was canceled. Messages were sent out to the disaffected regiments and workers telling them to stand ready to renew the demonstration in the morning. And in Kshesinskaya's house the formation of a new all-Bolshevik government was announced.

In the nature of things all these plans were very hastily contrived and that haste is apparent in the confusion of events that followed on July 17.

Early in the morning some six thousand sailors (other estimates give a much higher figure) set out from Kronstadt in two destroyers and other boats, and they landed on the quays of the Neva toward midday. Once again crowds of Red Guards, workers and soldiers appeared in the streets, most of them making for the Tauride Palace. Not all the regiments were in favor of the rising, but in the congested streets it was difficult to distinguish mutineers from men who were loyal to the government, and often friends opened fire on one another or shot wildly at people who were doing nothing more than idly standing by. A rough struggle developed outside the Tauride Palace when Chernov, one of the government ministers, tried to address the crowd. He was grabbed and might have been lynched on the spot had Trotsky not come running to his rescue. Meanwhile Lenin had hastily returned from Finland, and was haranguing the sailors from Kshesinskaya's balcony. It was an oddly careful speech. He applauded the sailors' revolutionary motives, but advised them against taking any definite action. The sailors took this with a grain of salt and went off to join the other demonstrators in the city. One group of them, apparently under orders, seized the symbolic Fortress of St. Peter and St. Paul—and prepared to resist a siege.

Petrograd at this moment was wide open to any kind of determined attack; any one of the contending groups could have seized the city's strongholds and dominated both loyal soldiers and police. But the situation was now entirely out of control and no leader came forward to mobilize the Bolshevik forces. There is even an element of comedy in the scene: at one point the mutinous 176th Regiment arrived from outside the city and made directly for the Tauride Palace, breathing fire against the government. The soldiers declared that they had come "to protect the revolution," but from whom they were not at all clear. The Menshevik leader Dan seized this opportunity: he persuaded the men that it was the Tauride Palace they were supposed to protect, and the regiment dutifully spent the rest of the day keeping back the crowds from the very members of the government they themselves wished to liquidate.

In the end, when some four hundred people were killed or wounded, it was a sharp shower of summer rain that probably did more than anything else to quash the rising. The people ran for shelter, and once dispersed they did not care to reassemble in their sodden clothes. Moreover, the loyal elements among the garrison began to assert themselves at last, and during the night they were reinforced by additional troops that were brought in from outside the city.

On the morning of July 19 the Kronstadt sailors found themselves isolated in the St. Peter and St. Paul Fortress, and after some hours of confused negotiations their leaders agreed to retire. This was the end of the organized resistance.

There is the quality of a summer thunderstorm about these two days of fighting in Petrograd—the commotion blows itself away just as suddenly and violently as it came—and in order to understand what happened next one must remember that the population of the city did not consist entirely of class-conscious workers or of excitable young men. Most of the citizens were perfectly normal people with families and jobs and responsibilities, and they had no desire at all to live dangerously or in a constant state of crisis: they recoiled from the idea, they hated it even more than they hated the hardship of their lives; and now that they had been so roughly disturbed they were furiously angry, as angry as only frightened people can be. Many of the Mensheviks and the Social Revolutionaries, even the Petrograd Soviet itself, must be included among these people. They had not called the rising. They strongly opposed it, and they had been badly shaken by what had happened. The authority of the non-Bolshevik party leaders had counted for nothing. A wild mob had been let loose in the streets, and somebody, they felt, must be to blame, somebody or some group of people who must now be hunted down and treated like common criminals.

This general feeling—this common desire for revenge on the disturbers of the peace—would not by itself have been able to create the remarkable tempest of anger that overtook the ordinary people in the city on the night of July 17 and on the succeeding days. Some spark was needed to ignite their resentment. That spark, however, was provided. The government released for publication a secret dossier that appeared to prove beyond any doubt that Lenin was a German agent. The immediate implication was that the Bolsheviks had deliberately provoked the rising on the instructions of the Germans.

The effect of this revelation was, in Kerensky's phrase, "shattering." In a moment the news spread around the town, and it dawned like a blinding light on the less politically-minded citizens that they had been made the victims of an elaborate plot. Here was treachery on a national scale, the complete and damning explanation of the whole sinister affair. A further shock was coming. On July 19 the Germans renewed their counterattack on the front at Tarnopol, and for the first time the public was made aware of the full extent of the Russian defeat. It was more than a defeat: the reverse at Tarnopol soon developed into rout. At this news many of those who had doubted the authenticity of the Lenin spy documents in the first place were completely won over; it seemed all too painfully clear that the Bolshevik rising had been timed to coincide with the German onslaught at the front.

From this moment the Bolshevik cause was lost. The Cossacks who had been brought into the city, and the loyal regiments in the garrison, were in a fighting mood, and they were out for reprisals. A company of armed men burst in upon the offices of *Pravda* early on the morning of July 18, and in a moment they had wrecked the interior of the building. The linotypes were smashed, the plates torn off the machinery and the machinery itself shattered beyond repair. Files, books and papers were torn up and scattered over the floor. Another detachment set off for Kshesinskaya's palace only to find that they were too late: Lenin and his followers had got wind of their arrival and had vanished, leaving only a few house servants behind. However, the soldiers took possession of the building just the same and posted sentries outside. Other raids were made upon Bolshevik centers on the Vyborg side. All over the city Cossacks and policemen were picking up suspects and taking them off to jail. On July 19 Kerensky got back from the front and writs were issued for the arrest of Lenin, Kamenev, Zinoviev and others. Trotsky at his own request was arrested later on.

And now one more proof of Lenin's guilt was added to the rest: he did not wait to answer the government charges as Trotsky and the others did. He went into hiding.

"In company with Zinoviev," Trotsky tells us, "Lenin passed a number of weeks in the environs of Petrograd in a forest near Sestroretsk. They had to spend the night and find shelter from the rain in a haystack. Disguised as a fireman Lenin then crossed the Finland border on a locomotive, and concealed himself in the apartment of a Helsingfors police chief, a former Petrograd worker." Meanwhile, the other Bolsheviks faced the music.

A vast library has been written on the subject of the Lenin spy documents, but it still seems doubtful whether we are ever going to get to the full truth of the matter. Some aspects, however, have been established beyond all doubt. One source of the information against Lenin was a Ukrainian officer named Ermolenko, who prior to the war had been an agent of the Czarist secret police. During the war he had gone over to the Germans, and had agreed to act as a spy on their behalf in the camps for Russian prisoners of war. In 1917 the Germans sent him back across the front line into the Ukraine to carry out acts of sabotage and espionage behind the Russian lines. Ermolenko promptly informed the Russian authorities about his mission. He declared to intelligence officers that the Germans had told him that Lenin was one of their agents.

General Denikin, the Russian general before whom Ermolenko was brought, was very much impressed by this information, and passed it on to Petrograd. But the Provisional Government decided to take no action; after all the evidence was not corroborated by other witnesses, and Ermolenko was a man of somewhat doubtful past. He was packed off into central Russia and told to remain in retirement. This was in May. Now, however, in July, matters looked very different: there were now good grounds for believing that a Bolshevik conspiracy was on foot. Ermolenko was brought back to the capital and although he was unable to produce any further evidence there were others who could. Kerensky himself had been warned about Lenin's activities earlier in the year. Some twenty telegrams that passed between the Bolsheviks and Stockholm had been intercepted and these telegrams made it clear that foreign money had been reaching the party in Petrograd. Now also, a certain Grigory Alexinsky, a former Bolshevik deputy, was ready to come forward; he too had information that Lenin had been in correspondence with Parvus, Ganetsky and other German agents in Stockholm, and had received money from them.

The government still hesitated to bring a charge, and the documents in the case were left with the Minister of Justice, Perevertsev. It was while Kerensky was at the front on July 16—the first day of the rising—that Perevertsev decided to issue the documents for publication. The Ex Com immediately protested that this was political blackmail, and they managed to persuade the newspapers to refrain from publication. One paper, however, defied the ban, and by the night of July 17 the news was all over Petrograd.

Trotsky fought a vigorous rearguard action for the reputation of his chief on July 18 and the days following, but this bombshell had started a fire which neither he nor anyone else could put out. All over Russia Bolsheviks were being labeled as German agents and Lenin by going into hiding had ruined his own case. Trotsky's defense boiled down to a simple denial that a revolutionary of Lenin's long standing could ever have joined hands with an enemy capitalist government. As for the money he was alleged to have received, where was it? The Bolsheviks were notoriously poor. Trotsky also defended Lenin's going into hiding on the ground that in the prevailing atmosphere of the city he would never have been given a fair trial, and might even have been lynched. Years afterward when he himself was a refugee from Stalinist Russia Trotsky renewed this defense of Lenin in one of the most scornful and trenchant chapters of his history of the revolution. He summed up:

"The unbroken chain of suspicions of Germanophilism and espionage, extending from the Czarina, Rasputin and the court circles, through the ministry, the staffs, the Duma, the liberal newspapers, to Kerensky, and a number of the Soviet leaders, strikes one most of all by its monotony. The political enemy seems to have firmly resolved not to overwork their imaginations: they simply switched the same old accusations about from one point to another, the movement being predominantly from right to left."

From his refuge in the haystack Lenin produced his own disavowals. In Gorky's *New Life*, and in the Kronstadt *Pravda* (the Petrograd *Pravda* had been banned) and in a specially printed leaflet he repudiated all the charges. Parvus, he said, he had cast off in 1915, and he had received no money from Ganetsky. He denied that Ganetsky was a party comrade. As for his having traveled to Russia in a German train, he pointed out, not without reason, that Martov and others had used the same route and no suspicion of disloyalty had fallen on them.

This was all very well in its way, yet we know from Lenin's own posthumously published letters that he was in close and continuous correspondence with Ganetsky in Stockholm (and Ganetsky incidently had a successful career among the Bolsheviks in Russia after the revolution). Moreover, as we have seen, there is abundant evidence in the Wilhelmstrasse files that during the early part of the war Lenin was in contact with the Germans through the agent Keskuela, and that he did receive assistance, financial and otherwise. The sealed train was part of that assistance. We also know from the German records that money was paid to the Bolsheviks in Petrograd fairly regularly from March right up to the second revolution in November, 1917. Kuhlmann, the German Foreign Minister, states in one document dated December 3, 1917, that it was only through German help that the Bolsheviks were able "to enlarge *Pravda*, their main organ, and to greatly broaden the basis of their party."

That there was some sort of dealing between Lenin and the Germans cannot any longer be a matter of doubt. It may have been expedient for him to deny it in 1917, but one wonders why his supporters should bother to cling to the denial at this late day, when it has long since been made apparent that Lenin was determined to take power in Russia by any means and at any cost. His attitude to the Russian masses was not unlike that of a Victorian missionary in darkest Africa; he had his Marxist faith and that was sacrosanct, nothing could touch it. The Russians were ignorant benighted children who had to be corrected and coaxed and led toward the light. Anyone who opposed him in this course was an agent of the devil, or if not the devil then whatever his equivalent is called in the Marxist anathema. And if he was obliged to be ruthless in this righteous course—if, for example, he found it necessary to hang a hundred capitalists and to resurrect the Okhrana in a form that was far more terrible than anything the Czars had contrived—then it was merely in order that he could save Russia and the world from the fatal heresy of non-Leninism. It was the surgical approach, and it was not only applied to the physical welfare of mankind; it applied to the human spirit as well.

These ironclad attitudes of mind were, in any case, bound to be revealed through the Russian nightmare of 1917 as Lenin moved closer to his goal. In order to be awakened to their danger the Russian public had no real need of spy documents. It had only to consult its own knowledge. From the moment of his return in April Lenin had taken the German line, even if he did so purely in his own interests. He had demanded that the Russians should break their allegiance to the Allies and sign a separate peace. He had urged the soldiers in the front line to befriend the enemy. He had called for civil war in Russia. He had publicly denounced the new offensive in July, and had openly tried to sabotage the operation by attacking the government and by urging workers and peasants to revolt.

On the question of whether or not Lenin provoked the July rising and tried then to seize power, we have an absorbing passage in Sukhanov's account of the revolution. Sukhanov's pages do not have the intellectual sparkle or the massive force of Trotsky's writing, but there is something about his racing mocking sentences that rings true while often Trotsky's words do not. Trotsky, of course, denies flatly that the Bolsheviks ever intended to carry out a *coup d'état* in July. Sukhanov, however, says this:

... Lunacharsky told me the unknown details of the July uprising. They were unexpected. According to him, on the night of July 17 Lenin was definitely planning a *coup d'état*. The Government, which would in fact be in the hands of the Bolshevik Central Committee, would officially be embodied in a "Soviet" Cabinet made up of eminent and popular Bolsheviks. For the time being three Ministers had been appointed: Lenin, Trotsky and Lunacharsky. This government would at once issue decrees about peace and land, thus attracting the sympathies of the millions of the capital and the provinces and consolidating its power. An agreement of this kind had been come to between Lenin, Trotsky and Lunacharsky. It was concluded while the Kronstadters were making their way from Kshesinskaya's house to the Tauride Palace. The *coup d'état* itself was to proceed in this way: the 176th Regiment [the same one Dan had posted on guard in the Tauride Palace], arriving from Krasnoe Selo, was to arrest the Central Ex Com, and at about that time Lenin was to arrive on the scene of action and proclaim the new Government. But Lenin was too late. The 176th Regiment was intercepted and became disorganized. The "rising" had failed.*

When Sukhanov was about to publish this account in 1920 he consulted Trotsky—and incidentally by that time Lenin, Trotsky and Lunacharsky were all ministers. Trotsky strongly contested the truth of the story, and shortly afterward Sukhanov had a letter from Lunacharsky:

Dear Nicolai Nicolayevich,
Yesterday I received from Comrade Trotsky the following note: "N. N. Sukhanov has told me that in his book on the revolution there is an account of the July Days in which he relates, in your words, that in July the three of us (Lenin, you and myself) wanted to seize power and set about doing so!?!?!?"

It is clear, Nicolai Nicolayevich, that you have fallen into a profound error, which may have disagreeable consequences for you . . . your memory has completely distorted our conversation. . . . I beg you to take this letter of mine into account in the final version of your history, so that you yourself do not fall into error or lead others into it.

People's Commissar
[signed] A. Lunacharsky.

Already in 1920 we have here the talk of "errors," the new bureaucratic cant, the threats, and a few years later Sukhanov was arrested and tried. Then he vanished. But in 1920 he was not dismayed. He went ahead and published. He was prepared to admit, he wrote, that Lunacharsky might have got his facts wrong at the time, but he was pretty sure he had not misreported him. He and

* This quotation and the following are from Joel Carmichael's translation of Sukhanov, *The Russian Revolution, 1917.*

Lunacharsky were sleeping in the same room during the July Days, and he remembered very well how on the night of July 20 he lay on his sofa listening to Lunacharsky telling him the story.

Somewhere in all this the truth lies hiding. On the facts available, however, it seems to be a fair assumption that the Bolsheviks did have a hand in the provoking of the rising, and that they had a plan to take advantage of it, and that in the midst of the crisis they lost their nerve. It was a mistake that Lenin did not intend to make a second time.

CHAPTER THIRTEEN

The Kornilov Affair

T HE VERY bitterness of the reaction against the Bolsheviks meant that it could not last; and yet for a few weeks after the July Days Russia had a chance—a last chance—of avoiding Communism. Everywhere, in the army as well as in the cities and the provinces, the membership of the Bolshevik party fell away. Those who had been about to join it drew back, others on the fringes of the movement melted away in thousands, and even at places like Kronstadt and the Vyborg district of Petrograd there were few who cared openly to demonstrate their faith in Lenin any more. Printing shops refused to handle Bolshevik literature, and for the first time in many months no Bolshevik newspaper appeared. Trotsky was in prison. Lenin, in hiding, saw very little chance of the party's immediate recovery, and he settled down to the writing of a book. "Aren't they getting ready to shoot us all?" he had asked Trotsky before he left Petrograd, and now at the end of July he wrote to Kamenev from Finland: "Strictly *entre nous*: if I am done in, please publish my notebook, *Marxism and the State*."*

Kerensky meanwhile was profiting from the anti-Bolshevik reaction. On July 20 he replaced Prince Lvov and formed a new government with himself as Prime Minister and Minister for War. It lasted about ten days in a welter of suspicion and disagreement, and Kerensky then felt strong enough to shake off some of his more trouble-

* This was subsequently published under the title *The State and Revolution*.

some left-wing supporters; he went through the gesture of resigning. There was no one to replace him: neither the Cadets nor the right-wing socialist parties could rule alone, nor could they combine under any other man. And so obligingly they urged him to come back. His next ministry took office on August 6, and although it was a coalition government of a sort the emphasis this time was predominantly on the right. The death penalty was reinstated in the army, and in the rear new restrictions were placed upon the press and public meetings. Lenin was formally indicted for treason, and General Kornilov, the soldier who in May had wanted to use force to disperse the mob in Petrograd, was elevated to the rank of Commander-in-Chief. At the same time some attempt was made to get the more disaffected regiments out of Petrograd and up to the front line.

If Kerensky could have enforced these measures with any thoroughness there is little doubt that the Bolshevik party could have been seriously and perhaps permanently weakened by early August, weakened enough at all events to enable the moderate parties to sink their differences and establish a firm hold on the government. But nobody really trusted or respected Kerensky. His prime ministership was an uncertain wavering, first to the left and then to the right, and he did not fall at once because for the moment nobody except the Bolsheviks wanted him to fall. This was not the sort of leadership that could enforce orders or inspire much confidence in a political crisis that had now gone on far too long. Moreover, the discrediting of the Bolshevik party had left a void among the masses which none of the other socialist parties were energetic enough to fill; and it was only natural for the masses to turn inward upon their own discontent.

Factories continued to close down because of the breakdown of transport; others that stayed open were soon paralyzed by another wave of strikes. And so wholesale unemployment was added to the other miseries of the war, and it was not very helpful, just at this time, that a leading Moscow industrialist named Ryabushinsky should have made a speech in which he said that, in the end, the workers would be brought back to their senses by "the bony hands of hunger." This was just the kind of provocation that was bound to halt the drift away from the Bolshevik party. The workers took careful note of that phrase about hunger; indeed, it became a political slogan among them. At a time when all controls and restraints were loosened it aroused a new and fiercer hatred of "the rich."

Then too the anger against Lenin was bound to die down. Even people who were anti-Bolshevik began to murmur that the vilification of his character had gone too far: after all, in politics everyone was bought in some degree. If Lenin had been bought by the Germans then Kerensky had been bought by the British, the Americans and the French. And meanwhile when was someone, anyone, going to do something to end the accursed and hopeless war?

By the end of the first week in August the anti-Bolshevik campaign had blown itself out so far as the mass of the population was concerned, and Kerensky's opportunity was gone. This was not at all apparent on the surface—the Bolsheviks were still much in disgrace—but it was made very plain at a surreptitious conference of the party that was held in Petrograd on August 8. At their previous conference in May, 151 Bolshevik delegates had turned up, representing 80,000 members. Now in August, despite the public distrust of Lenin, despite the suppression of the party newspapers and the imprisonment of its leaders, 175 delegates were returned, and they claimed to represent no less than 177,000 party members, mostly among the industrial proletariat. In other words, the July Days had only been a momentary check; the falling off of the party membership had now stopped entirely, and things were swinging steadily the other way. It was an astonishing recovery, and although the conference had to shift its meeting place from one house to another to avoid being broken up by the government police, a good deal of business was done.

Lenin was not present, but he was elected honorary president, and by letter he urged the comrades to abandon their old slogan "All Power to the Soviets" until such time as they had turned out their political rivals and got control of the Soviets themselves. Meanwhile they should prepare plans for an armed rising. This was accepted, and a new Central Committee was formed to control the party's activities. The most influential members of this body were Lenin, Zinoviev, Kamenev, Nogin, Alexandra Kollontai, Stalin and Trotsky (though Trotsky and Kamenev of course were in prison and Zinoviev was in hiding with Lenin). The July Days, Trotsky claims, had cleared the air; the waverers and the half believers had been weeded out from the Bolshevik rank and file and now it was a hard kernel of out-and-out Leninists that was moving into action.

It is doubtful, however, if any of these matters—the stealthy resuscitation of the party, the continuing hunger and discontent, even the steady demoralization of the army at the front—would have been enough to have restored Lenin's reputation and put the Bolsheviks back on their feet again. Something extra, something really forceful and dramatic, was needed to tip the balance in their favor. This additional requirement was provided by the incident that is known as the Kornilov affair. It is perhaps the most depressing event in the whole course of the revolution.

By August, 1917, there were very many people in Russia who had supported the revolution in the beginning, but who now looked back on the past with bitter regrets. The July Days had been a great awakening. To the big industrialists and landowners, to the right-wing Cadets and to large numbers of officers in the army, it now seemed that there was only one way to save the country: a dictator would have to be found. Kerensky was obviously too wordy, too emotional, too socialist for the post. None of the other older Duma politicians could have got a sufficient following. General Kornilov, however, presented interesting possibilities.

He was the son of a Siberian Cossack, and that to some extent made him acceptable to the rank and file of the army and the lower classes—indeed, he often made a parade of his humble origin—and yet there was no question that, politically, he stood to the right of the socialists. He had served most of his life in the army in the east, and by a combination of toughness and persistence had made his way up to the top. Early in the present war he had come west to a command on the Austrian front, and had been taken prisoner, but he had escaped shortly before the March rising against the Czar, and he had done well in Kerensky's recent abortive offensive. It was regrettable that the General was politically naïve—Alexeiev described him as "a man with a lion's heart and the brains of a sheep"—but what was needed in this emergency was a strong man who was not beset by doubts and hesitations; and there was no doubt that Kornilov was very strong, and personally very brave. He was forty-seven at this time, and although his physical appearance was not very reassuring—most of his contemporaries refer to his "dark Kalmuk face," his "slanting Mongolian eyes"—he had taken up his new post of Commander-in-Chief with great confidence. It was his practice to move about attended by an armed bodyguard of Asian warriors dressed in long red coats, and he issued his orders in the manner of a man who was accustomed to being obeyed. Lavr Georgievich Kornilov, in short, was one of those familiar figures who emerge in so many domestic crises in history when governments collapse and political parties begin to drift toward civil war; he was the sergeant-major on horseback, the patriot-hero from the ranks who lives by the military tradition.

Kornilov himself probably did not aim so far as military dictatorship at first—he was a sincere supporter of the revolution—but already in August he had traveled a certain distance along the road. On assuming his new duties he presented Kerensky with a demand that he should be given wide powers for disciplining the army. He wanted the right to shoot deserters and mutineers, and he proposed a far more rigid control of the political commissars and soldiers' committees at the front. In the rear he wanted to exercise military discipline on the railways, the arsenals and the munition factories: and there is no doubt he was justified in urging reforms. When Kerensky hesitated the general proceeded with his bodyguard to Petrograd to have the matter out, and everything in the capital, even Kerensky himself, filled him with anger and disgust. On his return to his headquarters at Mogilev on August 17 he declared to his staff that the only way to clean things up was to hang Lenin and disperse the Soviets before they could engineer another rising.

It was not altogether an empty threat. There were about a million Cossacks in Russia, and they were beginning to look to Kornilov as their leader. General Kaledin, the Ataman of the Don Cossacks, supported him, and it did not take the various liberal and right-wing parties long to discover that they had here a new champion of some promise. The British military attaché spoke warmly of the new Commander-in-Chief. Rodzianko, the old leader of the Czarist Duma, telegraphed him: "In this threatening hour all thinking Russia looks to you with faith and hope." A number of officers' clubs and rightist groups, which had been dispersed by the revolution, began to revive and look with new hope toward the future.

With this encouragement Kornilov started to concentrate the Third Cavalry Corps at a convenient point in the north from which it could advance upon Petrograd; and again he pressed Kerensky for authority to tighten up discipline within the army.

For all his failings, his vanity and his emotional egotism, one must sympathize with Kerensky at this moment. He could not in an instant abandon all his socialist convictions and throw in his lot entirely with Kornilov, and yet he wanted to combine with him so that together they could find a way out of the crisis. He believed that he had to try and rally the support of the moderates of all parties if his government was going to survive. This was an almost impossible feat; yet he felt bound to attempt it, and no doubt his vanity led him on. He called a State Conference together in Moscow. In retrospect this conference appears as a strained and artificial affair, yet it is difficult to see how else Kerensky could have found support. Some twenty-five hundred delegates were summoned, and they were supposed to represent a rough cross-section of Russian politics. There were delegates from the Soviets and from the four Czarist Dumas, from the trades unions and from the employers, from the army and other state institutions. However, it was the liberal, right-wing and property-owning classes who predominated, and the Bolsheviks took no part.

The opening on August 25 was not propitious. Moscow had been chosen as the meeting place in the belief that it was politically calmer than the capital, but this belief was mistaken. The Moscow workers boycotted the conference. They staged a lightning strike of such effectiveness that the delegates could find no public vehicle to take them to the opera house where the conference was being held, no restaurants in which to eat, and few shops willing to keep their doors open. It was the first definite sign that the Bolsheviks, after a month or more of political exile, were moving back to their old positions by way of the workshops and the factories.

In the conference itself Kerensky's opening speech cast a veneer of patriotic unity over the proceedings, but it soon wore thin when other speakers came down to the basic issue of whether or not they were to go on with the war; and when the right burst out with applause the left sat grimly silent. Yet on the whole the delegates wanted to combine, and the gathering might have been judged at least as an innocuous success had it not been overshadowed by the prospect of Kornilov's arrival. This was the event upon which all the delegates fixed their attention, and it happened with dramatic flourishes on August 26.

If anyone up to this point had been skeptical about Kornilov's pugnacity they were left in no doubt about it now. The general's first act on arriving by train in Moscow was to inspect his fierce red-coated guards on the railroad platform to the music of military bands. Next he proceeded to the Shrine of the Iberian Virgin, where in former days it had been customary for the Czars to pray before their coronation. This seems to have been a moment of awakening for Kerensky and from this point onward his distrust of Kornilov steadily increased. He managed to buttonhole the general in the evening and he demanded that, on his appearance at the conference on the following day, he should speak of nothing but military matters. Kornilov naturally refused, and when on August 27 he was called to the platform he received a tremendous ovation from the right-wing delegates. Milyukov describes the scene: "The short, stumpy, but strong figure of a man with Kalmuk features appeared on the stage, darting sharp, piercing glances from his small black eyes in which there was a vicious glint. The hall rocked with applause. All leapt to their feet with the exception of . . . the soldiers."

This was interesting. The general apparently found his real enemies within the army itself, and as the soldiers and the left-wing delegates continued in their seats the right shouted at them: "Get up, get up." A storm of abuse broke out, and it was Kerensky at last who brought them to order by insisting that they should listen to the "first soldier of the Provisional Government."

Kornilov's speech was less of a bombshell than had been expected. Evidently his main idea was to instill a sense of reality into his audience: "The enemy is already knocking at the gates of Riga," he declared, "and if the instability of our army does not make it possible to restrain him on the Gulf of Riga, then the road to Petrograd is open." The army, Kornilov continued, had been "converted into a crazy mob trembling for its own life," and he hinted that drastic measures might soon become necessary to correct the situation.

General Kaledin, who followed Kornilov to the speaker's rostrum, was more precise; he demanded that the soldiers' committees in the army should be disbanded.

The fundamental issues were now coming out fairly rapidly into the open. It was plain that 'a new political party was crystallizing around Kornilov, and it was determined to act while there was still time. It aimed quite simply at a *coup d'état* in Petrograd. Hesitating between the Bolsheviks and this new group (they soon became known as the "Kornilovists") was the great majority of Russian politicians, who still believed that you could govern by more democratic methods, by holding elections for a constituent assembly and by the appointment of a cabinet that was responsible to it. These people included most of the Cadets, who still had their faith in a parliament on the English model, and most of the Mensheviks and Social Revolutionaries, who still believed in socialism but thought that they could achieve it by peaceful means, by supporting a coalition government for the time being and by winning the elections later on. And so for the moment nearly all these moderates were prepared to put up with Kerensky and oppose Kornilov's strong-arm methods just as, in the July Days, they had opposed the Bolsheviks.

Kerensky wound up the conference with a speech of extreme theatricality—his voice descending and ascending through thunder to a whisper—and once again he stated the old impossible dilemma: we are in the midst of a crisis, even a fatal crisis. If you on the left push me too far with your demands for socialism I will collapse, and you will be left to the mercies of the Kornilovists. If you on the right try to force a reactionary policy on me it will be just as bad; the socialist mob will be let loose on you. You must have faith in me: the only alternative is chaos. He left the platform in a state of dazed exhaustion.

But already on August 29, the day the conference broke up, the movement around Kornilov had gathered too much impetus to turn back. The Bolsheviks had their fling in July; now it was the turn of the right wing.

The political fracas that now began resembles nothing so much as a vendetta between the Guelphs and the Ghibellines in medieval Italy, with Kornilov playing the part of the rebellious *condottiere* on the one side, and Kerensky some Machiavellian grand duke on the other. The struggle was just as bloodless as the Italian vendettas used to be, just as much bedeviled by chicanery and a kind of artless braggadocio, but it was a great deal more fateful in its consequences. Lenin alone stood to gain by this brawl; and in the game of seizing power out of the confusion of civil war no underground maffia in the Italian Middle Ages could hold a candle to the Bolsheviks.

Kornilov's plan, briefly, was to provoke a street disturbance in Petrograd and then, on the pretext that the government was in danger, march on the city from the north and from the south. The field force was to be assisted by a kind of fifth column within the capital itself; a cadre of some two thousand officers was posted to the Petrograd district, and they had instructions to arrest the socialist leaders and to seize the principal buildings as soon as the street disturbances began. Some day "not later than September 14" was named as the date for the attempt.

In the manner of such exploits in revolutionary Russia, Kornilov announced his intentions in advance. For the first few days of September emissaries flew back and forth between the general at Mogilev and the Prime Minister in the Winter Palace, and each made a great show of pretending that he had the other's best interest at heart. "Come to Mogilev," says Kornilov sweetly, "and I will protect you from the Bolsheviks. Then we can crush them together." "By all means," Kerensky replies, "but first keep your troops where they are and tell me all your plans." There may even have been some genuine complicity between the two men. Certainly through these preliminary days each thought he could use the other, each aimed for power, and each believed he could arrive there, in some vague way, with the other's agreement.

But it was obviously not a situation that could last, and on September 8, when Kornilov had already ordered his men to stand by for their swoop onto the city, Kerensky precipitated a crisis. He did this by staging a trap which was entirely in the *opéra bouffe* character of the whole affair. A certain Vladimir Lvov, the Procurator of the Holy Synod (who is not to be confused with Prince Lvov, the former Prime Minister) was acting as a go-between, and Kerensky induced him to write down Kornilov's aggressive proposals on paper. Lvov was then dismissed and Kerensky got through directly to Kornilov on the telegraph wire. Pretending at first to be Lvov, he asked Kornilov to confirm his proposals and then indicated that he

(Kerensky) was in favor of them. He said he (Kerensky) would come to Mogilev on the following day. Having thus lulled the General's suspicions (and Kornilov indeed went to bed well satisfied) Kerensky burst into furious activity. He secreted an army officer as a witness behind a curtain in his quarters in the Winter Palace and then recalled Lvov. Lvov now was asked to repeat the Kornilov proposals once again and directly he had done so the army officer emerged from hiding and placed him under arrest. The unfortunate Procurator was marched off and locked in a nearby room. Kerensky at this stage seems to have been beside himself; Lvov remembered later how, through the night, the Prime Minister paced about singing snatches of Italian opera.

The cabinet was now summoned and apprised of the situation. It was agreed that all the ministers should resign, or at any rate surrender their portfolios for the moment, in order to give Kerensky a free hand. The Prime Minister acted at once by telegraphing Kornilov to hand over his command to his subordinate, General Lukomsky, and to come to Petrograd. Kornilov replied to this by ordering his troops to march on the capital.

It is the element of irresponsibility that strikes one chiefly in following the events of the next few hours. Riga had fallen to the Germans on September 3, just as Kornilov had predicted it would, and presumably Petrograd was in some danger. But nobody could now think of anything but the internal crisis, and it was a crisis of the most elusive kind. Both the opposing camps were dealing in delusions. Kornilov behaved as though he were at the head of some sort of crusade, with a loyal army at his back, which was very far from being the case. He had the other generals and most of the officers on his side, but the Cossacks were not nearly as loyal as he imagined. Even if his orders reached their destination—and often they were deliberately mislaid—it was impossible for his subordinates to carry them out because of the hopeless inefficiency of the whole army machine. Transport broke down or simply failed to materialize. Weapons of every kind were missing, and many of the units that were being deployed were down to half their normal strength. It was the most unsoldierly operation conceivable.

Kerensky on his side was also living in a world of fantasy. He brushed aside an eleventh-hour attempt made by his own followers to bring about a reconciliation with Kornilov, and began sending out orders from the Winter Palace as though he too had great forces waiting to do his bidding. These orders in themselves were sensible enough: all troop movements in the direction of Petrograd were forbidden, and the city itself was put under martial law. A proclamation was issued denouncing Kornilov as a traitor and declaring that he had been removed from his command. But it was not possible at this stage for Kerensky to know whether or not any of his orders were being carried out; they simply flew into the void. The rebel troops were already marching on the capital and the general was busy getting out a counter-proclamation of his own. This proclamation was an extremely foolish document, for it declared that Kerensky was acting under pressure from the German General Staff and from the Bolsheviks, and this was manifestly nonsense which was not likely to deceive anybody except possibly a few of the more exuberant officers on Kornilov's own staff.

Neither man, in short, had any real power to control the situation they had so recklessly created; the real power lay with the soldiers themselves and the Petrograd Soviet and everything depended upon which side they supported. They decided against Kornilov. Men came pouring out of the factories and the barracks and they were determined to defend the city. The Red Guards appeared once more (in the end there were about twenty-five thousand of them), and soon barricades were being thrown up in the principal streets. The railway workers got to work rooting up the tracks and sabotaging the rolling stock along Kornilov's line of advance. Signalmen blocked the general's messages to his divisional commanders, and some thousands of Bolshevik Kronstadt sailors arrived in the Neva ready to fight.

The center of all this activity was not the Winter Palace but the Petrograd Soviet; it formed its own military committee for the defense of the capital, and it had the support of all the socialist parties, the Bolsheviks included. Lenin was still in hiding, but for once he was prepared to co-operate; indeed, he saw a great opportunity here. He would not fight for Kerensky, he said, but he was perfectly willing to fight against Kornilov. And now the Bolsheviks came forward to get their share of the arms that were being handed out from the government arsenals.

If Kornilov ever had any real chance of success it was now gone. On the night of September 9 his advance units came to a dead stop, and it was not long before the Petrograd Soviet had its agitators among them. A delegation was sent off to talk to the soldiers in the Savage Division, who were coming in from the south, and news soon arrived that they had agreed to defy their officers and remain where they were. The men of the Third Cavalry Corps, which had halted halfway between Pskov and Petrograd, did not even need persuasion; of their own accord they abandoned the operation and sent representatives in to the Petrograd Soviet for information and instructions. In the capital itself the two thousand Kornilovist officers dispersed without firing a shot, and those who were foolish enough to appear in public were quickly arrested.

There was worse news for Kornilov on the following day; unrest was spreading through the entire army, and General Denikin, one of the senior commanders, had been placed under arrest by his own men. In Moscow and most of the larger garrison towns hostile demonstrations against Kornilov were taking place. With bewildering rapidity the whole country was sweeping towards the left.

It was now Milyukov's turn to try his hand at saving the situation. The majority of the Cadets had not liked the idea of the Kornilov coup from the beginning, but they certainly did not welcome the idea of it ending in quite such a debacle as this. What was needed was a compromise: Milyukov proposed to Kerensky that he should step down and allow General Alexeiev, the former Czarist Commander-in-Chief, to form a government. To him at least Kornilov was ready to submit. It was a shrewd idea, and it had its attractions for Kerensky since he was none too sure of his own position. Kornilov may have been defeated, or at any rate held off for the time being, but the crisis in the army still existed. The thought of resignation was hateful to the Prime Minister, but how could he hope to carry on unless he had something more than the outward show of power? Salvation, however, was on its way. At this moment a delegation from the Soviet appeared at the Winter Palace with assurances of support from all the socialist parties, except the Bolsheviks. It was all that Kerensky needed, and the situation, if not exactly saved, took on at least a fairly definite pattern.

The events of the next few days can be related very quickly. On

September 12 General Krymov, the commander of the Third Cavalry Corps, was arrested by his soldiers and handed over to the government in Petrograd. He committed suicide almost at once. Kerensky, meanwhile, elevated himself to the rank of Commander-in-Chief of the army, and ordered Alexeiev to arrest the rebel Kornilov. On the 13th Alexeiev reluctantly and politely carried out these instructions, and Kornilov, in a state of high fever, was taken off to imprisonment in a monastery near Bikhov. Kerensky now formed a five-man "directory," with himself at the head (the other directors being Tereshchenko, the Menshevik Nikitin, and two officers, General Verkhovsky and Admiral Verderevsky, who in the past had displayed left-wing views). As a further sop to the socialists Russia was proclaimed a republic. By the 18th Alexeiev had resigned and many of the other Kornilovist generals had been dismissed or imprisoned, and with this the Kornilov affair can be said to be finally ended. Kerensky had not emerged from this encounter with much credit. Kornilov, after all, was a patriot and whatever one thinks of his methods his overriding aim had been to save Russia in a desperate crisis. When he failed the hopes of all moderate men in Russia failed as well. Indeed, from this point onward we are confronted with one of the great historical movements of modern times: the downslide into the Bolshevik revolution.

It is one of the peculiarities of the events in Russia in 1917 that so often the Bolsheviks seem to be on the very edge of success in their affairs, only to lose their grasp and fall away again. On Lenin's arrival in April, again in early May in the demonstrations against Milyukov and the Cadets, still again in the July Days, and even now in the Kornilov upheaval—on all these occasions one thinks one sees the beginnings of their rise to power. But always it is Kerensky who emerges.

Now, however, in September it was not quite so. Kerensky, it is true, had emerged again, and had even become a sort of dictator, but in the course of his recovery there had occurred an incident that was quite different from anything that had gone before: this was the arming of the Bolsheviks at the height of the crisis on September 9. It is doubtful if the government could have avoided this step at the time; the Bolsheviks had agreed to support the

Soviets and to defend the city. They had had as much right to the arms as any of the other political organizations. But now the crisis was over, and the new Directory lost no time in asking the Bolsheviks to return these arms to the arsenals whence they had been issued. In this the Directory were quite unsuccessful. They got no arms; the Bolsheviks were not only not in a giving mood, they very much resented any instruction whatsoever from Kerensky. Things had changed very much since their outcast days in July. Kornilov had brought them back into the arena again, and as propaganda to blacken the moderates and the right wing his name had magic. Kornilov, the Bolsheviks declared, had deliberately abandoned Riga in order to provoke an atmosphere of crisis in the capital. Kornilov stood for everything that was vile, treacherous and reactionary in Russia. Now at last the workers and the peasants knew who their true enemies were: not the Bolsheviks who wanted to make peace, but the Czarist generals who wanted to make war on the Russian people.

There was just enough truth in these charges to unsettle everybody, and the reaction against "Kornilovism" that now set in all over Russia was even stronger than the anti-Bolshevik phobia had been in July. Now it was the "monarchists," "the junker officer," anyone with the faintest hue of the Czarist past, who was hunted off the streets.

But it was upon the inner political structure of the socialist movement that the Kornilov fiasco had its really significant effect. By the end of September a new alignment was developing among the various left-wing groups. More and more the Menshevik following was confined to the government employees and the skilled workers in the trades unions. The Social Revolutionaries, on the other hand, were becoming rather less of a peasant party than they were before, and they were split into two groups: those following Kerensky toward the right and those who turned toward the left with people like Kamkov and Spiridonova. They were still the largest party, but according to Sukhanov it was made up of "the petty bourgeois democracy—peasants, shopkeepers, co-operators, minor officials, the Third Estate, the great mass of indigent intelligentsia and all the unthinking people and odds and ends who had been stirred and shaken up by recent events." It was left to the Bolsheviks to exploit the rest of the population, the city workers, the soldiers, the vast illiterate hordes who had nothing much to lose and a great deal to gain from the breakup of the established order.

Apart from direct action—the refusal to pay rents to landlords, striking in the factory and desertion from the army—there was only one way for all these people to express their political views, and that was through their local Soviets. These Soviets, it will be recalled, were very largely spontaneous organizations and they were only semi-official. They had begun by being strike committees, local popular parliaments. Any group of men were free to form a Soviet; it might be the workers in some textile mill in Moscow, the sailors in Odessa, the miners in the Donets Basin, and in a big city like Petrograd they grouped themselves into a combination of district Soviets called the City Soviet. In addition, large national groups like the peasants and specialized workmen like the railwaymen established Soviet systems of their own.

As a general rule all the main socialist parties—the Social Revolutionaries, the Mensheviks and the Bolsheviks—were represented in all the Soviets and contended for places on the executive committees and the presidiums, the presidium being composed of the leading men who sat on the platform and controlled the debates. The party that dominated the executive committee and the presidium had the right to send one or more delegates to the All-Russian Congress of Soviets that met in Petrograd from time to time.

This then, very broadly, was the principle on which the Soviet system worked, but in practice it was an extremely haphazard contrivance. Elections were conducted openly, often by a simple show of hands. There were no fixed dates and no particular rules for these elections, or if dates and rules did exist they were not observed. In the factories and barracks an endless political discussion went on, and according to how the discussion developed the men changed the delegates they sent as their representatives in their local Soviet. Thus an uncontrolled continuous election was going on, and the political make-up of many Soviets altered almost from week to week. Through late August and early September in a quite unobtrusive way the workers and soldiers began to return more and more Bolsheviks as their delegates.

On September 12, when the anti-Kornilov feeling was at its height, the full importance of this movement to the left suddenly became apparent: by 279 votes to 115 the Petrograd Soviet passed a Bolshevik resolution which demanded that Russia should be declared a republic, that the government should be made up entirely of socialists, that the land should be given to the peasant Soviets, that the workers should control industry, that the secret peace treaties should be annulled, and that peace should be concluded at once—in short, the whole Bolshevik program. It was a major victory, and Lenin did not lose a moment in following it up. He wrote to the party's Central Committee from Finland urging them to put all possible pressure on Kerensky, to extract concessions from him and to sabotage his government in every available way.

One of the first results of this new pressure was that Trotsky and Kamenev were released on bail from prison. Trotsky seems to have emerged much refreshed from his confinement, and he plunged at once into the fray. His reappearance was the signal for a direct challenge of the Mensheviks and the Social Revolutionaries in the Petrograd Soviet. The Bolsheviks demanded that there should be new elections for the presidium, and they won their motion by 519 to 414 with 67 abstentions. From this it was only a short step, on October 8, to the setting up of a new presidium that was dominated by the Bolsheviks. The Menshevik Chkheidze, who had been chairman for the past six months, was out, and Trotsky took his place. The rest of the presidium consisted of thirteen Bolsheviks, six Social Revolutionaries and three Mensheviks. These changes also meant that Trotsky and his followers were able to use the Petrograd Soviet's influence among the military garrison—an important factor. They immediately announced that the Soviet's support of Kerensky was withdrawn, and this was followed by a demand that the order for Lenin's arrest should be suppressed.

A similar overturn was now taking place all over Russia. In many places, even in the most distant towns and villages, local Soviets were setting themselves up and voting for Bolshevik resolutions. On September 23 the Moscow Soviet swung left and elected the Bolshevik Nogin as its chairman. Inside the other socialist parties the same contagion was at work; Tseretelli, the rightist leader of the Mensheviks, was dropped in favor of the more revolutionary Dan, and the Social Revolutionary party conference also indicated a sharp incline toward the left. For all this Kornilov's failure was a good deal to blame.

It is some measure of the importance of these moves that the Germans took the liveliest interest in them; a search of the Wilhelmstrasse files reveals that even as early as September 25 Ludendorff was recommending to the Foreign Office in Berlin that the Bolsheviks should be supported "by any means—even the most radical."

The Bolsheviks now demanded that a meeting of the Second All-Russian Congress of Soviets should take place in Petrograd, and the date was fixed for November 2. With a majority in the congress the Bolsheviks would be well placed for forcing their program on the government, and perhaps even for seizing control of the government itself.

This program, however, was not nearly drastic enough for Lenin. He was consumed with impatience. From his haven in Finland he bombarded the Bolshevik Central Committee with instructions, admonitions and even outright taunts. He wanted not conferences but action. On September 25 he wrote a letter urging the committee to start organizing at once for an armed rising. There should be a staff to co-ordinate plans, he wrote, and the first object was to seize Petrograd. Special squads should be ready to take over the telephone exchange and other important buildings. Plans should be made to put the General Staff under arrest.

The committee was a little aghast. They burned the letter.

On September 30 Lenin moved from Helsingfors to a new hiding place in Finland just outside the capital, and from here he kept up a close-range fire on his subordinates. "The crisis is here," he wrote. "It is criminal to delay." Not only Russia but all Europe was on the edge of revolution. They must strike at three places: in Petrograd, in Moscow and in the Baltic fleet. They must have plans to assault the Winter Palace, to seize the bridges across the Neva, to isolate the capital from the hinterland. Why won't the Central Committee act? Can't they see that the party has the power NOW and that there is no point in waiting for the All-Russian Congress of Soviets in November?

The committee still demurred, and in a rage Lenin threatened to resign so that he would be free to agitate independently "in the lower ranks of the party." And in fact he did go over the heads of the Petrograd Central Committee by approaching the Bolshevik leader in Helsingfors, instructing him to prepare for a rising, and by writing violent articles for the press. The following is a fair example of his style in one of his calmer moods:

And when the last unskilled laborer, every unemployed man, every cook, every impoverished peasant sees—not from the newspapers but with his own eyes—that the proletarian power does not grovel before the rich, but helps the poor, that it does not shirk from revolutionary measures, that it takes surplus products from the idlers and gives them to the hungry, that it forcibly settles the homeless into the apartments of the rich, that it compels the rich to pay for milk, but does not give them one drop of milk until the children of all poor families are adequately supplied, that the land passes to the toilers, the factories and the banks under the control of the workers, that immediate and serious punishment awaits the millionaires who hide their riches—when the poor see and feel this, then no power of the capitalists and kulaks, no power of world finance capital, that has stolen billions, can conquer the people's revolution. On the contrary it will conquer the whole world, because the socialist upheaval ripens in all countries.

That was for public consumption. Privately he kept hammering away at the committee "Delay means death." And on October 22, like some predator closing in on its quarry, he moved secretly into Petrograd itself.

The moderates in Russia had not exactly huddled together like a flock of sheep during these eventful days of the reaction against Kornilov, but their movements did indeed have a certain nervousness and lack of direction. Kerensky was in an impossible position. The failure of the Kornilov coup had demoralized the army, and Kerensky was hated by the officers for the part he had taken in the affair. The Allies were of no support to him; in fact, it was the other way about. They threatened to cut off their supplies to Russia unless she renewed her struggle against the Germans, a thing she was patently incapable of doing. But the most serious aspect for Kerensky was that he no longer had the backing of the Soviets, and although he reshuffled his cabinet once again to bring in some of the leading Mensheviks and Social Revolutionaries it was not the same thing as before. These moderates had lost their grip on the Soviets and to some extent on their own parties. The Bolshevik organization had been too strong for them.

Yet the Bolsheviks were still a long way from dominating the entire country. If a general election were to have been held—an election that took in not only the socialist voters but those of the center and right-wing parties as well—there is no doubt whatever that the Bolsheviks would have been overwhelmed. The correct tactics for the moderates, therefore, were surely to by-pass the Soviets and to return to the form of government which they had all so ardently desired for so many years: a government by parliament, a Constituent Assembly.

Kerensky began to move along this path toward the end of September. He called together a "Democratic Conference" in Petrograd with the dual purpose of getting support for his government and preparing the ground for the elections to the Constituent Assembly, which were to take place in November. In some ways it was a re-creation of his State Conference in Moscow in the previous month, though rather more weighted on the socialist side. Some twelve hundred delegates attended, and they represented in a general way a grouping of the organized opposition to the Bolsheviks in Russia. Yet it was a confused and indecisive gathering. Even at this eleventh hour the moderate socialists could not or would not see that their one hope of escaping civil war was to combine with the liberal groups, and Kerensky was given a vote of confidence only on condition that he excluded the Cadets from his administration.

The only other result of the conference was that it was agreed that, pending the elections for the Constituent Assembly, a temporary body should be set up under the name of the "Pre-Parliament," and this at least was some small guarantee that the moderates in Russia would have a meeting place and not be scattered or intimidated by the Bolshevik threats. The opening of the Pre-Parliament was fixed for October 20.

It was a cold wet day when the delegates assembled in the late afternoon in the Mariinsky Palace in Petrograd. There were about 550 of them in all, and the right-wing parties were outvoted by roughly three to one by the socialist parties. About 60 Bolsheviks attended, very much against the wishes of Lenin, and they came in late, after Kerensky had finished his opening speech.

Trotsky asked leave to make an emergency statement and was granted ten minutes. There was much eagerness to hear him. Many of the delegates only knew of this notorious rabble-rouser by name, but it had become a resounding name, perhaps even transcending that of Lenin. In the past few weeks Trotsky had instilled among the Bolsheviks a purpose and a discipline that had been very much lacking before, and now the delegates saw in the thin cruel face an aspect of definite menace.

The propertied classes . . . [the speaker said], are openly steering a course for the bony hand of hunger, which is expected to strangle the revolution and the Constituent Assembly first of all. Nor is their foreign policy any less criminal. After 40 months of war the capital is threatened by mortal danger. In response to this a plan had been put forward for the transfer of the government to Moscow. The idea of surrendering the revolutionary capital to German troops does not arouse the slightest indignation among the bourgeois classes; on the contrary it is accepted as a natural link in the general policy that is supposed to help them in their counter-revolutionary conspiracy.

There was an uproar. Some of the delegates sprang on to their seats and there were shouts about Lenin and the sealed train followed by counter shouts from the Bolsheviks.

When the noise had died down a little Trotsky was heard saying, "We, the Bolshevik faction of the Social-Democratic party, declare that, with this government of national treachery . . ."

Another angry outburst drowned his voice but he kept going:

. . . that we have nothing in common with them. We have nothing in common with that murderous intrigue against the people which is being conducted behind the official scenes. We refuse to shield it either directly or indirectly for a single day. . . . Petersburg is in danger, the revolution is in danger, the nation is in danger. The government is intensifying that danger. The ruling parties are increasing it. Only the nation can save itself and the country. We appeal to the people: Long live an immediate, honorable, democratic peace, all power to the Soviets, all land to the people, long live the Constituent Assembly.

It was a rousing declaration and there was very little in it either of realism or the truth. Lenin did not intend to allow the Constituent Assembly to last ten minutes if he could help it, nor any other democratic institution. He did not even care two straws about Petrograd and intended to abandon it. Yet as a declaration of war this speech was very clear, and it was followed by an action which has become time-honored practice down to the present day: the Bolsheviks got up from their seats and walked out of the conference. They intended to have nothing more to do with conferences and parliaments.

There remains one other incident that must be recorded here in the account of these agitated days before the final upheaval. Nicholas—now known to the socialists as Citizen Romanov—and his family had been living quietly since the spring under guard at Tsarskoe Selo. The Kronstadt sailors, however, had been threatening to raid the palace, and in early August the government decided that it was essential to move them to a safer place. The British cabinet under Lloyd George had cooled toward the idea of granting asylum to the family; there was much opposition to it from the British socialists and Nicholas was informed that the earlier offer had been withdrawn.

It was now decided that the family should be secretly removed to the quiet provincial town of Tobolsk in Siberia. The Empress was ill, but it was thought unwise to delay. On August 14 Nicholas, his wife, the five children (the girls were now grown up and the Czarevich was thirteen), their French tutor Pierre Gilliard, and others of the domestic staff boarded a train under a Japanese flag, and traveled to Tyumen, in the Urals. Here they were transferred to the steamer *Rus*, in which they sailed past Rasputin's home at Pokrovskoe to their destination. The house at Tobolsk where they were to be interned was not ready, and there was a seven-day wait on the river before they went ashore on August 26.

The Tobolsk population was largely Menshevik and not unsympathetic. Nuns from the convent brought the family food, and they were allowed to worship in the local church; the Empress now lived for her faith and her family and little else.

It was in this rural backwater that Nicholas lived through the critical months ahead, and if he had plans to escape then nothing came of them. He was almost as much forgotten as Lenin himself had been when he too had been sent as a prisoner to Siberia so many years ago. The ruthless politics of the revolution now dominated everybody's mind.

CHAPTER FOURTEEN

The Bolsheviks Seize Power

O N THE NIGHT of October 23 Lenin, wearing a wig and with his beard shaved, made his way secretly into Petrograd for a meeting with the Bolshevik Central Committee in Sukhanov's apartment. It was a strange place for the Committee to assemble, for Sukhanov was no Bolshevik and knew nothing about the matter; his wife, however, was a party member, and she had persuaded him to stay away for the night. Besides Lenin there were present Zinoviev, Kamenev, Trotsky, Stalin, Sverdlov, Uritsky, Dzerzhinsky, Kollontai, Bubnov, Sokolnikov and Lomov, in fact, the whole inner group of the party. It was the fate of some of these people to be outlawed and assassinated by Stalin in the years ahead, but just now they were a close conspiratorial circle, and the object of the meeting was to decide whether or not they should revolt against the Russian government.

The debate continued for ten hours. Lenin spoke up for an immediate rebellion and finally demolished all his opponents except Kamenev and Zinoviev. These two thought that the party was not yet strong enough, and that it was wrong to stake its whole future on a single desperate move; if the rising failed there would be no reprieve such as there had been after the July Days. This time they would probably all be destroyed. However, in the end Lenin had his way, and with only Kamenev and Zinoviev dissenting it was agreed that "an armed uprising has become inevitable and acute," and that all the party organizations should be urged to act accordingly. A political bureau of the Central Committee was also established at this meeting, and the members elected to it were Lenin, Trotsky, Stalin, Sokolnikov, Bubnov, and, surprisingly, the two weaker brethren, Kamenev and Zinoviev. At 3 A.M. the gathering broke up, and Lenin again vanished into hiding.

He had won a very definite victory here, and Trotsky quickly followed it up. On October 25 the Ex Com passed a resolution to the effect that plans should be made to defend Petrograd against "Kornilovist pogroms"—which was an inverted way of saying that it intended to prepare the workers and the soldiers for aggressive action against the government—and a few days later Trotsky signed an order on the Sestroretsk factory for the delivery of five thousand rifles to the Bolsheviks. He had no authority whatever for issuing such an order, but the factory workers handed over the weapons without ado.

And yet the last word had not been said. The Mensheviks and the Social Revolutionaries still controlled the Central Executive Committee of the All-Russian Congress of Soviets (the new congress was not due to meet until November 2), and on October 27 they turned down a Bolshevik motion that the Soviets should now take the power from the Kerensky government. They also expressed concern at the tense situation which was developing in the capital, and warned the workers against taking any part in an illegal rising.

Within the Bolshevik party itself there were also misgivings. When the experts got down to the practical problems of a *coup d'état* there was much disagreement. It was accepted that terror was necessary, and that the rising must take place before the Constituent Assembly met in December. It was even agreed that the Bolsheviks could be fairly sure of Petrograd; but no one could speak with any finality about what would happen in Moscow and the provinces. There were also serious doubts about the attitude of the railwaymen and of the employees of the telephone department and the post office, and these people always occupied a key position in a rising. Finally, there was the danger that Kerensky would bring into the capital new front-line troops who were hostile to the Bolsheviks. On the whole the party's military committee was inclined to think that they were not yet ready to act.

On October 29 there was a further meeting of the Bolshevik Central Committee, and Lenin with great energy set himself to quash these fears. Once again he demanded instant action, and it was pointed out by the extremist faction that the party could now count on the support of some 400,000 members throughout Russia: a huge advance. Once again Kamenev and Zinoviev were in opposition—they argued that action should be delayed at least until the new All-Russian Congress had assembled—but they were overborne.

The capital was now alive with rumors. In every political camp the prospects of the coming rebellion were debated, and indeed, among the welter of fantastic events that were about to happen, nothing is more astonishing than the way in which the Bolsheviks made no secret of their plans. They openly discussed them in the press. On October 31 Kamenev wrote an article in the *Novaya Zhizn* in which he explained his and Zinoviev's position: to provoke a rising "a few days before the opening of the All-Russian Congress of Soviets" he said was quite wrong. Lenin's answer to this was to denounce the two culprits to the Central Committee of the Bolshevik party, and on November 1 he too wrote an article for the press explaining *his* position. "The famine will not wait . . ." he wrote, "the war will not wait."

The newspaper *Dyen* also discussed the matter on October 31. It stated that the Bolsheviks had planned a rising for the previous night. There were to have been three assaults, one on the Tauride Palace, another on the Winter Palace and other nearby buildings, and a third on the Fortress of St. Peter and St. Paul, but the attempt had been called off because of the defensive measures which had been taken by Colonel Polkovnikov, the military commandant of the city. Other papers professed to have information that the coup was now to take place on November 4.

Trotsky blandly denied all this in a meeting of the Petrograd Soviet. He said it was incorrect to say that the Bolsheviks were planning a rising within the next few days. However, if the government insisted on sending away certain units of the Petrograd garrison, replacing them by troops from the front, the Bolsheviks might be forced to take action. (This was an important point: Trotsky's Military Revolutionary Committee had canvassed the Petrograd garrison very thoroughly and had discovered that only two regiments were against them.)

Everyone now began to take a hand at this strange game of threats and counterthreats. The non-Bolshevik Executive Committee of the All-Russian Congress postponed the meeting of the new Congress (which was likely to have a Bolshevik majority) from November 2 to November 7, and demanded that no arms should be handed out to anyone without its consent. Colonel Polkovnikov posted a guard round the Winter Palace, and all street demonstrations were forbidden. The United States Ambassador, Francis, sent a wire to Washington saying that he was beginning to think that the Bolsheviks would not make a demonstration. "Sentiment," he said, "is turning against them." On November 2 Kamenev resigned from the Bolshevik Central Committee.

The field of action, however, was now beginning to clarify itself somewhat in the manner of one of those Shakespearean battlefields in the Middle Ages, where the opposing armies take up their positions in full view of one another, while the generals ride about from place to place making declamatory speeches. The government forces were a good deal dispersed. Kerensky himself and his cabinet were ensconced in the Winter Palace; the Pre-Parliament was meeting in the Mariinsky Palace; and the headquarters of the Petrograd Military District was established in yet another building.

As for the old Central Executive Committee of the All-Russian Congress of Soviets (which could be fairly called a government organization in this crisis) it found itself most uncomfortably situated in the midst of the Bolshevik camp in Smolny Institute, on the banks of the Neva and at some distance from the center of the city. Smolny is one of the landmarks of the Russian revolution. It had been built as a nunnery for orphan girls in 1748, but was later converted into a select school for the daughters of the nobility. It consisted of a convent topped by graceful blue cupolas and an adjoining institute, a huge barrackslike building, three stories high and two hundred yards long. The imperial coat of arms carved in stone stood over the entrance.

In July the Soviets, with all their network of bureaus and committees, had been asked to leave the Tauride Palace so that it could be got ready to receive the Constituent Assembly, and they had taken roost at Smolny (the daughters of the nobility having, of course, already flown). There were more than a hundred large rooms in the building, and it suited well enough. Through October Smolny had become more and more overrun by the Bolsheviks, and now at the beginning of November it was a Bolshevik stronghold.

Between the two opposing forces—the Bolsheviks at Smolny and the government forces grouped about the Winter and Mariinsky Palaces in the center of the city—lay a no man's land of the wide flat streets themselves, the bridges crossing the Neva to the islands, the scattered garrisons of the soldiers, the workers' district on the Vyborg side, and, on an island in the river just upstream from the Winter Palace, the ancient Fortress of St. Peter and St. Paul.

On November 2, Zinoviev made a public recantation in the press of his opposition to Lenin (Kamenev was soon to follow suit), and the Bolsheviks began to close their ranks in preparation for direct action. It was now Trotsky's chief purpose—and we must consider Trotsky as the commanding general of the Bolsheviks through the next few days—to tighten his grip on the Petrograd garrison. With this object Soviet commissars were appointed to all the regiments. In some cases these commissars were rejected by the soldiers, but for the most part they were accepted, and a continuous liaison between Smolny and the garrison now began. The next step was to send off a delegation to Colonel Polkovnikov to demand that the commissars should be given official recognition. Polkovnikov increased his Cossack patrols in the streets and refused.

Sunday, November 4, was in the nature of a dress rehearsal for the clash ahead. The Petrograd Soviet—that is to say, the Bolsheviks—called on their followers to demonstrate in their own districts, not violently, but simply to make a show of strength. There was no serious incident, but the meetings were crammed with soldiers and workers who clearly were only waiting for a signal, and through the course of the day the Bolshevik Military Committee sent messages to the regiments that in future they were to obey no orders but those of their commissars.

On Monday, November 5, negotiations with Polkovnikov were resumed, and the Bolsheviks now demanded that they be given a place in the staff conferences of the Petrograd Military District. When this was refused telegrams were sent out from Smolny to the regiments ordering them to occupy strategic points in their areas with machine guns.

Now at last the government began to take serious action. Kerensky called a cabinet meeting late in the evening of November 5, and an emergency was declared. Polkovnikov was put in command of all forces in the city, with orders to take drastic action against disturbances. The Soviet Military Revolutionary Committee was declared illegal, and an order was sent out for the arrest of Trotsky and other Bolshevik leaders. Bolshevik newspapers were banned. Kerensky continued to be confident; he said he knew all about the Bolshevik plans. He would be glad if they did attempt a rising; he had ample forces to deal with it. Even now loyal troops were being summoned from outside the city. Yet Polkovnikov took no drastic action on this night. He sent off a Women's Battalion* to strengthen the guard inside the Winter Palace, but he made no attempt at all to attack the real center of the trouble, Smolny. And in fact the government had already suffered a major reverse on this day without a single shot being fired.

The garrison of the Fortress of St. Peter and St. Paul was made up of gunners and a bicycle battalion, and they had been none too friendly to the Bolsheviks. They had rejected the Bolshevik commissar who had been sent to them, and it was clear that if they did not actually oppose a rising they would remain neutral. As a last resource Trotsky was asked to address the men. Trotsky in his own account passes over this incident with a fair show of modesty, but it seems clear that he must have risen to heights of oratory, for he won the garrison over, and that meant control of the arsenal as well. During the night about ten thousand small arms were handed out to the Red Guards, who were now organized in battalions of five to six hundred men in all the larger factories.

The last hours of political maneuvering were running out very quickly. Early in the morning of November 6 Polkovnikov cut the telephone lines to Smolny, and detachments of loyal troops attempted to occupy the printing shops of the Bolshevik newspapers. The cruiser *Aurora*, always a doubtful center of loyalty, was ordered to leave the Neva for the open sea. Officer cadets from Oranienbaum

* This was a volunteer force of patriotic women who had sworn to fight to the death against the Germans.

and other troops which were reputed to be reliable were instructed to march into the city. The Bolsheviks, however, were not so easily cut off. Red Guards stood sentry over the printing shops, and the Bolshevik papers came out at noon with inflammatory appeals for action. In Smolny Trotsky and his Military Revolutionary Committee still had the use of other means of communication, and a stream of defiant orders was sent out to the military garrison: the *Aurora* was not to move, the regiments which had been ordered by the government into the city were to stay where they were, and the Petrograd garrison itself was to stand ready for action. A further call went out to Kronstadt urging the sailors to come to the capital without delay.

It was a situation of extreme confusion, since the generals in both camps were in effect pretending to be in command of the same army and navy, and no one yet could say whose will would prevail. All through the day (November 6) the streets remained quiet, but it was an ominous quiet, and in the Mariinsky Palace where the Pre-Parliament had been sitting since 1 P.M. the delegates made no attempt to hide their fears. Kerensky had opened the proceedings by declaring a "state of insurrection," and by denouncing Lenin as "a state criminal." As a proof of the Bolsheviks' guilt he read out to the assembly a copy of the latest order issued by the "Military Revolutionary Committee" inside Smolny. "The Petrograd Soviet of Workers and Soldiers Deputies is menaced," it declared. "We order the regiments immediately to mobilize on a war footing and to await new orders. All delay and nonexecution of this order will be considered as an act of treason to the revolution."

This was obvious rebellion, and yet as the debate went on it became increasingly clear that the majority of the delegates were not in favor of the government using force. They did not want a civil war. They still thought they could find another way out. The Menshevik leader Dan proposed an interesting solution: he suggested, in effect, that they could circumvent the rising by taking over the Bolshevik program, or at any rate that part of it that called for an immediate peace with Germany and Austria. The discussion dragged on until late at night, with no definite result.

At Smolny the Bolsheviks were making their final plans. Posts were assigned to the chief men: one man to be in charge of the railway workers, another of the food supplies, another of the postal and telegraph workers and so on. A representative was sent to the Bolsheviks in Moscow asking them to co-ordinate their actions with the capital; no other Bolshevik leader was allowed to leave the building. A message arrived from Lenin with a final appeal for action. "The matter," he wrote, "must be absolutely decided this evening or tonight." Toward midnight he himself arrived at Smolny. For a time the sentries would not let him in—he was disguised by a dirty bandage he had wound round his face and was carrying a Bolshevik pass that was out of date—but he managed to slip by in the end and he made his way to the room where Trotsky was working.

The American correspondent John Reed has left us a remarkable description of Petrograd through these critical days. In his *Ten Days That Shook the World*[*] he makes us feel as no one else has done what it was like to be there, especially if you happened to be a foreigner and an avid supporter of the Bolsheviks.

Under dull gray skies [he says], in the shortening days, the rain fell drenching, incessant. The mud underfoot was deep, slippery and clinging, tracked everywhere by heavy boots, and worse than usual because of the complete breakdown of the municipal administration. Bitter damp winds rushed in from the Gulf of Finland, and the chill fog rolled through the streets. At night for motives of economy as well as fear of Zeppelins, the street lights were few and far between; in private dwellings and apartment houses the electricity was turned on from six o'clock until midnight, with candles forty cents apiece and little kerosene to be had. It was dark from three in the afternoon to ten in the morning. Robberies and house breaking increased. In apartment houses the men took turns at all-night guard duty, armed with loaded rifles.

Food queues began to assemble before dawn, and fantastic prices were paid for fruit, sugar and even bread.

The ladies of the minor bureaucratic set took tea with each other in the afternoon, carrying each her little gold or silver or jewelled sugar-box, and half a loaf of bread in her muff, and wished that the tsar were back, or that the Germans would come, or anything that would solve the servant problem. . . . The daughter of a friend of mine came home one

[*] Published 1919 by Boni & Liveright, 1926 by International Publishers.

afternoon in hysterics because the woman streetcar conductor had called her "Comrade."

Waiters in hotels refused tips, and the statue of Catherine the Great before the Alexandrinsky Theater had a little red flag in its hand. Yet there was still much to remind you of prerevolutionary and even prewar Petrograd. Everybody, says Reed, still wore uniforms according to the old Czarist Table of Ranks, with the imperial insignia still on it. Gambling for very high stakes continued in the clubs all night, and the champagne, the prostitutes and the gypsy singers were all still there. At the Mariinsky Theater—and the theaters and the moving picture houses remained open throughout the revolution—Karsavina was appearing in a new ballet. Chaliapin was singing. At the Alexandrinsky there was a revival of Meyerhold's production of *Death of Ivan the Terrible,* and at the Krivoye Zerkalo a "sumptuous version" of Schnitzler's *Reigen.*

One odd change had overtaken the streets: the Salvation Army had recently been admitted into Russia, and the city walls were plastered with its announcements.

Reed went out to Smolny on a streetcar, "moving snail-like with a groaning noise through the cobbled muddy streets, and jammed with people."

He was allowed inside the school, and roamed among the ghosts of the departed schoolgirls. Their rooms were

white and bare, on their doors enameled plaques still informing the passer-by that within was "Ladies Classroom Number 4," or "Teachers' Bureau"; but over these hung crudely-lettered signs, evidence of the vitality of the new order, "Central Committee of the Petrograd Soviet," etc. The long vaulted corridors, lit by rare electric lights, were thronged with hurrying shapes of soldiers and workmen, some bent under the weight of huge bundles of newspapers, proclamations, printed propaganda of all sorts. The sound of their heavy boots made a deep and incessant thunder on the wooden floor.

The refectory downstairs with its low ceiling was still a dining room, and for two rubles Reed obtained a ticket for dinner. He stood in line with a thousand others while women ladled out cabbage soup from huge caldrons and served hunks of meat, *kasha* and slabs of black bread. One grabbed a greasy wooden spoon from a basket and sat down to eat wherever there was a place. The comrades wolfed their food and shouted jokes and pleasantries to their companions while they ate. There was another dining room upstairs for the members of the Central Ex Com and visitors, but anyone could go there. Here the bread was thickly buttered and one consumed endless glasses of tea.

The Soviet's meeting hall was the former assembly room in the south wing on the second floor, a lofty, white-painted room, lit by glazed white chandeliers holding hundreds of ornate electric bulbs and divided by two rows of massive columns. At one end there was a dais, and an empty gold frame from which the Czar's portrait had been cut.

The delegates for the new All-Russian Congress were assembling at the time of Reed's visit. By November 2 only 15 had arrived, but 100 more turned up on the following day and 175 on the day after that. By November 6, the day before the opening, a total of 560 had arrived, and 250 of these were Bolsheviks. For the most part these delegates were heavy, bearded soldiers in their uniforms or workmen in black blouses, with a few long-haired peasants among them. They slept in the corridors, on benches, on the floor, anywhere they could find a place. "The depths of Russia had been stirred up," Reed says with approval, "and it was the bottom which came uppermost now."

Throughout the first days of November the Petrograd Soviet was in continuous session, and its meetings were tumultuous. Trotsky was the orator they all wanted to hear, and he addressed the crowds for as long as four or five hours a day. There were continual shouts and interjections, rising occasionally to an uproar of approval or protest when some messenger came in with the news that this or that regiment had joined the Bolsheviks or had sided with the government. Everyone demanded the right to speak, and sometimes it would be an illiterate peasant, who would bow politely to the four corners of the room before he began and who would address his audience as "my dears." Then it would be Trotsky's turn again.

John Reed was not the only one who was captivated by these scenes. Many of the Bolsheviks themselves seem to have been caught up in a sort of frantic excitement at the prospect of getting the better of their enemies at last. It was the atmosphere of election night except that this was no ordinary election; at one mighty bound they were going to bring in the millennium and put an end to all the miseries of mankind.

And yet the Bolsheviks were a long way from being sure of themselves or of their success. Every account of their activities inside Smolny makes it clear that from day to day, often from hour to hour, neither the leaders nor anyone else knew precisely what was going to happen. Every messenger starts a new alarm or a sudden wave of enthusiasm, and every meeting is an agitation of nervous hopes and fears. In Room 10—the headquarters of the Military Revolutionary Committee—Trotsky and his followers live from minute to minute, each order that goes out is an *ad hoc* affair, hurriedly decided upon, and none of them can guess what the result will be. An official bursts into a meeting: "Fifteen agitators wanted at once to go to the Semenovsky Regiment"—or to St. Peter and St. Paul, or to the Finland Station—and up jump a group of volunteers, no one knows who exactly, none can say what they are supposed to do, but off they go; and another speaker rushes to the platform, "on an emergency." It is all an enormous gamble, gloriously exciting. And it can quite easily end in disaster.

In the evening of November 6, Reed tells us, the Second All-Russian Congress of Soviets, as a sort of curtain raiser to the opening of the conference on the following day, held a preliminary meeting in the Smolny assembly hall. "As night fell the great hall filled with soldiers and workmen, a monstrous dun mass, deep-humming in a blue haze of smoke." It was not until after midnight, however, that the meeting actually got under way. In deep silence Dan, the Menshevik leader, got up to speak, but an angry protest broke forth when, with his first words, he began to attack the Bolshevik rising. There was, Reed says,

immense continued uproar, in which his voice could be heard screaming, as he pounded the desk, "Those who are urging this are committing a crime!" . . . Then for the Bolsheviks, Trotsky mounted the tribune, borne on a wave of roaring applause that burst into cheers and a rising house, thunderous. His thin pointed face was positively Mephistophelian in its expression of malicious irony. "Dan's tactics prove that the masses—the great, dull, indifferent masses—are absolutely with him!" (Titanic mirth). . . . "No. The history of the last seven months shows that the masses

have left the Mensheviks. The Mensheviks and the Socialist Revolutionaries conquered the Cadets, and then when they got the power, they gave
it to the Cadets. . . . Dan tells you that you have no right to make an
insurrection. Insurrection is the right of all revolutionists! When the down-
trodden masses revolt, it is their right. . . ."

And so it went on: howls, shouts and catcalls as the rival speakers
followed one another to the platform, until at last, sure of getting
a majority at the opening of the Congress on the following day, the
Bolsheviks walked out of the meeting.

Toward four in the morning (of November 7) Reed went into
the outer hall of the building, and there met one of the Bolsheviks
with a rifle slung from his shoulder.

"We're moving," he said calmly but with satisfaction. "We pinched
the assistant minister of justice and the minister of religions. They're down
in the cellar now. One regiment is on the march to capture the telephone
exchange, another the telegraph agency, another the state bank. The Red
Guard is out. . . ."

On the steps of Smolny, in the chill dark, we first saw the Red Guard—
a huddled group of boys in workmen's clothes, carrying guns with bayonets, talking nervously together.

Far over the still roofs westward came the sound of scattered rifle fire,
where the yunkers were trying to open the bridges over the Neva, to prevent the factory workers and the soldiers of the Viborg quarter from
joining the Soviet forces in the center of the city; and the Kronstadt
sailors were closing them again. . . .

Behind us great Smolny, bright with lights, hummed like a gigantic
hive.

The events of the next twenty-four hours in Petrograd must surely
be among the strangest in all Russian history. In the nature of things
this should have been a day of terrible and serious drama, and so it
was in many ways; and yet there was also a high, strained note of
absurdity in much that happened, almost an element of farce. Philip
Jordan, the American ambassador's Negro butler, perhaps summed
it all up as well as anyone. In a letter he sent home to the United
States he wrote, "On last Tuesday the Bolsheviks got the city in their
hands and I want to tell you that it is something awful."* By Tuesday
(November 6) he meant Wednesday (November 7), but this does

* See George F. Kennan's *Russia Leaves the War.*

not matter in the least: "got the city in their hands" is perfect. It admirably conveys the infiltrating process, the stealthy almost accidental way in which the Bolsheviks pounced on one stronghold after another until like a house that has been eaten out by white ants, like a house of cards, the whole edifice of the government collapsed.

The people of Petrograd themselves were by no means fully aware of what was happening. Many of them went to work in the usual way on November 7; the shops stayed open, the streetcars ran, the movie theaters had their audiences, and the crowds were normal in the principal streets and except for the firing that broke out briefly in the evening, there was nothing much to show that this raw cold day marked the end of an era.

A good deal of the white-anting had been done during the night. By daybreak the Bolsheviks had seized the railway stations, the state bank, the power stations, the bridges across the river and finally the telephone exchange. Dawn disclosed that the cruiser *Aurora* was still in the Neva; with two torpedo boats she had come up to the Nicholas Bridge and had put ashore a party of sailors. There had been no resistance anywhere except for a few shots along the river, and the Cossack patrols were behaving with that air of appearing to notice nothing which usually overtakes policemen and soldiers who, in a crisis, are without leadership or definite orders.

Kerensky held an emergency cabinet meeting during the night and it was far from satisfactory; he appears to have suspected that Polkovnikov, instead of stamping out the rising, was deliberately allowing it to go forward so that he could eventually attempt a *coup d'état* of his own. Whether this was true or not it was now quite clear that reinforcements were needed, and during the morning Kerensky himself set off to find them. He hoped at Gatchina to rally the Third Cavalry Corps, that same corps which had served Kornilov so badly in September, and bring it into the city. However, nothing more was heard from Kerensky in the course of the day, and during his absence he lost the city. Once again, to use Sukhanov's phrase, "the break was accomplished with a sort of fabulous ease." It was even less eventful than the first rising in March.

At 10 A.M. on November 7 a proclamation was issued by Trotsky's Military Revolutionary Committee stating that the Provisional Government had fallen, and that power had passed to itself. This was nothing more than a piece of political bluff, but it was rapidly becoming true, at any rate as far as Petrograd was concerned. The government ministers whom Kerensky had left in the Winter Palace were quite powerless. While they sat and debated one district after another went over to the Bolsheviks, and still the Cossacks did nothing. By midday it was apparent that there was nothing much they *could* do: almost all of the rest of the garrison was either neutral or actively supporting the rising, some twenty thousand Red Guards were in the streets, and a squadron of seven rebel warships was on the way from Kronstadt. In addition, several trainloads of armed sailors came in from Helsingfors in Finland, where the Bolshevik party was very strong.

The Pre-Parliament might have made a center of resistance, but it was outmaneuvered by simple violence; a gang of soldiers and sailors walked into the Mariinsky Palace with their rifles and ordered the delegates to disperse. The delegates had no course but to obey. After this the collapse became general, and by seven o'clock in the evening only the Winter Palace was holding out. Its position was precarious. Throughout the day there had been a steady stream of desertions from the garrison, and those that were left numbered barely a thousand, of whom 130 were women and the rest mainly officer cadets, an absurdly small force to hold a building that covered an area of 4½ acres. After Kerensky's departure for the front the thirteen remaining ministers in the government had continued in session in one of the rooms on the river side. They had dismissed Polkovnikov and had placed their faith instead in the expected arrival of loyal troops from outside the city. A direct wire connected the palace with General Dukhonin, who was now acting as chief of staff of the army at the front, and the general had sent reassuring messages in reply to the ministers' appeals for help. He had sounded out the political feeling in the armies along the front, and all except the northern army—that is to say, the one nearest to Petrograd —had declared that they would support the government. He promised that detachments of Cossacks and other reinforcements would soon arrive. Upon this the ministers decided to hold out. But they were not comfortable. Through the windows of their room they could see the rebel cruiser *Aurora* in the river, and the guns of St.

Peter and St. Paul lay just beyond. By 6 P.M. the palace itself was invested by Bolshevik troops on every side, and artillery could be seen taking up positions in the main courtyard.

At 6:30 two messengers arrived from the Bolshevik forces with an ultimatum: either the ministers and their garrison must surrender within twenty minutes or the assault would begin. After a further consultation with Dukhonin on the teletype the ministers decided to continue their resistance. They removed themselves to a room in the interior of the building.

Two blank shots fired, one from the *Aurora*, the other from the Fortress of St. Peter and St. Paul, at 9 P.M. were the signal for action, and a desultory shelling of the palace began. It was not very effective—a few windows were smashed, a few stones were knocked down—but it was too much for the Women's Battalion. They came out to surrender and were soon followed by other deserters. Small parties of Red Guards now began to break into the outward rooms of the huge building, and those who did not become lost in the ornate corridors that stretched away like streets into the distance were engaged in a series of hand-to-hand skirmishes with the officer cadets. Neither side seems to have been very certain of itself: at one stage a Red Guard suddenly found himself confronted with the reflection of a painting of a horseman in a huge mirror, and with a horrified cry of "The Cavalry" he turned and bolted with his men. Huge crowds had gathered now in the Nevsky Prospekt, and all who could surged toward the palace. Armored cars with Bolshevik insignia daubed on their sides cruised about before the main entrance, but Reed and some friends with the aid of their American passports had no difficulty in getting into the building. The porters on duty at the door, wearing brass-buttoned uniforms with red and gold collars, politely took their coats.

After a pause of about an hour the shelling was resumed at 11 P.M. by the gunners in St. Peter and St. Paul, but not with much accuracy. No one was hurt. The psychological effects, however, were considerable. The slow solemn booming of the cannon seemed to many citizens to be an intolerable thing, and toward midnight the members of the Petrograd City Duma decided that they could stand it no longer. They carried a motion that they would march on the palace in a body and die with the Provisional Government; and in fact the mayor of the city, G. N. Schreider, armed with an umbrella and a lantern, did set out with a few followers. At the palace, however, Red sailors brusquely told them that they could not pass and eventually they returned to their homes.

At 1 A.M. on November 8 the last phase of the siege began. Red Guards began to infiltrate the corridors in earnest, and soon after two they rushed the inner room where the civilian ministers of the cabinet—the military members had already surrendered—were meeting. These men, who had behaved with some courage and dignity throughout the day, were arrested and taken off to the dungeons of St. Peter and St. Paul. Casualties caused by the whole operation hardly amounted to twenty men and none of the defenders were seriously hurt.

While these events were going on the conspirators at Smolny had had a momentous day. Lenin had appeared at a meeting of the Petrograd Soviet in the afternoon—a rapturous moment for his followers—and Trotsky had announced triumphantly that the revolution was proving bloodless. Telegrams had been sent off to the front announcing the fall of the government. Late in the evening the Second All-Russian Congress opened, and it was hardly possible for the delegates to breathe as they stood in one solid congested mass, a dense cloud of tobacco smoke floating over their heads. But they were living on excitement now. The result of the election of the new presidium was no surprise to anybody—the Bolsheviks came in with an overwhelming majority; the old presidium stepped down and the new one moved onto the platform: fourteen Bolsheviks, seven Left Social Revolutionaries and one representative of the Ukraine. Three Mensheviks and one Menshevik Internationalist who had also been elected refused to serve. Kamenev took the chair. For the first time in its existence the word Bolshevik ceased to be a lie: at this meeting at least the party had a genuine majority at last. "The hall," Reed says, "rose, thundering."

Kamenev announced the order of the day. They would first discuss, he said, the organization of power—or, in other words, the setting up of a new Russian government—then war and peace, and finally the elections for the Constituent Assembly.

From outside the booming of the cannon firing on the Winter Palace could be heard quite plainly, and Martov sprang up on behalf of the Mensheviks: "The civil war is beginning, comrades. The first question must be the peaceful settlement of the crisis." From all parts of the hall speakers rose up to support him. They made a bitter denunciation of the rising, and although the Bolsheviks howled them down there was some considerable force in this attack.

The Bolsheviks were by no means secure as yet. No reply had been received to the telegrams which Trotsky had sent out to the army, and it was still entirely possible that the soldiers would not acknowledge this revolution. No one had any news of what Kerensky was doing. It was simply rumored that he had mustered a force that was now marching on the city. Even inside Petrograd itself the opposition was recovering from its initial surprise; a Committee for the Salvation of the Country and the Revolution was being formed, and it had the support of all the right-wing elements, all the moderates, all those who might normally have remained neutral but now detested the Bolsheviks because of the violence that was being done at the Winter Palace. It was all very well for the meeting ("roaring," Reed says, "like the sea,") to gloat over the announcement of the names of the government ministers who had been arrested; the Bolsheviks had aroused fierce antagonism inside the socialist movement itself. The Mensheviks and other moderates walked out of Smolny and joined the Committee of Salvation.

A curious stillness settled on Petrograd during the remaining hours of darkness. On this of all nights no holdups or robberies occurred, and except for the continuous commotion at Smolny no move of any consequence was made by either side. Bright searchlights played on the walls of the Winter Palace, and a mob of soldiers tramped through the halls and corridors within, but there was no further disturbance. In the morning, Sukhanov says, the newspapers came out as usual, most of the editorials thundering against the Bolsheviks. But there was very little news in them. A panic began on the stock exchange, and the banks and the shops did not open their doors; yet no one believed that the revolt would last. In the government offices employees held meetings to decide what they would do if the Bolsheviks appeared. "And so," Sukhanov writes, "on November 8 the man in the street was given into the power of rumors. And of course he was extremely excited."

By midday, however, certain definite information was available and it was important. A bicycle battalion which had been advancing on the city to defend the government—and at this stage one battalion might have made all the difference—had halted and had come over to the Bolsheviks. In Moscow the garrison had risen against the government. And from the front there was a message to say that the Twelfth Army supported the rising. All this was great encouragement for Smolny; indeed, when the news about the Twelfth Army came in pandemonium broke out and the delegates flung their arms round one another, weeping with relief.

But there was bad news for the Bolsheviks as well, and it came chiefly from the worst possible quarter, from the workers themselves. The Union of Railway Workers declared that it was opposed to the Bolshevik coup and demanded that the new government should be a coalition of all the socialist parties. The union also threatened to tie up the whole railroad system of Russia if the Bolsheviks precipitated a civil war. This was a serious threat, and it was all the more serious because the post and telegraph workers had also announced their opposition to the Bolsheviks. A general strike began to spread through all the government departments. Inside Smolny Lenin and Trotsky spent most of this day, Thursday, November 8, in rallying those weaker elements in the Congress and inside their own party who were beginning to think that some sort of compromise ought to be patched up with the moderate socialist groups. But it was with the army that both Lenin and Trotsky were most deeply concerned; with the army on their side their cause was won, without it they were finished. Appeal after appeal went out to the Cossacks, to the city garrisons and to the front-line regiments, urging the soldiers to acknowledge the fall of the government.

The Bolsheviks would have been a good deal comforted if they had known more about Kerensky's movements at this critical moment. He had met great treachery at the front. At Gatchina he had found no troops, and he had continued to Pskov, where General Cheremisov, the new commander of the northern front, had his headquarters. Cheremisov had been a protégé of Kerensky's, but in this crisis he discovered other loyalties. He was influenced no doubt by the fact that a Military Revolutionary Committee had been set up in Pskov, and it was an organization that had influence not only along the front but with the new masters in Petrograd. Cheremisov at all events decided to co-operate with the committee and not with Kerensky, who was his commander-in-chief. Kerensky on November 7 had given orders to General Krasnov, who was loyal, to lead a cavalry corps into Petrograd. Cheremisov now countermanded these orders and reported to General Dukhonin, the chief of the General Staff, who was at Mogilev, that he had done so on Kerensky's instructions. He also told Dukhonin that Kerensky had relinquished his post as commander-in-chief and expressed a desire that Cheremisov himself should take his place. When Dukhonin asked to speak to Kerensky over the telephone to confirm this news he was told that that would not be possible. It was an effective piece of double-dealing, and at this moment it was decisive. Kerensky, who seems to have been in ignorance of what was going on, went off with General Krasnov to his headquarters at Ostrov, and while they traveled the vital hours slipped away.

Meanwhile at Smolny the Bolsheviks were proceeding with their tactics of rushing ahead before their opponents could guess what was happening. At 8:40 on the evening of November 8 the Congress assembled for another meeting, and this time Lenin himself went onto the platform with the presidium. There was the usual commotion, and at last Lenin got up to speak. He stood there, says Reed, "gripping the edge of the reading stand, letting his little winking eyes travel over the crowd . . . apparently oblivious to the long-rolling ovation, which lasted several minutes. When it finished he said simply, 'We shall now proceed to construct the Socialist order.' Again that overwhelming human roar."

Trotsky does not remember Lenin uttering that lapidary phrase about the socialist order, but it seems hardly likely that Reed could have invented it; and in fact the words indicated precisely what Lenin now proceeded to do, except that it was Lenin himself who did the constructing in his own fashion and not the overwrought delegates, who stood jammed in the body of the hall. He read a proclamation. There was to be peace, immediate peace, peace without annexations or indemnities. The secret treaties with the Allies were to be repudiated and the self-determination of peoples was to be guaranteed.

It was a proposition that could hardly fail to please the meeting, and when it was approved by a unanimous vote something like delirium seized the crowd. Sobbing, with shining eyes, they sang the "Internationale," and when someone cried, "The war is ended," it really seemed to be true. There was another shout, "Remember dead comrades," and this was the signal for the singing of the Funeral March.

Lenin continued impassively. His next proposal was that the meeting should approve of a decree by which all private ownership of land in Russia was abolished. No compensation was to be paid to the landowners. This also was put to the vote and after a long debate was passed with only one dissenting voice.

It was now half past two in the morning, but the Bolsheviks had not finished yet; indeed, they had only now approached the important part of their work. Kamenev read out a "constitution of power." It provided for a "Council of People's Commissars" which was to rule Russia until the Constituent Assembly met. There were some unexpected and unknown names among the new commissars, but all got a cheer as Kamenev read out the list: President: Lenin. Foreign Affairs: Trotsky. Education: Lunacharsky. Finance: Skvortsov. Labor: Shlyapnikov. Agriculture: Miliutin. Minority Nationalities: Stalin. Army and Navy: Antonov, Krylenko, Dybenko. Interior: Rykov. Industry and Commerce: Nogin. Justice: Lomov. Supply: Teodorovich. Posts and Telegraphs: Glebov.

There was a significant absence of a Commissar for Railways; that post apparently was to be held open until the railwaymen adopted a less recalcitrant attitude toward the Bolsheviks. Kamenev was appointed chairman of the Central Executive Committee of the Congress, and Zinoviev editor of the Soviet paper *Izvestiya*, which now, of course, became a Bolshevik organ.

Since few of the new ministers had any experience whatever in government or even in the industries and organizations they were supposed to control, these appointments were not so solid as they looked. Indeed, nothing was solid. The meeting had reached the stage where a little cool thinking was required, and this, unexpectedly, was now supplied by a young journalist named Avilov, who was attached to Maxim Gorky's paper *Novaya Zhizn.*

We must ask ourselves where we are going [he said]. . . . The ease with which the coalition government was upset cannot be explained by the strength of the left wing of the democracy, but only by the incapacity of the government to give the people peace and bread. And the left wing cannot maintain itself in power unless it can solve these questions. . . .

Can it give bread to the people? Grain is scarce. The majority of the peasants will not be with you, for you cannot give them the machinery they need. Fuel and other primary necessities are almost impossible to procure. . . .

As for peace that will be even more difficult. The Allies . . . will never accept the proposition of a peace conference from *you*. You will not be recognized either in London or in Paris, or in Berlin. . . .

You cannot count on the effective help of the proletariat of the Allied countries, because in most countries it is very far from the revolutionary struggle. . . .

The isolation of Russia will fatally result either in the defeat of the Russian army by the Germans, and the patching up of a peace between the Austro-German coalition and the Franco-British coalition at the expense of Russia—or in a separate peace with Germany.

I have just learned that the Allied ambassadors are preparing to leave, and that Committees for Salvation of Country and Revolution are forming in all the cities of Russia. . . . No one party can conquer these enormous difficulties.

And the speaker proposed a government of coalition with the non-Bolshevik parties.

In the event much of this speech proved to be incorrect—few people in Russia as yet had anticipated how ruthlessly the Bolsheviks were going to enforce their will by terror—but it was a clear and courageous utterance and it sobered the meeting. Trotsky, who rose to reply, needed all his eloquence to reassure the comrades that they were not isolated and that they must go on along the road they had chosen. He concluded: "There are only two alternatives: either the Russian revolution will create a revolutionary movement in Europe, or the European powers will destroy the Russian revolution!"

Here Trotsky too was wrong, and he remains wrong to this day. But it was not wrongness or rightness which counted in Smolny on this night; it was the reckless and exhilarating emotion that overtakes the gambler when for the moment he seems to be winning the game. The delegates turned down the motion for a peaceful settlement with the other parties, and then adjourned the Congress and went off to get what sleep they could.

Friday, November 9, the third day of the rising, was the beginning of an awakening throughout Russia. By now the news of the happenings in the capital had spread to the more remote towns and military garrisons, and a vast debate was going on: to support the rising or oppose it, to go over to the Bolsheviks or join the Committee for Salvation? Everywhere men began to drift into one or other of these two camps, and a stream of propaganda poured out from the rival headquarters. It was not easy for the *moujik* or the illiterate soldier to make up his mind. Reed describes one typical meeting that took place at the Mikhailovsky Riding School in Petrograd. Two thousand men of an armored car regiment which up to now had remained neutral were gathered in a compact mass around one of their vehicles which served as a platform. Under a single arc light speaker after speaker got up to put the opposing sides of the case. "Never," Reed says, "have I seen men trying so hard to understand, to decide. They never moved, stood staring with a sort of terrible intentness at the speaker. . . ." In this case it was the Bolsheviks who won the day—Krylenko, a new commissar for military affairs, managed to swing the meeting—but it was not so among the civil servants in Petrograd. The employees in most of the ministries came out on strike, and both the railwaymen and the post and telegraph staff remained adamant. Nor was it so in Moscow, where loyal troops struck back at the insurgents in the Kremlin and forced them to surrender.

At Smolny the new ministers were at work. Comrade Trotsky, the People's Commissar for Foreign Affairs, sent off a note to all the belligerents in the war proposing an immediate armistice. At the instance of Lenin a decree was passed suppressing the "bourgeois" newspapers "temporarily," and squads of Red Guards were sent to occupy their printing presses. A further decree announced that elections for the Constituent Assembly would be held on November 25.

But it was one thing to issue notes and decrees and quite another to make them effective. The Allies elaborately ignored Trotsky's note and refused to recognize the Bolshevik government. Nor was it possible to kill free speech with such dispatch; all Russia wanted to join in this great debate, and it was beginning to look as if the immediate future held something far more drastic than an election of a Constituent Assembly: in short, a civil war.

The next three days were a period of continuous suspense in Petrograd. It was now known that Kerensky had joined General Krasnov, and with a force of Cossacks was advancing on Tsarskoe Selo. In actual fact this force of Cossacks numbered only seven hundred men, but no one knew that in Petrograd and fantastic rumors flew about. A whole army was said to be bearing down on the city, and there was a rush to dig trenches and to throw up barricades in the streets. It was hoped that Kerensky would be stopped in the open plains to the south of the capital, and a force of Red Guards and sailors had gone out to do battle there, somewhat in the manner of General Gallieni, who had saved Paris from the Germans at the beginning of the war: anyone who wanted to fight went off, cars and cabs were grabbed by the soldiers off the streets, volunteers manned the locomotives of the troop trains, and there was an atmosphere of desperate resolution about it all. But would they succeed? Even at Smolny the comrades were beginning to ask, "What chance has a mob got against trained soldiers?"

On November 11 fighting broke out again in the city. It was a short but extremely savage affair; a group of officer cadets rushed the telephone exchange (which meant that Smolny was cut off once more), and all day went by before the Red forces could get them out. This time there were something over one hundred casualties. The situation was even more serious for the Bolsheviks in Moscow; after a short armistice heavy fighting had begun again, and the government forces still dominated the Kremlin.

Now too the strike of civil servants was beginning to take its effect. The telephone girls refused to work for the Bolsheviks, the post offices refused to transmit their messages and the banks refused to pay out money. It was all very well for Smolny to threaten that they would blast the bank vaults open with dynamite and send Red Guards and volunteers to man the public services; you could not turn a factory hand or a sailor into a bank clerk or a telegrapher overnight.

Trotsky in his reminiscences is perfectly frank about the danger that threatened the Bolsheviks through these three days: it was touch and go. With every day that went by more and more people were gathering around the Committee of Salvation, and from the banks the Committee had all the money it wanted. The weather turned cold and gloomy with a touch of snow in the air, and through the long dark hours there was now one overriding thought in everybody's mind: when will Kerensky come?

It was not until Tuesday, November 13, that this state of tension was broken. Trotsky himself had gone to the front, and it was he who sent the news. "The night of November 12/13," he wired to Smolny, "will go down in history. . . . Kerensky . . . has been decisively repulsed. Kerensky is retreating. We are advancing. . . ." There had been a short battle at Tsarskoe Selo but the Cossacks, like almost everyone else in this revolution of words, had succumbed to the speeches of the Bolshevik agitators; they had agreed to negotiate and that was as good as a victory. Petrograd was saved. A great wave of relief swept over the Council of People's Commissars at Smolny. The triumphant order went out: "To all army, corps, divisional and regimental committees, to all Soviets of workers, soldiers' and peasants' deputies, to all, all, all: we demand that Kerensky be arrested."

But Kerensky had already gone. Disguised as a sailor he had slipped away from Gatchina in the night,* and it was left to General Kornilov and others who had escaped from their internment in the confusion to carry on the struggle. For the moment, however, the Bolsheviks in Petrograd were secure, or at any rate secure enough to reject the pressure on them to form a coalition government with the other socialist parties. With the defeat of Kerensky all negotiations on that score came to an end. On November 15 the government forces in the Kremlin surrendered; the Bolsheviks shelled them out of their last stronghold in the arsenal, and with this all serious opposition in Moscow collapsed.

Heavy snow had begun to fall, and there was a bright and sparkling quality in the air. To the more poetical Bolsheviks it was a symbol of their inner joy. They had had an unbelievable success. Not much more than a week had elapsed since Lenin with his bandage around his face had come secretly into Smolny to urge them into action, and now they had usurped an empire.

* With the aid of the British agent Bruce Lockhart he eventually escaped from Russia.

CHAPTER FIFTEEN

The Constituent Assembly

THE ASTONISHING thing about the Bolshevik seizure of power in Petrograd is not that it happened so quickly and bloodlessly—the main crisis had lasted only from November 7 to November 16—nor that it so easily could have failed, but that the Russian state could have been in a condition of such utter weakness. It was like a body with no bones in it, like a mind with no will. E. H. Carr, in his *History of Soviet Russia*, points out that from July onward the collapse of the state was "inevitable"; it was waiting only for its successor to appear. Bolshevism succeeded to a vacant throne.

Yet still one feels that somewhere, somehow, there ought to have been some center of organized power capable of striking back. It was not as if the government was taken by surprise. All the Bolshevik plans were known in advance. Lenin had announced them more clearly even than Hitler was subsequently to announce his plans in *Mein Kampf*. The Military Revolutionary Committee at Smolny issued its orders openly over the telephone, and at any moment during the insurrection almost anyone could have walked into the building and discovered what was going on. It is also certainly true that Smolny itself could have been seized by a single regiment of loyal troops under a competent leader; it could have fallen almost as easily as the Winter Palace fell, and the Bolshevik leaders could have been captured with just as much dispatch as the members of Kerensky's government were captured. But no such loyal troops existed. A kind of trance seems to have fallen upon the opposition parties, and by the time they recovered from their bewilderment it was too late.

For the Bolsheviks, of course, it was like the March rising all over again. "All around me," says Sukhanov, "was a mood bordering on ecstasy"; but this did not mean that the Bolsheviks, having won a victory in the two biggest Russian cities, knew what they were going to do with it. They very much feared the days ahead, and they were divided among themselves as to the way in which they were going to proceed. No one, not even Lenin, knew what was going to happen, and Trotsky as good as admits this when he says: "If we had not seized the power in November we would not have seized it at all. . . . If they [the masses] had seen any vacillation at this moment on our part, any delay, any incongruity between word and deed, then in the course of two or three months they would have drifted away from us. . . . It was just this that made Lenin decide to act. From this sprang his uneasiness, his anxiety, his mistrust and his ceaseless hurry. . . ."

It had been, as Trotsky himself says, a revolution "by telegraph." Petrograd and Moscow might have been subdued, but there remained the rest of Russia and the dependent states, a vast area, one-sixth of the earth's surface, to settle with. The telegrams saying what had happened in the capital had gone out to the Baltic States, to Finland, to the Ukraine, to the Black Sea, and to the vast hinterland that stretched across the Vladivostok on the Pacific Ocean 4,500 miles away, but there was no guarantee whatever that the inhabitants of these regions, 175 millions of them, were going to submit to the orders of 240,000 Bolsheviks. In fact, there was every evidence that the great majority of them would not. In the Ukraine an independent government had been set up, and it was hostile to Lenin. Finland and the Baltic States soon demanded independence. Poland was already occupied by the Germans. Along the trans-Siberian railway tens of thousands of German and Austrian prisoners of war were behaving more like an occupation force than defeated enemies. In the south, in the Don areas, the most serious situation of all was developing. General Alexeiev and General Kornilov had gone there, and so had Milyukov and Rodzianko. These had grouped themselves under the leadership of Kaledin, the Ataman of the Don Cossacks, and a volunteer army was being raised to fight the Bolsheviks. It had very good prospects of getting the support of Britain, France and the U.S.

The Allied ambassadors in Petrograd would have nothing to do officially with the Bolsheviks; like thousands of the Russians themselves they were considering the possibility of leaving the country, and the capital began to take on that spiritless and dejected air of a city that has recently fallen to the enemy. The bread ration went down to one-eighth of a pound a day, and the Bolsheviks resorted to the desperate measure of sending out armed gangs into the country districts to forage for food. Trains laden with iron and other city manufactures went off to Siberia, and it was hoped to barter these goods for grain and potatoes. The fuel crisis became acute; theaters and restaurants were deprived of light, streetcars were cut down and Red sailors emptied the coal bunkers of the warships, but still there was not enough power to keep the factories going. Now more than ever Petrograd became a place of conspiracies, and it was a common thing for servants to inform against their employers. The old Okhrana had been abolished but a new Cheka was being formed under the Polish Bolshevik Dzerzhinsky, and it was soon to find ways of demoralizing its victims, and of extorting money from the rich; they were arrested and kept in prison until they agreed to contribute a "loan" to the Bolshevik government.

On November 23 a Congress of Peasants' Soviets met in Petrograd, and only one-fifth of the delegates were Bolshevik. "On the third day," Reed says, "Lenin suddenly mounted the tribune; for ten minutes the room went mad. 'Down with him,' they shrieked." Yet he won them round in the end, and this was an important gain. The railroad men, however, continued to hold out, and there was a serious split inside the Bolshevik cabinet itself. Lunacharsky, the Commissar for Education, was the first to go. He was appalled at the Bolshevik shelling of the Kremlin in Moscow: "I can bear no more," he wrote in an emotional letter of resignation, and his lead was soon followed by four other senior party members—Kamenev, Zinoviev, Rykov and Nogin—and a number of others. They protested against terrorist methods and demanded that some attempt should be made to form a coalition government with the other socialist parties. This split in the inner party council was not very serious—

eventually all these men came tamely back to their posts again—but it was clear that Lenin had every reason for his "uneasiness, his anxiety, his mistrust and his ceaseless hurry."

The Germans were not hurrying him as yet; they were fairly confident of his assurance that he was going to make peace and they held their hand at the front so as not to increase his difficulties. But haste, real haste, was needed in consolidating support behind the new government inside Russia before the inevitable reaction set in. Lenin's peculiar method of handling this situation was to act as though the support already existed. For twenty years he and his followers had been hammering out their Marxist code. Now it was suddenly thrust upon Russia as the law.

For six hours every day the Soviet Council of People's Commissars met under Lenin's chairmanship, and a fantastic stream of decrees began to pour out of Smolny. Nothing like it had been seen in the world before; it was a program that uprooted every institution and tradition in Russian life. The abolition of private ownership in land was followed by the nationalization of the banks, of the merchant marine and of all industrial enterprises. The stock market was swept away, and so were the rights of inheritance. All state debts were annulled, and gold was declared a government monopoly. Wages of the People's Commissars were pegged at 500 rubles a month for single people with additional payments for families. The old criminal courts were supplemented or replaced by "revolutionary tribunals" made up of a president and six peasants, workers and soldiers, and any citizen could appear as a lawyer. Men and women were declared equal in law, and the strict Czarist code governing marriage and divorce was abolished; a civil marriage now took the place of the church ceremony and divorce could be obtained by either party of the marriage merely asking for it. All titles were submerged into the universal "Citizen" or "Comrade." The church was permitted to continue but in a drastically truncated form; its lands—and they were enormous—were confiscated and religious teaching was forbidden in the schools. The state religion was now Leninism. The Western calendar, which was now thirteen days ahead of the old Russian calendar, was declared law, and even the alphabet was pruned of various letters and signs. Later on strikes were declared to be treason.

Lenin as yet had no means of seeing that these new Soviet-made laws were carried out. The strike in the government ministries was still on, and the most grotesque situations were developing; in the Foreign Office the employees hid their books and refused to hand over their keys to Trotsky; in the banks half-literate volunteers were trying to make sense out of ledgers and cash books that were quite beyond them. "All were against them [the Bolsheviks]," Reed says, "—businessmen, speculators, investors, landowners, army officers, politicians, teachers, students, professional men, shopkeepers, clerks, agents. The other socialist parties hated the Bolsheviks with an implacable hatred. On the side of the Soviets were the rank and file of the workers, the sailors, all the undemoralized soldiers, the landless peasants, and a few—a very few—intellectuals."

But none of this made much difference to the men who were making a new world in Smolny Institute, nor did it count in the least with Lenin that he had not the flimsiest show of legal authority for his decrees. The country had not elected him, and the Congress of Soviets was not a legislature; it represented only the left-wing political parties. But for the moment he had control of the strongest party machine in Russia, and he was ruthless—more ruthless than any of the others. Speaking of the repeal of the death sentence he had said, "It is a mistake, an inadmissible weakness . . . a pacifist illusion." Later he added, "Do you think we can be victors without the most severe revolutionary terror?" And so the death sentence was reinstated in fact if not by law and the Cheka began its work of exterminating all political rivals. The Cadet party was outlawed, and orders were given for the arrest of men like Dan and Tseretelli, who had fought just as hard as the Bolsheviks for socialism—but not socialism of this kind, socialism imposed by terror. Long before this Dostoevsky had written, "Starting from unlimited liberty it [the Russian revolution] will arrive at unlimited despotism." Russia was now beginning to discover the terrible truth of that prophecy.

It was the opportunism of Lenin which most disconcerted his rivals. None, for example, had cried out louder than the Bolsheviks when Kerensky had proposed to move the capital to the safer and calmer atmosphere of Moscow. They did this because it was easier to stage their *coup d'état* in Petrograd. But now that the Bolsheviks had seized the power Lenin changed his mind: he decided that the move must be made. Not all his followers were in favor of this; they felt that the party had built up its reputation in Petrograd, and that there was a certain propaganda value in remaining there. Lenin's answer to this was worthy of Machiavelli.

Lenin [Trotsky says] was literally beside himself and replied to these objections, "Can you cover the question of the fate of the revolution with that kind of sentimental stupidity? If the Germans at a single bound take possession of Petrograd with us within it, the revolution is lost. If, on the other hand, the government is in Moscow, then the fall of Petersburg would only mean a serious part-blow. How is it possible that you do not see and comprehend that? Besides, if we stay in Petersburg under the present conditions we increase its military danger and at the same time rouse the Germans to occupation of Petersburg. If, on the contrary, the government is in Moscow the temptation to take Petersburg is incomparably less. . . . What is that stupid speech about the symbolic meaning of Smolny? Smolny is only Smolny because we are in it. And when we are in the Kremlin all their symbolism will be transferred to the Kremlin."

The logic here is the same logic that had won Lenin his battles in all the earlier party conferences, but the tone has changed: it is impatient, almost petulant, and it is the accent of an anxious man. And indeed Petrograd was not altogether a safe place for the Bolsheviks. The continuing disorders in the streets were a reflection of the chaos that was spreading all over Russia. At every rising in the past eight months the jails had been flung open, and it was not only the political prisoners who were released; the criminals got out as well. Through the last week in November there were constant disturbances, and these culminated in a major brawl when the mob broke into the wine shops. Drunken soldiers fought with drunken Red Guards, and the Military Revolutionary Committee at Smolny had to send out a squad of machine gunners to fire on the rioters before order was restored. It was not entirely drunkenness that was at the root of this affair. A certain bitterness was growing up between the military garrison and the Red Guards. Several of those very regiments which had supported the Bolsheviks at first were beginning to discover that they liked their new masters no better than the old, and in particular they resented the growing power of the armed workmen, the political squads. At Smolny the Bolsheviks were quick to notice this change, and once more they set about doing the thing they said they would not do: they ordered several of the disaffected regiments out of the capital and replaced them with foreign soldiers, who were more politically reliable. Through the critical days ahead the Bolsheviks in Petrograd were guarded by Lettish troops and Estonian and Finnish sailors.

And now at last the real issue was put to the test. On November 25 the elections for the Constituent Assembly began. For forty years at least the Russian people had been waiting for this day, and the idea of a freely elected parliament had been at the basis of every political program in every party from the moderate right to the extreme left. The Bolsheviks had supported it. "Long live the Constituent Assembly," Trotsky had cried as he walked out of the Pre-Parliament in October, and it was with this slogan that the Bolsheviks had risen against Kerensky.

The results of the election were startling. Out of a total of 41.7 million votes only 9.8 million were polled for the Bolsheviks—24 per cent or, at the most, 29 per cent if you counted the Left Social Revolutionaries in with them. Even in Petrograd and Moscow, even in the army and the navy, Lenin had less than half the vote. The Social Revolutionaries with nearly 20.8 million votes, or 58 per cent of the total, were the big winners. As for the Mensheviks, they had all but vanished from the scene, and the bourgeois parties polled only 1.99 million votes between them.

This was a tremendous clarification. Directly the results became known all the anti-Bolshevik parties began to group themselves together so as to ensure that when the Assembly met it would be acknowledged as the source of true government of Russia. The Bolsheviks just as quickly discovered that they had no faith in freely elected parliaments after all. It was now "Down with the Constituent Assembly." Lenin, with some perspicacity, had foreseen how the voting would go, and had tried to postpone the elections, but he had been overborne by his colleagues. Now, however, being in the position of saying, "I told you so," he launched himself upon the work of sabotaging the new parliament with all the passionate and fanatical determination at his command. He hated the Constituent Assembly more even than he had hated the Czars. In order to destroy it he was ready to do anything. The long and careful preparation which he had made for the Marxist party congresses in the old days was nothing compared to the arrangements which were now made to demoralize and discredit the deputies even before they arrived in Petrograd. The outlawing of the Cadet party and the orders for the arrest of the Menshevik and other leaders were just a small part of these measures.

The immediate thing to do, Lenin realized, was to try to prevent the Assembly from meeting at all, and the opening was postponed from early December to some vague day in January. However, he could not prevent the deputies from drifting into the capital from all over Russia, and they decided to meet on December 11 anyway. Sorokin, one of the deputies, records:

The legal opening day of the Constituent Assembly dawned beautifully clear. Blue sky, white snow, an auspicious background for the huge placards everywhere displayed. "Long Life to the Constituent Assembly, the Master of Russia." Crowds of people, bearing these standards, welcomed the highest authority of the country, the real voice of the Russian people. As the deputies approached the Tauride Palace, thousands of people hailed them with deafening cheers. But when the deputies reached the gates they found them closed and guarded by Bolshevik Lettish soldiers, armed to the teeth.

Something had to be done, and at once. Climbing the iron fence of the palace I addressed the people while other deputies climbed up and scrambled after me. They managed to unlock the gates and crowds rushed in filling the courtyard. Staggered at the audacity of this move, the Lettish soldiers hesitated. We attacked the doors of the palace, also guarded by Lettish soldiers and officers behind whom appeared Uritsky and other Bolsheviks. Again speaking to the people, I concluded by thanking the Lettish soldiers for their welcome to the highest authority in Russia and their apparent willingness to guard its liberties. At last I even embraced the commanding officer. The whole lot wavered in confusion and as a result the doors were opened and we walked in, many of the citizens following. In the passage Uritsky, an exceedingly repulsive Jew, demanded that we go to his office to register but we contemptuously pushed him aside saying that the Constituent Assembly stood in no need of his services. In the hall of the palace we held our meeting and called upon the Russian nation to defend its Constituent Assembly. A resolution was passed that the Assembly, in spite of every obstacle, should open on January 18.*

* This quotation and the following are from P. A. Sorokin, *Leaves from a Russian Diary*, E. P. Dutton, 1924.

Other meetings and demonstrations followed this protest, and an attempt was made to bring out the Petrograd garrison against Lenin. To quote Sorokin again:

Today at a meeting of representatives of the Petrograd garrison, the subject under discussion was the relation of soldiers to the Constituent Assembly. Speakers of all parties were present. The garrison was inclined to assume a passive attitude, not inimical of course, but not aggressively defensive. Exasperated by this cursed pacifism, I burst out, begging the soldiers to remember how many generations of Russian people had dreamed of the Constituent Assembly as the greatest blessing that could ever happen. "Thousands of men and women," I told them, "have sacrificed their lives for the realisation of this dream. Now when the great dream is about to come true, when the Constituent Assembly is about to open, you dally with the idea of a Bolshevik paradise, you refuse to do your duty. Traitors to your country. If you cling to this mad delusion you will reap its certain fruits. Within a few months you will face starvation, tyranny, civil war, and horrors which you cannot even imagine. Remember then whose voices warned you of what this treachery would certainly bring. That is all I have to say." Two regiments promise to be active in defending the Assembly. Of the others I have no hope.

It was splendid rhetoric and once again one is reminded of some Shakespearean tragedy, *Julius Caesar* perhaps; the citizens in the forum declaring their faith in liberty but not accomplishing very much in the way of action. Lenin moved very swiftly. All printing presses that published anti-Bolshevik literature were seized and declared government property. House-to-house searches were made by the Cheka at night, and the number of arrests was redoubled. On December 26 Lenin issued a direct threat in an article in *Pravda*: the interests of the revolution, he said, "stand over the formal rights of the Constituent Assembly." This was followed by still another Smolny decree that "the Russian Republic is vested with the Soviets. . . . Every attempt to usurp government authority . . . will be suppressed."

Yet the Assembly had to meet. By the second week in January, 1918, some five hundred deputies had arrived in Petrograd, and Russia was not quite a dictatorship as yet. Of these deputies 267 were Social Revolutionaries (as against 161 Bolsheviks), and they threatened to storm the Tauride Palace once again if the doors were not opened for them. Moreover, inside the Bolshevik party itself there was still a large faction which wanted the Assembly to meet. They not only had a conscience about it, they also felt that the Bolshevik government could not legally rule until it had the backing of the country through the new parliament. It had been agreed that the opening should take place on January 18 at noon.

For the next few days the atmosphere in Petrograd was almost as tense as it had been at the height of the November rising. On January 15 an attempt was made on Lenin's life: a shot was fired at him while he was riding in a car and he was only saved from serious injury by his companion, Fritz Platten, pushing his head down in time. Platten was wounded in the hand.

On January 17 Smolny ordered the Petrograd garrison to stand ready for action. The Tauride Palace was surrounded by Lettish guards, and artillery was drawn up in the neighboring streets. Foreign representatives were advised to remove themselves to safer quarters out of the center of the city. Once again it was a situation where everyone expected trouble but no one could say exactly how or where it would begin.

It began on the morning of January 18. Once more huge crowds appeared in the streets to demonstrate in favor of the Assembly, and when they advanced upon the Tauride Palace the Bolshevik guards opened fire. It says something for the courage of the non-Bolshevik deputies that they did not turn back. Some of them faced an order for arrest, but they emerged from hiding and ran the gauntlet between the jeering ranks of the Red soldiers guarding the approaches to the palace. Once inside they quite expected to be besieged, and so they brought food with them and candles in case the Bolsheviks should switch off the electric current. "Thus," says Trotsky, "democracy entered upon the struggle with dictatorship heavily armed with sandwiches and candles."

The dictatorship, as Trotsky prefers to call it, had come to the meeting much better prepared. It had packed the corridors and the galleries of the main hall with Lettish guards and sailors from the *Aurora* and the battleship *Respublika*. All these men carried loaded rifles in their hands. Hand grenades and cartridge belts were stacked in the anterooms.

By 1 P.M. all the opposition parties were present but they were kept waiting four hours before the Bolsheviks arrived. Lenin was among them and he too had come armed (though someone stole his revolver from his coat pocket in the cloakroom).

Just as an elderly Right Social Revolutionary deputy rose to fulfill his duty as senior representative present and make the official opening remarks, there was an uproar and the Bolsheviks surged toward the platform. One of them seized the speaker's bell and handed it to Jacob Sverdlov, the chairman of the Congress of Soviets Executive Committee (Sverdlov had replaced Kamenev in November). Sverdlov himself made the opening speech. Then the Bolsheviks led the assembly in singing the "Internationale." Despite this move, however, the Right Social Revolutionaries stood their ground, and their leader Victor Chernov was elected to the chair by 244 votes to 151.

The debate that followed bordered on lunacy. Every speech was interrupted by Bolshevik howls, catcalls and jeers: "Judas . . . hangman . . . shoot him down . . . traitor." Men put their fingers in their mouths and whistled as though they were at a football game. During most of the speeches Lenin lolled about on the steps leading to the platform and at one point curled up on a bench and pretended to go to sleep. After six or seven hours of this a Bolshevik motion that the Assembly should recognize the Congress of Soviets as the government of Russia was defeated by 237 votes to 136. A recess was then called, and when the meeting was resumed at 1 A.M., the Bolsheviks announced that they would leave the Assembly. Some began to drift up into the galleries to watch the proceedings, and an hour later they were followed by the Left Social Revolutionaries.

The Lettish guards and sailors were now getting entirely out of hand. Some jumped down into the body of the hall and tried to break up the meeting. Others amused themselves by aiming their rifles directly at the deputies, and it was a huge joke among them when they selected one unfortunate man with a gleaming bald head as their favorite target.

Yet still the Right Social Revolutionaries and a handful of Mensheviks held on. They rushed through one resolution after another against a rising tide of hoots and jeers from the soldiers and the sailors. These resolutions have been all but forgotten in the rush of events that subsequently swallowed up democracy in Russia, but they have a certain importance, for they dispose entirely of the Bolshevik contention that the Assembly was a counter-revolutionary body. The Assembly was very revolutionary—almost as revolutionary as the Bolsheviks. In these last frantic minutes of its existence it approved of the armistice with the Germans, it passed a land decree that was fully as radical as anything the Bolsheviks had devised,* it supported the convocation of an international socialist conference and it declared Russia to be a republic. The one thing the Assembly would not do was to acknowledge the dictatorship of the Bolsheviks.

It was while Chernov was reading out the land decree that a sailor came up and putting a hand on his arm told him that the meeting must now disperse as the guard was tired. Chernov replied that the deputies also were tired but that the work they had to do would not wait. He was still trying to speak when the lights were turned off.

Things had now reached the point where a chance shot from a rifle could precipitate a massacre, and it was the Bolsheviks themselves—apparently acting on orders from Lenin—who saved the situation. Those who still remained in the corridors managed to hold back the sailors and the soldiers, while in small groups the Social Revolutionaries were escorted from the building. They scattered into the freezing night, some of them to go immediately into hiding, others to leave Russia for good.

On January 19 the Executive Committee of the Congress of Soviets passed a resolution dissolving the Assembly, and guards were posted on the doors of the Tauride Palace to prevent any of the deputies from returning. The Assembly never met again. "The simple, open, brutal breaking-up of the Constituent Assembly," Trotsky wrote later, with some satisfaction, "dealt formal democracy a finishing stroke from which it has never recovered." This is very true.

The wheel had now turned almost full cycle from Nicholas to Lenin, from autocracy back to autocracy again. The Bolsheviks had now betrayed or were about to betray nearly every political slogan that had brought them into power. They had promised the freedom of the individual and instead had censored the press, forbidden

---

* In fact the Bolsheviks had stolen the Social Revolutionaries' land program in the first place.

strikes and set up a secret police. They had undertaken to respect the rights of minority states and already they had an army on the move to crush the independent republic of the Ukraine. They had cried for a freely elected Constituent Assembly and now they had abolished it by force.

"Bread and Peace" had been at the heart of the party's program from the beginning. What Russia was now about to receive was famine and civil war.

It could be argued, of course—and Lenin did use the argument very forcibly at the time—that no government could have stayed in office unless it imposed these repressive measures; they were necessary so long as the crisis lasted. The answer to this presumably is that like King Charles II this crisis has been an unconscionable time a-dying, for none of these restrictions on human liberty have been lifted in Russia even yet.

There remained, however, in January, 1918, one field in which the Bolsheviks could make good their promises: they could come to terms with the Germans. And this in haste and even with desperation they now proceeded to do; indeed, they saw no hope of their own survival unless they brought the war to an end.

CHAPTER SIXTEEN

Brest-Litovsk

EVEN as early as the end of November, 1917, the Bolsheviks had begun to sue for peace with Germany. Soon after Kerensky was defeated at Tsarskoe Selo they sent a message to General Dukhonin, the officer who was in charge at Mogilev, ordering him to open up negotiations with the Germans at once. Dukhonin hesitated. No one could assure him that the Bolsheviks were the legal government of Russia; but if not the Bolsheviks then who else? Kerensky had vanished. Three leading generals, Kaledin, Alexeiev and Krasnov, had gone off to Novocherkassk in the Don area and could be of no help to him; and his own army, the huge force of over a hundred divisions, was breaking up around him. The government issued orders on November 22 to the Russian regiments along the entire front that they should fraternize with the Germans and open truce negotiations wherever they could.

After delaying for a day Dukhonin defied the Bolsheviks. Smolny's answer to this was to announce that the general had been dismissed, and on November 23 Ensign Krylenko, one of the new commissars for military affairs, set out for the front to take over the command. The matter was still further complicated when the Allied military missions at Mogilev delivered an official note to Dukhonin warning him of the consequences of making a separate peace with the Germans. On November 25 Krylenko arrived at Dvinsk, accompanied by a bodyguard of fifty Red sailors, and dismissed some of the generals in the northern sector.

On November 26 a Russian delegation, preceded by a trumpeter and a white flag, crossed into the German lines opposite Dvinsk with a formal request for an armistice. They came back on the following day with a favorable reply: the Germans were willing to open negotiations at the city of Brest-Litovsk at 5 p.m. on December 2. Upon this Krylenko ordered an immediate ceasefire. He added, apparently on the insistence of the Germans, that there should be no further fraternization on the front line in the meantime.

Dukhonin, however, had not quite given up as yet. From Mogilev he had appealed to the troops and instructions had been issued that Krylenko's guard be stopped before it reached Mogilev. It was the old fiasco of rival commanders issuing rival orders to the same troops, but the significant difference now was that the army was entirely demoralized; and being demoralized it came over haphazardly to the Bolshevik side. Bolshevik political committees had sprung up in every regiment and in every divisional and corps headquarters, even in general headquarters itself. On December 3 Krylenko and his fifty sailors arrived at Mogilev and the military establishment there collapsed without a struggle. Dukhonin was grabbed by his own soldiers, and although Krylenko later claimed that he tried to save him he was lynched.

It was still the attitude of the Bolsheviks at this time that they did not want to sign a separate peace. Trotsky, the Commissar for Foreign Affairs, was furious with the Allied embassies for having addressed their protest to Dukhonin, a dismissed general—it was, he said, an outrageous interference in Russia's domestic affairs—but at the same time he made it clear that the Bolsheviks would be very ready to accept an Allied delegation at Brest: the conference could then discuss a general peace for all the belligerents. The Allies of course had no intention whatever of going to Brest.

The Russian delegation that arrived on December 3 at the German headquarters at Brest was headed by Adolf Joffe, an old associate of Trotsky's from his Vienna days, and he was accompanied by Kamenev, Sokolnikov and a number of others. For Germany (and also for the Austrians, Bulgarians and Turks who were taking part in the conference) the principal spokesman was General Max Hoffmann, the German chief-of-staff on the eastern front. Hoffmann, not surprisingly, seems to have dominated the proceedings. He refused the Russian proposal for an immediate armistice of six months and refused to evacuate German troops from the three strategic islands they had seized at the mouth of the Gulf of Finland. But he did agree to a suspension of hostilities until December 17, to allow both sides to prepare their terms for peace; and with this the meeting broke up on December 5.

There was now a ferment of activity behind the lines, and none of it was either clear or simple. Among the Allies there was a general feeling that, in some way or another, Russia had to be kept in the war so as to prevent the Germans from moving troops from the east to the west, and that the best way of doing this was to unseat the Bolsheviks. The Brest conference had to be boycotted, and immediate aid had to be given to the anti-Bolshevik forces inside Russia, chiefly to the Kaledin volunteer army on the Don. Early in December the British arranged to send ten million pounds to Kaledin, and soon afterward both the Americans and the French also undertook to furnish him with clandestine support.

Sir George Buchanan, the British ambassador at Petrograd, was probably speaking for all the Allies when on December 10 he made a statement to the Russian press saying that England regarded the Brest conversations as a violation of the agreement Russia had signed with the Allies at the beginning of the war. The British government, he said, wanted a democratic peace, but thought it wrong to conclude first an armistice and then to elaborate the peace conditions. On the contrary the Allies wanted to work out the peace conditions first, and then agree upon an armistice. The Brest negotiations were being conducted with the Kaiser and not with the German people, and the Kaiser would only sign an imperialistic peace.

Once a permanent government was established in Russia, Buchanan went on, the Allies would be ready to discuss war aims. Meanwhile the Allies were helping Russia by keeping the German armies engaged in the west. If Britain had abandoned Russia there would have been no revolution. Britain would be glad to help Russia in her present crisis, but asked that Russia should have similar feelings toward Britain. Yet reading the Russian press one might have thought that Russia was at war with Britain, not with Germany.

He ended by warning the Bolsheviks against their attempt to stir up revolution in other countries.

This was the official British view, but it was not the only one. The Inter-Allied Conference had recently met in Paris, and while Clemenceau was implacably opposed to the Bolsheviks and the Brest conference, neither Colonel House nor Lloyd George was so sure about the matter. They thought that there was something to be said for letting Russia have a free hand at Brest. Even inside the Allied embassies in Petrograd there was disagreement. The French, British and American ambassadors had no official contact with the Bolsheviks and future negotiations were to be carried on very largely through Raymond Robins, of the American Red Cross unit in Russia, Bruce Lockhart, the British agent, and Captain Jacques Sadoul of the French military mission. These three men all believed that the best way of saving the situation was for the Allies to treat with the Bolsheviks and so strengthen them that they would be able to resist the Germans. To provoke civil war in Russia by supporting Kaledin and the independent republic in the Ukraine they thought was foolish, since it would only lead to the Germans overrunning the country.

The German position was just as complicated. They were investing a huge sum in the Russian revolution—it was something like fifty million marks in the end—and now they wanted to get their money's worth. But was Lenin going to stay in power long enough to put through the separate peace? And could he be trusted? Already the Bolsheviks were fomenting trouble: fraternization had begun again on the front line, and there was some danger that direct contact would be made with the German socialists. Parvus was behind a movement for holding a joint German-Russian socialist peace conference at Stockholm, a conference that would take the place of the official meeting at Brest—and a group of the deputies in the German Reichstag were in favor of an interparliamentary meeting with the Russians. The German High Command did not like these moves at all. They did not want a soft friendly peace with Russia, and they did not want the German socialists to interfere. They wanted a tough military peace and the complete obliteration of the Russian forces, so that they could turn the full weight of their war effort upon the Allies in the west.

For the Bolsheviks, on the other hand, it was a matter of playing a double game out of extreme weakness. Lenin had his understanding with the Germans; they had sent him back to Russia in order to seize the power and make peace, and they had financed him. In his own interests too he needed peace desperately in order to subdue the anti-Bolshevik forces that were growing up around him. But not all his own followers were ready to make peace at any price. They wanted a "just democratic peace without annexations or indemnities," and they hoped very much that a revolution would occur inside Germany. "We began peace negotiations," Trotsky says, "in the hope of arousing the workingmen's party of Germany and Austro-Hungary as well as of the Entente countries." There was some truth in this. The Bolsheviks had a good deal to hope from the German socialists and center parties and by concerted action with them might possibly have outmaneuvered the German High Command. And so while Lenin wanted to push on and force through an immediate peace many of his followers preferred to hold back and prolong the negotiations as long as possible, so that the German workers would have time to revolt.

All these various rival tendencies were developing fast when the delegations of the Russians and of the Central Powers again assembled at Brest on December 13. There was a brief but not unfriendly conference; one of General Hoffmann's main concerns at this stage was to stop the fraternization that was going on along the front line, and when this and other points at issue were agreed to the armistice was signed. It was to come into force on December 17, and continue until January 14—time enough, it was thought, for the full peace treaty to be negotiated—and both sides undertook not to move their troops from their present positions.

The next three weeks were in the nature of a political honeymoon between the Germans and the Bolsheviks. There were disputes and misgivings, but in the main both sides appear to have believed in each other's good faith. At Brest the delegations dined together, and the Germans issued a conciliatory statement saying that, in general, they respected the Bolshevik's peace aims. Count Mirbach arrived in Petrograd at the head of a German commission which was to deal with such matters as the exchange of prisoners of war, and the future financial and commercial relations between the two countries. Similar commissions were sent to Riga and Odessa by Germany and Austria. Along the dark frozen front hardly a shot was fired, and there was silence for the first time in more than three years.

In reality the deep unbridgeable gap remained between the two sides. The Germans continued to make their arrangements for a hard peace. The Bolsheviks professedly continued to agitate for world revolution, and even made a show of voting a sum of two million rubles for this object. The question of Stockholm also remained; the Bolsheviks were now coming round to the idea that it might be to their advantage to move there from Brest for the negotiations. At Stockholm it would be easier for their propaganda to reach the socialists of the world. None of these moves, however, had led to much more than a cooling off when, on January 9, the delegations assembled once more at Brest for the second full discussion of the peace treaty. Trotsky himself now headed the Russian delegation. The Central Powers were represented by the German Foreign Minister, Baron von Kuhlmann, the Austrian Foreign Minister, Count Czernin, representatives of Bulgaria and Turkey, General Hoffmann and others.

Now finally the moment had come to lay the cards on the table and the Germans wasted no time. They rejected the Russian proposal that the conference should move to Stockholm, and stated forcibly that the Bolshevik agitation behind their lines had to stop. As for the peace terms themselves there was to be no talk of German concessions or withdrawals. The German forces were to remain in occupation of the ground they had already conquered. They were to have full liberty to move their troops wherever they wished, and the Russians were to come forward with substantial indemnities. Russia, in short, was to be treated as a defeated enemy. Von Kühlmann summed it all up with the phrase: "The only choice they [the Bolsheviks] have is as to what sauce they shall be eaten with."

Trotsky played for time. For a week he prevaricated and made difficulties, and it was plain that his arguments were mainly intended to rouse the mass of the German people against the war; and by January 18 the Germans had had enough. Hoffmann showed Trotsky a map which set forth the Germans' territorial demands and they were enormous: most of Poland and all of Lithuania were to be separated from Russia as well as sections of the other Baltic States, and large areas inhabited by the Ukrainians and White Russians. Trotsky's comment was an evasive protest. He suspended the negotiations and left for Petrograd on January 18—that same day on which Lenin already had enough trouble on his hands with the meeting of the Constituent Assembly.

The last half of January was not the best of times for the Bolsheviks to try and make a stand. In Petrograd and Moscow they were surrounded by the hatred engendered by the breaking up of the Constituent Assembly. In the Ukraine civil war was starting, and although *Pravda* was advocating a plan for holding off the German invasion by adopting guerrilla tactics, it was perfectly clear that, as an effective force, the Russian army was nearly finished.

And yet there were certain grounds for optimism. It was hardly likely that after the respite of the last few weeks the German soldiers would be very willing to take up the struggle again. In both Austria and Germany socialist antiwar propaganda was taking effect; strikes were starting to break out, and there were serious public demonstrations against the failure of the government to conclude peace. Kühlmann himself and all but the diehard German imperialists had doubts about pressing the Bolsheviks too hard. Both the German and the Austrian foreign offices were in favor of a compromise. They feared that Lenin might soon be turned out of office. Germany, they argued, was in no position to invade Russia on a large scale; she needed the soldiers in the west, and in any case there was a definite feeling against a resumption of the campaign among the German public.

These views made very little impression upon the Kaiser's military advisers. Only a few months now divided Germany from her own collapse but the dream of conquest still persisted. Both Hindenburg and Ludendorff argued that if the negotiations broke down they were bound to invade Russia to prevent the United States and England from landing armies there.

There was similar disagreement inside the Bolshevik Central Committee. Lenin was all for peace: peace at any price, peace with annexations and indemnities, immediate peace. There was no hope at this moment, he said, of their being saved by a revolution inside Germany. If the Germans attacked again, the Bolshevik government

might fall, and in any case they were bound to sign a peace treaty
sometime or other, probably on far worse terms than they were
being offered now. Zinoviev and Kamenev supported Lenin on
this issue. They were opposed by other party leaders who appear
to have been fired by the notion that the Russian soldier could still
be roused to fight a "revolutionary war" in defense of Russia. These
people were indignant at Germany's ruthlessness, at her "betrayal"
of Russian good faith, and there may have been some flickering here
at last of old-fashioned patriotism. Certainly too they had it in mind
that a revolutionary struggle against the Germans would spread
dissatisfaction in the German army. Between these two groups stood
Trotsky. He wanted to break off negotiations entirely, and only
renew them again if the Germans attacked. When the matter was put
to the vote, it was decided that Trotsky should return to Brest and
string out the conference as long as possible. If the Germans
threatened an ultimatum he was to fall back on a formula of his own
creation: "No war—no peace." This meant that Russia would neither
sign the peace treaty nor would she continue the war.

On January 30 Trotsky was back at Brest again with his strange
brief, but it was obvious that the game could go on only a few days
longer. On February 9 the Germans signed a separate peace treaty
with the Ukrainian Government which was being attacked by the
Bolsheviks, and toward the Bolsheviks themselves they adopted
a much tougher attitude. On February 10, when he was practically
faced by an ultimatum, Trotsky at last made his announcement. "We
withdraw from the war," he said, "but we are obliged to refuse to
sign the peace treaty"; and with this he led his delegation back to
Petrograd once more. At the same time it was announced that the
Russian army was to be demobilized, a measure which may have
been a ruse to placate the Germans or merely a final *cri de coeur* to
the proletariat of the world: if Russia was to be raped she would not
defend herself. It was an eloquent gesture, but it failed in any way
to disturb General Ludendorff or General Hoffmann; on February
17 they ordered a general advance into Russia. The Red army fell
back with little show of resistance.

The panic that now seized Petrograd can be best illustrated by
describing the behavior of the Bolsheviks themselves. The majority
of the Central Committee had been opposing Lenin's every attempt

to get a resumption of the negotiations. But now on the 18th, when the appalling news of the German attack arrived from the front, they collapsed; Lenin and Trotsky were authorized to send a radiogram to Berlin saying that Russia would now accept the peace terms without further dispute. On the following day Hoffmann replied that he was not prepared to accept a radio message; he wanted a signed document and he wanted it delivered to the German commander at Dvinsk. Meanwhile the German advance would continue.

There was some little flame of resistance left among the Bolsheviks, and perhaps it was generated mainly by fear—the fear that the Germans would no longer listen to reason; and indeed it seemed at this moment that Ludendorff was determined to settle the whole issue by brute force. An outburst of feverish activity marked the Bolsheviks' actions through the next few days. A proclamation was issued calling for a "People's War" to resist the invader. Bridges and dumps were to be blown up in the path of the German advance. Traitors were to be shot out of hand. Every village was to sacrifice itself as it had done in the days of Napoleon.

Trotsky performed a startling political somersault: he told Bruce Lockhart and the other Allied agents that Russia would carry on the struggle if the Allies gave them support. It was a futile proposition—there was nothing the Allies could do at this eleventh hour —but it seems to have been made genuinely enough. Even Lenin wavered. There is some dispute as to the exact manner in which he agreed to receive help from the Allies, but the most widely circulated Bolshevik version is that he wrote a note saying that he agreed "that Comrade Trotsky be authorized to accept the assistance of the brigands of the French imperialism against the German brigands."

The Germans allowed the Bolsheviks to stew in their juice for two more days, and then on February 23 they produced their new peace terms. As Lenin had predicted, they were much stiffer than before. Germany was now to occupy Estonia and part of Latvia, and the Russians to withdraw from Finland and the Ukraine. The Turks were also to have a bigger slice of the booty. Three hundred million gold rubles were to be paid for the repatriation of Russian prisoners of war, and Russia was to give an undertaking that she would abandon her revolutionary propaganda. These terms were to be accepted within forty-eight hours and the peace treaty was to be signed within three days of the arrival of the delegates at Brest. Ratification was to take place within two weeks thereafter.

It was harsh enough to make the Bolsheviks break out into furious argument amongst themselves once more, and no doubt the dispute might have continued indefinitely had not the German army been getting steadily nearer to Petrograd with every hour that went by. Lenin in any case forced the issue to a decision on February 23 by threatening to resign unless the German offer was accepted. This was enough to get him a favorable vote in the Central Committee of the party, and when the question was put to the Central Executive Committee of the Soviet Congress he won by 116 votes to 85, with 26 abstaining. In the early morning of February 24 Lenin and Trotsky sent a message to the Germans saying that they would sign.

Four more days were to elapse before the delegations reassembled at Brest, and the Russians would have signed there and then. But the Germans were in no hurry—their troops were still pushing deeper into Russia all this time—and it was not until 5 P.M. on March 3 that the signatures were finally affixed to the treaty. Trotsky spared himself this last indignity; he sent Sokolnikov in his place, and Sokolnikov is said to have permitted himself the gesture of not even reading the document before he signed.

It was a crushing defeat. Russia lost one-third, or sixty-two millions, of her population, one-quarter of her territory, one-third of her crop lands, twenty-seven per cent of her income, and more than half her industries. She was left defenseless.

The Bolsheviks quite rightly anticipated the current of anger and disgust that was bound to run through the country when the news of this humiliation got out. Trotsky even went so far as to approach Raymond Robins again and ask him what the attitude of the Allies would be if Russia refused to ratify the treaty. But this was so much moonshine. Trotsky himself was about to resign his office and become Commissar for Military Affairs. They were all on the run. All over western Russia the German armies were creeping forward toward Odessa on the Black Sea, Kharkov in the Ukraine, and were poised in Estonia at the very approaches to Petrograd. It was now, in the second week of March, that the move of the government to Moscow was made, and on March 14 the Congress of Soviets assembled there to ratify the treaty.

Lenin in his speech said that it was impossible for the Russians to fight on; they had no army, they had to have a rest. The revolution, he said, had gone through three periods. At first the workers and the bourgeoisie had combined in March to overthrow the monarchy; then came a transition period when the power of the bourgeoisie was sustained by the Mensheviks and the Social Revolutionaries. In November the third stage had been reached; now Russia had to abandon the international revolution for the time being while she consolidated her strength.

"We must . . . say to ourselves," he went on, "whatever the respite, however precarious, however short, however burdensome and humiliating the peace, it is better than war, for it will give the national masses an opportunity to have a breathing spell. . . . We shall prove ourselves capable not only of heroic attack, but also of heroic retreat. We shall know how to wait until the international socialist proletariat comes to our aid, and we shall then start a second socialist revolution on a world scale."

There was a bitter debate, and the group of Left Social Revolutionaries who had recently joined the government resigned. But when the vote was taken the ratification of the treaty was agreed upon by 784 to 261, with 115 abstentions. Russia now descended by rapid stages into the nightmare of enemy occupation, of famine and of civil war.

Brest-Litovsk was not by any means the last word in the Bolshevik revolution, and in any case the treaty was annulled in the general collapse of Germany and the Central Powers eight months later, in November, 1918. Yet it must be regarded as an historical dividing line, the end of one evolutionary process and the beginning of another.

By April, 1918, the strikes and absenteeism in the government ministries had petered out. In the same month the Bolsheviks had established Joffe as their ambassador with a staff of three hundred in Berlin, and Count Mirbach was installed as the German representative in Moscow; thus the party had a firm link with the only people in the world who were actively supporting them—the Germans. By June Trotsky had already gone a long way toward building up the new Red army, and in comparison with the old army it was a fairly efficient machine; he made no bones about employing professional officers of the old regime and German prisoners of war. These and other moves enabled the Bolsheviks to face their major crisis in the summer of 1918.

Even so it was a touch-and-go affair. When the Fifth All-Russian Congress met in the Bolshoi Theater in Moscow on July 4 the Left Social Revolutionaries, led by Maria Spiridonova, still had one-third of the votes, and they launched a violent attack on the Bolsheviks' foreign policy. Mirbach, sitting in the ambassadors' gallery, had to face a storm of hooting and booing. This was not merely a political demonstration: it represented the hatred of vast forces that were rising against the Bolsheviks and the Germans all over Russia. The British had landed at Murmansk, and with the other Allies were about to land at Vladivostok. A civil war was being fought in Finland, and the Ukraine was both hostile and independent (except that German occupation forces were there). In the south Kaledin had committed suicide and Kornilov had been killed, but General Denikin had taken their place at the head of the rebellion; and Victor Chernov was setting up another center of resistance on the Volga. The Czech Legion, which had fought on the side of the Allies in Russia, had turned on the Bolsheviks and was making its fantastic march across to the Pacific, taking control of the Trans-Siberian Railway along the way. Siberia itself was held by the Social Revolutionaries.

On July 6 Mirbach was assassinated by Left Social Revolutionary terrorists, and street fighting broke out in Moscow, Petrograd and Yaroslavl. It was a foretaste of the civil war that lay ahead, and it was only through the disunity of their opponents that the Bolsheviks managed to survive.

The Brest treaty had another significance; it had revealed to the Allies just what sort of treatment was in store for them if the Germans won the war, and it stiffened their determination to fight on. More particularly it had the effect of drawing the United States much nearer to her European partners.

Speaking at Baltimore on April 6, President Wilson said:

I do not wish, even at this moment of utter disillusionment, to judge harshly or unrighteously. I judge only what the German arms have accomplished with unpitying thoroughness throughout every fair region they have touched. . . . For myself, I am ready . . . to discuss a fair and just and honest peace at any time that it is sincerely purposed—a peace in which the strong and the weak shall fare alike. But the answer, when I proposed such a peace, came from the German commanders in Russia, and I cannot mistake the meaning of the answer. I accept the challenge— Germany has once more said that force, and force alone, shall decide whether Justice and Peace shall reign in the affairs of men. . . . There is therefore but one response possible from us: Force, Force to the utmost, Force without stint or limit, the righteous and triumphant Force which shall make Right the law of the world, and cast every selfish dominion down in the dust.

In short, the United States now pledged herself to victory to the last dollar and the last man; and when the end came in November Wilson was among the first to insist that the Germans should immediately evacuate their forces from Russia. It was an obvious decision to make, and it was not wise. As soon as the German army retired the Bolsheviks were left with a clear field of action. The Red army not only seized the weapons the Germans left behind; it was also left as the undisputed master of great areas of Russia that were vital to the survival of the Bolsheviks during the civil war.

Churchill, now British Secretary of State for War, tried to awaken the western Allies to their danger, but they had no heart for another struggle, and the twenty-five thousand French, Italian, British and American soldiers who had been sent to Russia were soon withdrawn.

But the civil war and its end in Bolshevik victory is another story. Here, at the conclusion of this account of the Bolsheviks' rise to power, we need only take note of two final events in the lives of the two men who, more than any others, represent the rival forces that were at work.

In April, 1918, Nicholas and his family were taken to Ekaterinburg in the Urals where there was a strongly hostile local Soviet. They were imprisoned in a merchant's house, and it was just one of the many humiliations to which they were submitted that they were put on soldiers' rations. Let us again follow Bernard Pares in his account of the last few months of Nicholas's life. "The family," he says, "now had to take their meals out of a common pot, into which the chief of the guard, Andeyev, a not entirely ungenial drunkard, would also dip his spoon, leaning over between Nicholas and his wife."

Through the succeeding weeks other captured members of the Imperial family were brought into the Ekaterinburg district, and on June 12 the Grand Duke Michael and his secretary were shot. By now the Czech Legion was approaching, and no doubt this had the effect of increasing the Ekaterinburg Bolshevik's hatred of their helpless prisoners. Nicholas had not altogether given up hope, and indeed there were several bungled attempts by Royalists to rescue him. Once, for example, he received a letter telling him to unfasten the window of the room in which he was sleeping and to hold himself ready to escape. The family waited all night but nothing happened.

On July 16 the nightmare in which they were living became a brutal reality. On that day the family were told that they were to be moved again and they did not go to bed. Late in the evening they were ordered into the cellar of the house, and Nicholas was obliged to carry his son downstairs for the boy had fallen seriously ill. In the cellar the family asked for chairs, which were brought. The new head of the guard, a Captain Yurovsky, entered with a band of armed men, and he read out a sentence of execution which, he said, had been passed by the Ekaterinburg Soviet. Nicholas was then shot dead, and a volley demolished the rest of the family. The sick boy did not die at once, and Yurovsky emptied his revolver into his body. Anastasia, the youngest daughter, also continued to show some signs of life, and was killed with the bayonet. Then the children's spaniel dog was dispatched.

Litters were now produced, and on these the bodies were conveyed to a lorry and driven off to a deserted mine shaft outside the town, known as the Four Brothers. In the mine shaft vitriol was poured on the bodies, and fires were lit to obliterate the last traces. On the following day, July 17, the Grand Duke Sergius and his wife were murdered, together with other members of the Imperial family; and further murders followed on succeeding days. On July 25 Ekaterinburg was captured by the Czechs, and the Bolsheviks were routed for a time.

According to Trotsky, the party leaders in Moscow were too busy to be much interested when the news of the massacre reached them; but eventually twenty-eight of the murderers were arrested and five were executed.

Some six years later it was Lenin's turn. He died after a series of brain hemorrhages at Gorky, near Moscow, at 6:30 P.M. on January 21, 1924, at the age of fifty-three.

Churchill subsequently claimed that Lenin might have saved Russia from the extremities and the violence that lay before her: "He alone could have found the way back to the causeway. . . . The Russian people were left floundering in the bog. Their worst misfortune was his birth . . . their next worst—his death."

It is a controversial point, and it will never be settled. Perhaps the only safe comment is the one that Lenin himself made so often when he quoted Napoleon: "*On s'engage, et puis—on voit*"—"You commit yourself, and then—you see."

Lenin committed not only himself but all Russia. But he did not live to see.

DR. POSSONY's exhaustive study of the Russian revolution, and in particular his recent research into the German Foreign Office files, has provided the main foundation of this book. More specific reference follows to other sources which are not always mentioned in the text:

CHAPTER ONE: The description of Petrograd at the end of 1916 is taken from contemporary Russian newspapers, guidebooks, and from eyewitnesses who are still living. An account of the economic conditions of the Russian people under the Czars can be found in Michael F. Florinsky's *The End of the Russian Empire*, Yale University Press, 1931. The quotation from Leon Trotsky is taken from the preface to his *History of the Russian Revolution*, Simon and Schuster, 1936.

CHAPTER TWO: Bernard Pares's two works, *A History of Russia*, Knopf, 1953, and *The Fall of the Russian Monarchy*, Knopf, 1939, are the principal sources of the account of Russia through the second half of the nineteenth century, and of Nicholas's early years, marriage and accession to the throne.

CHAPTER THREE: Bertram D. Wolfe's *Three Who Made a Revolution*, Dial Press, 1948, has been most valuable in tracing the early careers of the chief revolutionary figures both in this chapter and in Chapter 6. Trotsky's short life of Lenin has also been useful. The Turgenev quotation is from his *The Threshold*. Mr. Edmund Wilson's description of Lenin is taken from his *To the Finland Station*, Harcourt, 1940; and the John Reed quotation is from *Ten Days That Shook the World*, Boni & Liveright, 1919, International Publishers, 1926. Maurice Paléologue's *Les Précurseurs de Lénine*, Plon, 1938, and Lenin's own letters, translated by Elizabeth Hill and Doris Mudie, Harcourt, 1937, have also been consulted.

CHAPTERS FOUR & FIVE: The account of the 1905 rising, and of the subsequent years to 1914, follows Pares in the main. The Empress's letter to Rasputin is taken from Trufanov Illiodor's *Zapiski o Rasputiny*, page 31. Illiodor says that he obtained this letter from Rasputin when he visited him in Pokrovskoye on December 8, 1909.

CHAPTER SIX: Bertram Wolfe's *Three Who Made a Revolution*, Lenin's letters, William Henry Chamberlin's *The Russian Revolution*, Macmillan, 1935, and Edward Hallett Carr's *The Bolshevik Revolution*, Macmillan, 1954, are all valuable guides to the activities of the revolutionaries in the pre-1914 war years.

CHAPTER SEVEN: Quotations from Paléologue, Pares and Trotsky have been acknowledged in the text. In addition Sir George Buchanan's *My Mission to Russia and other Diplomatic Memoirs*, Little, Brown, 1923, has been consulted. The correspondence of Nicholas and his wife has been published by Duckworth (1923) and the Bodley Head (1929).

CHAPTER EIGHT: This chapter is based mainly upon Dr. Possony's search of the German archives.

CHAPTER NINE: A large library exists on the March rising. The sources here most frequently consulted are Pares, Chamberlin, Trotsky and N. N. Sukhanov's *The Russian Revolution, 1917*, edited and translated by Joel Carmichael, Oxford University Press, 1955.

CHAPTER TEN: Sukhanov, Trotsky and the memoirs of the French and British ambassadors, Paléologue and Buchanan, all throw light on the aftermath of the March rising. Another eyewitness, Milyukov, has also described the scene in his *History of the Second Russian Revolution*, Sofia, 1921. George F. Kennan in his recent *Russia Leaves the War*, Princeton University Press, 1956, has given an absorbing description of the United States Embassy in Petrograd and it has been drawn on here.

CHAPTER ELEVEN: The well-known facts of Lenin's return to Russia have been supplemented by reference to the German archives, his own correspondence, and Sukhanov.

CHAPTERS TWELVE & THIRTEEN: The "July Days," Lenin's disgrace and the Kornilov adventure have all been chronicled with varying degrees of partisanship by Kerensky, Milyukov, Trotsky, Sukhanov and many other Russian eyewitnesses. The German archives throw some new light on these events. An investigation into the German spy documents has also been made by Dr. Kennan, and can be read in his *Russia Leaves the War*.

CHAPTER FOURTEEN: John Reed's vivid reporting in *Ten Days That Shook the World* has been acknowledged in the text, and almost all the sources quoted above have been consulted in compiling this account of the Bolshevik *coup d'état* in November.

CHAPTERS FIFTEEN & SIXTEEN: The abortive meeting of the Constituent Assembly and the Treaty of Brest-Litovsk are dealt with in all the standard histories of the revolution.

FINE WORKS OF NON-FICTION AVAILABLE IN QUALITY PAPERBACK EDITIONS FROM CARROLL & GRAF

- ☐ Anderson, Nancy/WORK WITH PASSION $8.95
- ☐ Athill, Diana/INSTEAD OF A LETTER $7.95
- ☐ Berton, Pierre/KLONDIKE FEVER $10.95
- ☐ Blanch, Lesley/THE WILDER SHORES OF LOVE $8.95
- ☐ Conot, Robert/JUSTICE AT NUREMBURG $10.95
- ☐ Cooper, Lady Diana/AUTOBIGRAPHY $12.95
- ☐ Haycraft, Howard (ed.)/THE ART OF THE MYSTERY STORY $9.95
- ☐ Lansing, Alfred/ENDURANCE: SHACKLETON'S INCREDIBLE VOYAGE $8.95
- ☐ Maurois, Andre/PROUST: PORTRAIT OF A GENIUS $10.95
- ☐ McCarthy, Barry & Emily/SEXUAL AWARENESS $9.95
- ☐ Poncins, Gontran de/KABLOONA $9.95
- ☐ Rowse, A.L./HOMOSEXUALS IN HISTORY $9.95
- ☐ Roy, Jules/THE BATTLE OF DIENBIENPHU $8.95
- ☐ Salisbury, Harrison/A JOURNEY OF OUR TIMES $10.95
- ☐ Werth, Alexander/RUSSIA AT WAR 1941–1945 $15.95

Available from fine bookstores everywhere or use this coupon for ordering:

Caroll & Graf Publishers, Inc., 260 Fifth Avenue, N.Y., N.Y. 10001

Please send me the books I have checked above. I am enclosing $_____ (please add 1.75 per title to cover postage and handling.) Send check or money order— no cash or C.O.D.'s please. N.Y. residents please add 8¼% sales tax.

Mr/Mrs/Miss _____

Address _____

City _____ State/Zip _____

Please allow four to six weeks for delivery.